ANALYZING SOCIAL AND POLITICAL CHANGE

ANALYZING SOCIAL AND POLITICAL CHANGE

A Casebook of Methods

edited by

Angela Dale and Richard B. Davies

SAGE Publications
London • Thousand Oaks • New Delhi

First published 1994

 SAGE Publications Ltd
6 Bonhill Street
London EC2A 4PU

SAGE Publications Inc
2455 Teller Road
Thousand Oaks, California 91320

SAGE Publications India Pvt Ltd
32, M-Block Market
Greater Kailash – I
New Delhi 110 048

British Library Cataloguing in Publication data

Analyzing Social and Political Change:
Casebook of Methods
    I. Dale, Angela II. Davies, R. B.
    300.7
ISBN 0–8039–8298–4
ISBN 0–8039–8299–2 (pbk)

Library of Congress catalog card number 94–065543

Typeset by Poole Typesetting (Wessex) Ltd, Bournemouth
Printed in Great Britain by The Cromwell Press Ltd, Broughton
Gifford, Melksham, Wiltshire

Contents

Preface

The aim of this book is to provide the non-statistician with an awareness of the kinds of methods that are available and the different problems to which they may be applied. We hope that the book will be of value to a wide range of quantitatively oriented social and political scientists and will provide the stimulation for seeking a greater depth of information.

Each chapter begins with a general introduction to the method and its applicability, moves into a more detailed methodological discussion and then presents a worked example using that method. The chapter concludes by highlighting any shortcoming of the method and also pointing out particular software packages available. Inevitably there is variation in the technical complexity of the chapters. In order to help the reader we have written short introductions to each chapter which provide an overview of the content and alert the reader to any technical issues which may cause problems in the text. We also indicate whether more difficult sections can be skipped without losing the sense of the chapter.

The book is the result of collaboration between a sociologist, Angela Dale, and a statistician, Richard Davies. Whilst the editors are in alphabetical order, there was considerable division of labour and, inevitably, the brunt of editing the statistical content was borne by Richard Davies.

Some of the papers were first presented at an ESRC-funded seminar on statistical methods of analyzing change, held at Nuffield College, Oxford in 1989, and we would like to acknowledge the support of the ESRC in this context. We would like to thank all the contributors for bearing with us over the time-consuming process of checking and correcting the text. We also thank Denise Lievesely, Director of the ESRC Data Archive at the University of Essex, for reading the draft manuscript and providing helpful suggestions. We would also like to thank Steve Barr of Sage for his support and enthusiasm and Doreen Hough from Lancaster University who provided assistance with typing.

Contributors

John Bynner worked on studies of young people at the Central Council for Health Education and at the UK Government Social Survey before moving to the Open University, where he was Professor of Education and Dean of the School of Education. He joined the Social Statistics Research Unit of City University (London) as Director in 1989. He was National Coordinator of the ESRC 16–19 Initiative and now directs the British Cohort Studies Programme at SSRU.

Angela Dale is Director of the Census Microdata Unit and Professor of Quantitative Social Research at the University of Manchester. She is the co-author (with Sara Arber and Mike Procter) of *Doing Secondary Analysis* (1988), and joint editor (with the late Cathie Marsh) of *The 1991 Census User's Guide* (1993).

Richard B. Davies is Director of the Centre for Applied Statistics and Professor of Social Statistics at the University of Lancaster. He has published extensively in the area of longitudinal data analysis.

Anthony Heath, FBA, is an Official Fellow in Sociology at Nuffield College, Oxford. He has been Co-Director of the 1983, 1987 and 1992 British Election Studies. His publications include *How Britain Votes* (1985) and *Understanding Political Change* (1991).

Rolf Langeheine is Research Associate at the Institute for Science Education in the Department of Educational and Psychological Methodology, University of Kiel. Over many years his interest has been in the analysis of categorical data by log-linear and latent class models, more recently focusing on the analysis of change by Markov chain models for sequential categorical data.

John Micklewright is Associate Professor of Economics at the European University Institute, Florence, and Reader in Economics at Queen Mary and Westfield College, University of London. He has published widely in the areas of education and young people using both longitudinal and cross-sectional data sources.

Clive Payne is Director of the Computing and Research Support Unit in the Social Studies Faculty of Oxford University and a Fellow of Nuffield College. His interests lie in the application of statistical models to the analysis of social and political data, and election forecasting. He is joint editor of the *GLIM4 Manual* (1993).

Joan Payne is Senior Fellow at the Policy Studies Institute. She has published widely in the field of labour market sociology including, *Off-the-Job Adult Skills Training: an Evaluation Study* (1990) and *Women, Training and the Skills Shortage: the Case for Public Investment* (1991).

Ian Plewis is a Senior Research Officer at the Thomas Coram Research Unit and a Senior Lecturer in the Department of Child Development and Primary Education at the Institute of Education, London. His main interests are the analysis of longitudinal data of all kinds and the academic progress of young children.

David Sanders is a Professor of Government at the University of Essex. He has published widely in the fields of comparative politics, international relations and political economy. His current research seeks to effect a synthesis between individual-level and aggregate-level analyses of political support.

Nancy Tuma, Mellon Professor of Interdisciplinary Studies at Stanford University, has been visiting the Department of Sociology, Cornell University. Her interests include developing models to investigate the global diffusion of national policies and to study interdependent events in the evolution of populations of organizations. She continues to engage in research on the life course and her empirical applications are currently focused on life careers in former state socialist societies.

Frank van de Pol is Research Associate at the Netherlands Central Bureau of Statistics and is Chief Editor of *Kwantitatieve Methoden*. He has written about design and analysis of panel surveys and recently developed a weighting method for panel data that produces only one set of weights for cross-sectional and longitudinal purposes.

Hugh Ward is a Senior Lecturer in the Department of Government at the University of Essex. He has published in a number of areas relating to rational choice theory and electoral behaviour. His current research centres on the application of formal modelling to international environmental politics.

1

Introduction

Richard B. Davies and Angela Dale

Whilst qualitative researchers have long been concerned with process, limitations of data and method have confined many quantitative researchers to cross-sectional studies with inferences about process requiring bold assumptions or heavy reliance upon untested substantive theory. However, the social and political sciences are moving through a period of rapid methodological development. Increasingly both the concepts and the tools are becoming available to ensure a more rigorous and thorough approach to empirical research. Much of this progress has been stimulated by a growing recognition that analyses of social life based upon static, cross-sectional data are partial at best and misleading at worst. This changing emphasis has also brought about a corresponding increase in the longitudinal data available for secondary analysis.

While there has long been pioneering work by a few, there is still a gap between the developmental work by statisticians and the everyday practice of social science research. The aim of this book is to provide the foundation for a bridge across that gap. Each chapter takes a particular method of statistical analysis and explains how it can be applied to the analysis of process. In the space available, there is no attempt at providing a complete description of the method. Rather, the aim is to alert the reader to some of the possibilities that exist, to the general principles that underlie the method, and to its strengths and limitations. In this introductory chapter we provide an overview of the way in which introducing a temporal element can increase the explanatory power of empirical analysis. All the data used in the book are longitudinal in some sense, whether panel data or time series using different cross-sections; it is the temporal element and the way that this can be used to provide explanations of change and process that is the focus of the book.

Why use longitudinal data?

To overcome problems of inferring process from cross-sectional data

Women's employment status presents very vividly the problem encountered when inferring life-course change from cross-sectional data. Successive cohorts of women have shown marked changes in their level of labour market participation, whilst there are also strong age or life-course effects *within* each cohort. Cross-sectional data that record level of labour market participation by age confound these two effects and may give a misleading impression of life-course changes. Surveys which record full work history data for women across a wide range of ages enable successive cohorts to be traced across the life course, thereby highlighting how ageing effects vary between cohorts. In Britain the Women and Employment Survey (Martin and Roberts, 1984) incorporated retrospective work histories for over 5,000 women aged 16–59. In the US, the National Longitudinal Study drew samples of men and women from three different age cohorts and recorded their labour market experience over a lengthy period (Center for Human Resource Research, 1981). Such data often include information on life events – for example, births, marriages, divorces – and allow analyses between cohorts which relate to the way in which women's decisions over the timing of first births and the interval between births have changed between cohorts and, also, how they are related to other characteristics such as education and occupation.

Where individuals are surveyed at successive time points, then it is possible to investigate how individual outcomes or responses are related to the earlier circumstances *of the same individuals*. This provides the framework for very powerful analyses of the processes experienced by individuals; it enables a model to be constructed which explicitly takes into account the earlier circumstances suspected to have an effect which carries through into later life. Variables such as school leaving age, educational qualifications, parental class and first job are often measured retrospectively, and appropriate questions can be included in cross-sectional surveys as easily as in longitudinal ones. However, retrospective information on a wider range of life- and work-related variables is difficult to collect accurately because of problems of recall (Dex, 1991). For example, respondents may have vivid recollections of recent short spells of unemployment but tend to overlook spells in the more distant past, even with careful prompting (Morgenstern and Barrett, 1974). Repeated sweeps of data collection are unavoidable for some areas of interest: attitude measures cannot be reconstructed and it is not usually feasible to ask for information on income retrospectively; many measures related to health – height, weight, blood pressure – must be recorded precisely at an exact time. Repeated surveys, which also contain retrospective questions to obtain information about the gaps between the surveys, obviously combine the best of both worlds.

Prospective, birth cohort studies are often used to analyze developmental processes because, particularly at younger ages, it is important to control very precisely for age. Often the concern is with exogenous factors that are thought to influence the developmental process, for example the effect of early education on later occupational attainment, or the effect of bad housing conditions on later health. For this kind of analysis, it is important to have individual longitudinal data which are collected throughout the life course, providing baseline measures against which to assess subsequent change. For developmental or life-course processes recorded for a single cohort, there is obviously no scope to examine variation between cohorts. A comparison between cohorts allows one to establish whether there has been change across time, for example whether children born to a cohort 20 years later are taller and heavier, age for age, than the earlier cohort. Measures of children's height and weight taken from cross-sectional samples will show age-related changes, but do not allow these to be distinguished from cohort effects.

The drawback, of course, with all prospective studies is that it is difficult to change the direction of the research in later years whilst still retaining the full longitudinal power of the data. Nevertheless, there are many examples of questions which have turned out, either through luck or foresight, to have unexpected relevance. One example is the inclusion of a question on smoking in the 1958 British Cohort Study (the National Child Development Study). At that time (1958) there had been no indication of the relationship between mother's smoking and low birth weight that later turned out to be so important.

Inertia effects

A recurrent theme throughout the social sciences is that behaviour is characterized by strong temporal dependencies. Thus the decision to quit a job, to divorce, or to migrate depends upon the interval since commencing the job, marrying, or previously moving. How a person votes, the brand of food purchased, or the mode of transport for travelling to work, each depends upon the choice made on the previous occasion. The former are examples of duration dependence while the latter are examples of state dependence (or, more formally, 'Markov' effects) and, methodologically, this proves to be a convenient distinction. Most of the factors creating such temporal dependencies generate inertial effects in behaviour. These include social, economic, and community ties which progressively inhibit change and prompted McGinnis (1968) to propose an 'axiom of cumulative inertia' for social processes. Similar but involuntary dependence may arise through constraints created by previous choices. For example, existing housing tenure can constrain alternative tenure opportunities (Short, 1978). The theory of cognitive dissonance (Festinger, 1957) also suggests continuity over time in choice behaviour: after people make a choice between alternatives they tend to align their attitudes to that choice, upgrading their satisfaction with both positive and negative attributes of the chosen alternative and downgrading those of the rejected alternative. Having made a choice, a person is therefore more likely to make a similar choice in the future. However, although inertia effects often dominate, some factors operate in the reverse direction. These include progressive mismatch between aspirations and current status (e.g. Huff and Clark, 1978: 'cumulative stress') and the postulated increase in the probability of obtaining a job as the unemployed reduce their reservation wage with duration of unemployment (Keifer and Neumann, 1979).

It will be evident that longitudinal data are essential if the temporal dependencies in micro-level behaviour are to be investigated in any analysis.

Omitted effects

With longitudinal data it is possible to achieve improved control for the myriad of variables which are inevitably omitted from any analysis. Indeed, this is sometimes claimed to be the main advantage of longitudinal data. In general terms, longitudinal data allow models to be constructed that are better able to take into account some of the complexities of the way in which people conduct their lives and of the influences on that process. An example may help to demonstrate this. Because of our limited ability to model human behaviour, there is always considerable heterogeneity in the response variable, even among people with the same characteristics on all the explanatory variables. Thus women with the same education, marital status and number of children will show considerable differences in their level of labour market participation. Clearly, there are other influences, which differ between these women, which have not been measured and which cannot therefore be taken into account in the model. Omitting these variables may lead to misleading results, particularly if the variables omitted are correlated with one of the explanatory variables. When this occurs the model will be misspecified. Using longitudinal data the effects of omitted variables can be explicitly accounted for in the model, thereby improving considerably the accuracy of the estimated effects of the explanatory variables. The ability to incorporate omitted effects is an important improvement in modelling sophistication.

One aspect of this general problem which is particularly important and which has received extensive attention in recent years is that inertial effects in behaviour tend to be systematically overestimated if the analysis does not include explicit control for omitted variables. Continuing our example of female labour force participation, women with a history of paid employment are more likely to be in work at a given time than women who do not have such a history, after taking into account other factors known to explain participation levels. In this case one would observe 'state dependency' between a woman's earlier work history and her current employment status. It may be postulated that women who are in work have been able to obtain child-care and otherwise to organize their lives around a paid job, and so there is an 'inertia' effect that operates to reinforce a woman in her current status. Conversely, a woman not in the labour force faces costs in a return to work. However, some of the observed state dependency may be a spurious consequence of residual heterogeneity with, in particular, more highly motivated women tending to remain in employment and less motivated women tending to remain out of the labour force.

Using a model which incorporated both residual (unobserved) heterogeneity and state dependency, Heckman (1979) showed that recent labour market experience does have a significant positive effect on one's current situation, but the effect of failing to include unobserved heterogeneity in the model increased the apparent impact of past work experience by a factor of 10. In the context of residential mobility, Davies and Pickles (1985) demonstrate that similarly misleading results can occur for duration dependence if there is no explicit representation of residual heterogeneity. They also show that cross-sectional analyses, where these effects cannot be incorporated into the model, can give misleading answers for some parameter estimates.

It is now possible to use statistical methods to model, and thereby disentangle, the various effects discussed above, with either retrospective or prospective longitudinal data. In the following section we review the process of statistical modelling, before moving on to examine the variety of types of data which contain a temporal dimension.

Statistical modelling

All the methods considered in this volume fall within the general inferential framework of statistical modelling. This is primarily a consequence of the complexity of longitudinal data. Statistical modelling is important because it enables researchers to make informed judgements about the systematic relationships in complex survey data. The problem is, of course, that empirical associations in survey data may be misleading without allowing for the effects of control variables, the sampling scheme used, and variation due to other, possibly unsuspected, features of the process of interest. This is precisely the issue that statistical modelling addresses by permitting many interrelationships to be considered simultaneously within a single analysis together with an error structure to represent unmeasured effects. The researcher is therefore able to distinguish systematic relationships from each other and from obscuring detail. Statistical modelling is also very attractive to social scientists because it makes explicit the role of substantive theory in the inferential process. Moreover, fitted models may be used for prediction, enabling researchers to provide at least tentative answers to the 'what if' questions that are so important in evaluating policy alternatives.

Statistical modelling consists of the sequence of procedures shown in Figure 1.1. At the first stage, a probability model is proposed as a description of the process of interest. This formulation will involve a number of assumptions but will be guided by substantive theoretical considerations.

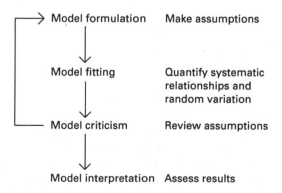

Figure 1.1 *Statistical modelling procedures*

It may even be possible to devise the probability model formally from theory. There is an example in Chapter 4 where Micklewright uses a theoretical latent variable specification in the derivation of a model of early school leaving. This should not be confused with the structural equation methods discussed by Bynner in Chapter 5; in this case, the latent variables appear in the model. Model formulation must also allow for the characteristics of the sampling scheme used in data collection. There will often be a response variable and a set of explanatory variables, and the type of measurement of the response variable, in particular, is likely to be an important factor in determining the probability model proposed. Thus, whereas a conventional linear regression model may be the obvious first choice if the response variable is continuous, a logistic, probit, or similar formulation may be suggested for a binary response variable. A variety of different response variable types occur in the following chapters.

At the second stage, the probability model is fitted to the observed data; the data are used to quantify the systematic relationships and random variation postulated by the model. This is achieved by estimating the unknown parameters of the model. With maximum likelihood estimation we ascribe to the parameters the values for which the observed outcomes are most likely to have occurred if the model is correct. Measures of the precision of these estimates (e.g. standard errors) will also be obtained.

At the model criticism stage, an assessment is made of the adequacy of the fitted model as a parsimonious representation of the observed process; some of the assumptions and simplifications made at the model formulation stage are put to the test. This may involve goodness-of-fit measures, analysis of residuals, and comparisons with simpler or more complex models. If the model is judged to be seriously flawed, the modeller may seek improvement by recycling through the sequence of procedures with a reformulated model. The model criticism stage receives comparatively little emphasis in this volume to avoid over-complicating the analyses which are intended to illustrate, rather than provide comprehensive examples of, the different methods discussed.

The model interpretation stage concludes the whole process with consideration given to the substantive significance of the results. Model interpretation methods are neglected in standard statistical texts but this tends to be the most interesting part of the exercise for the social scientist. Methods used in this volume include sample enumeration for assessing the impact of specific variables (Davies, Chapter 2) and graphical display of systematic relationships identified (Tuma, Chapter 7).

It will be evident from this description of the sequence of procedures that statistical modelling is a very general, coherent methodological approach which embraces what are often thought of as quite distinct methods including, for example, linear regression, log-linear modelling, and structural equation modelling. Indeed, a major advantage of statistical modelling is its emphasis upon the similarities rather than the differences between different methods and the analysis problems associated with different data. Some notable efforts have been made to standardize notation, terminology, and, perhaps most importantly, methods of conceptualizing the modelling task so that the researcher may focus less upon methodological questions about alternative techniques and more upon substantive questions about the characteristics of the process which generated the data (see, for example, McCullagh and Nelder, 1989; Aitkin et al., 1989). The software package GLIM (Francis et al. 1993) was, and remains, pioneering in this respect and is used in two of the chapters which follow.

However, the reader is warned that standardization has had little impact to date on the longitudinal analysis literature. The methods discussed in this volume therefore vary widely, not only in the specific research and data problems they address, but also in the terminology and notation used to describe their technical features. The main reasons for the diversity lie in the different genesis of the methods; for example, terminology and notation tend to vary between mainstream statistics, econometrics, and biostatistics and are often influenced by major areas of application in the past. In order to overcome the inevitable confusion that this causes, each chapter has an editors' introduction which tries to clarify any problems of terminology or notation used in the chapter and to provide an overview of the methods used and how they relate to other contributions.

All the data sources used in this volume have a temporal dimension, but in other respects they differ markedly. To clarify these differences, the following sections provide a classification of data types (summarized in Table 1.1), all of which may be classified as 'longitudinal'. For each type distinguished we discuss the ways in which the data may be collected, the research questions which the data may address and the statistical methods that may be appropriate. However, it is important to emphasize that there is no necessary one-to-one correspondence between the type of data and the method of data collection used.

Types of data and methods of modelling

Cross-sectional data, repeated across years, for different individuals or cases

Data structure Cross-sectional data are recorded at one point in time only (and should be distinguished from cross-sectional surveys which may also collect retrospective data). However, it is common for cross-sectional data to be collected in a succession of surveys with a new sample on each occasion. Where cross-sectional data are repeated over time with a high level of consistency between questions, sequences of measures may be created in *discrete* time and it is possible to incorporate a time trend into the analysis.

Recurrent government surveys often provide this kind of data structure. The British General Household Survey, the Family Expenditure Survey and the Labour Force Survey have all been carried out annually for many years and are used by several of the contributors to this book. Whilst the sampling unit is the household, information is recorded for all household members.

Table 1.1 *Data typologies*

GENERAL TYPOLOGY	
Cross-sectional data, repeated across time, for different individuals or cases:	
-micro-data at the individual level	Chapter 4
-macro-data, individuals aggregated across categories within tables	Chapter 3
Aggregate cross-sectional data, repeated across time, where each cross-section represents a single case	Chapter 9
Cross-sectional data repeated across years for the same individuals (or cases), e.g. panel data, cohort data measured in discrete time	Chapters 2, 5, 6, 8
Data recorded in continuous time, e.g. event history data	Chapters 2, 7
AGGREGATE VERSUS DISAGGREGATE	
Aggregate: time series, with a single aggregate measure at each time point	Chapter 9
Disaggregate:	
-same individuals at each time: panel or cohort	Chapters 2, 5, 6, 8
-different individuals at each time: cross-sectional	
-macro (grouped)	Chapter 3
-micro (individual)	Chapter 4
DISCRETE VERSUS CONTINUOUS TIME	
Discrete time: usually repeated surveys at fixed or varying intervals, may include retrospective data to fixed time point, e.g. one year ago, as well as current data; includes income, attitudes, employment	Chapters 2, 3, 4, 5, 6, 8
Continuous time: usually collected retrospectively but events must be dated; includes employment histories, births, deaths, housing histories	Chapters 2, 7

Because of their high level of consistency over time, their large and nationally representative samples, and the regularity of their data collection, these surveys may be very effective for studying trends over time. In the US, the General Social Survey, carried out by the National Opinion Research Center (NORC), provides a long and consistent record (Davis and Smith, 1992). Such data need not be confined to individuals or households; for example, repeated cross-sections of data may be collected where the sampling unit is firm, a school or a hospital.

There are two alternative ways in which this kind of data may be organized for analysis: (1) as micro-data at the individual level; or (2) as macro-data, where individuals (or cases) are aggregated across categories within tables. Each is discussed in turn.

Micro-data Cross-sectional, individual-level records, with the same variables but measured at one of several different time points, may be pooled to form a single data file. Each individual record includes a variable to represent time (usually year) of data collection. Although the population sampled (e.g. Great Britain) remains the same, a new sample is drawn at each time point.

Provided that the same variables are available for each time point and the method of sampling remains the same, it is straightforward to use pooled cross-sectional analysis at the individual level. By comparison with cross-sectional analysis for one time point only, this increases the sample size, thereby allowing analyses of small groups, and also injects a temporal dimension. For example, in assessing the reasons for early school leaving this method can incorporate the effect of rate of unemployment .which may have changed markedly over the relevant period. In Chapter 4, Micklewright estimates the way in which changing levels of unemployment (for which year represents a proxy) affect decisions over school leaving. Currently, pooled cross-sectional analyses are more widely used by economists than other social scientists, but there is probably no intrinsic reason why this should be the case.

Macro-data Alternatively, macro-level data may be used as multi-way tables. Individual-level data are grouped into the categories of interest, with year used as one of the tabulation variables. Whilst this type of data does not allow individual change over time to be modelled, it provides a relatively accessible way of incorporating a time dimension into otherwise cross-sectional data and thereby making inferences about trends, on the assumption that other things are equal.

Chapter 3 by Payne et al. shows how such data (with categorical variables) can be used to establish the way in which the labour market value of school qualifications has changed over time. Rather than making inferences from cross-sectional data, where rapidly changing labour market conditions may lead to misleading interpretations if results are based upon a one-year 'snapshot', the effect of such changes over time can be explicitly incorporated into the analysis. Similarly, the effect of declining class allegiance on voting behaviour can be modelled.

Where the response variable of interest is binary – which is often the case with categorical variables – then a logistic or probit model is commonly used to estimate the effect of the explanatory variables, continuous and/or categorical, on the probability of a given response occurring. Thus one may wish to model the effect of educational level, sex, age and year on the probability of being in paid work. In effect, the cases in each cell of this multi-way table are treated as a group of identical individuals, and there is no important methodological difference between this and micro-level analysis.

Where there is no assumption of causality, and so it is not appropriate to set up an equation with response and explanatory variables, log-linear modelling may be used to explore the relationships between categorical variables. An example is given in Chapter 3 where change in voting behaviour over time is modelled. The same formulation is also often used when a response variable has been defined which has more than two unordered categories. This is equivalent to a multinomial logistic model.

Aggregate cross-sectional data repeated over time Aggregate cross-sectional data represent summary information on a set of variables, collected on a number of different occasions for the same population. The data are typically collected as part of a time series and each time point represents a case. Thus data may be collected by government from administrative sources to represent the gross national product, the level of inflation, or unemployment for the country. Such data are widely used by economists to model time trends and to produce economic forecasts. Alternatively, data may be collected by business to record sales levels, for example an airline may record the number of passenger flights each month; or data may represent the level of support for a political party, with monthly recordings over many years. With this kind of data one of the usual aims is to model the temporal dependencies in the data and then to use this information to predict changes in the future. Data such as those collected by airlines may show strong seasonal effects, together with longer-term trends and periodicities both in the mean and in the degree of irregularity. Time-series data therefore present some complex and distinctive methodological challenges but, as data with similar characteristics are common in the physical and engineering sciences, many specialized statistical techniques and appropriate software are available. It is possible for social scientists to perform extremely sophisticated analyses of time-series data almost as a matter of routine, although, as emphasized in chapter 9, important questions remain about the relative merits of alternative formulations.

Figures on voting preference are often used by political scientists to gauge the way in which voting behaviour is affected by economic circumstances such as the buoyancy of the economy. In this book, Sanders and Ward (Chapter 9) use aggregate opinion poll data to model change in the voting intention of the electorate over time. With these time-series data they show the different ways in which the effect of an exogenous variable such as the 'Falklands factor' can be modelled – for example whether the effect of the war starts and ends abruptly or starts suddenly and ends gradually. However, as Sanders and Ward demonstrate, it is important not to be seduced by the apparent rigour of the methods available because the results obtained can be heavily dependent upon the assumptions that the modeller is prepared to make. An important feature of statistical modelling is the facility for model criticism, using goodness of fit, analysis of residuals, and other methods to review the appropriateness of the assumptions made. The basic problem with time-series analysis is that, with just one measure at each time point and with typically strong serial correlation (i.e. similar values for successive time points), there is comparatively little information in the data and there is limited scope for testing assumptions.

Cross-sectional data, repeated across years for the same individuals or cases

As before, this type of data is collected with reference to a particular point in time, but is repeated at intervals for the same individuals (or cases). For example, variables such as marital status, employment status or current income may be recorded at a number of times for the same respondents. These data are all recorded in *discrete time*: that is, they refer to one particular time point and all respondents are asked to record their condition or characteristics at that point.

In some cases such information can be recorded retrospectively: one might collect information on usual residence one year ago, as is asked in the British Census. The UK Labour Force Survey includes questions on employment and geographical location one year ago. Often, though, retrospective data are not appropriate for the research problem and repeated surveys of the same individual (or case) are necessary. In these circumstances the usual method of data collection is through panel or cohort surveys. In both cases, the length of the study may vary from a few weeks (for example, a panel study of shopping behaviour) to a lifetime. The interval between repeated sweeps may be regular (e.g. annual) or irregular depending upon both the nature of the research question and also pragmatic considerations like funding. The interval between sweeps may be chosen in relation to the speed of change in the response variable. Change may occur at different speeds at different stages of an individual's life, depending upon both developmental factors and also external factors. During adolescence attitudes may be expected to change and crystallize in response to external circumstances and the design of a study may capitalize on this by making repeated sweeps at quite short intervals (Banks et al., 1991). Thus a study would focus on one restricted age group (or cohort) followed over the period of the life course of most interest to the research (and thereby also maximizing the amount of variation in the response variable).

Cohort studies Cohort studies may begin at birth, as in the case of the three British birth cohort studies: the 1946 National Health and Development Survey (Wadsworth, 1987), the 1958 National Child Development Study (NCDS) (Davie et al., 1972; Fogelman, 1983) and the 1970 British Cohort Study (Butler et al., 1986). All three British birth cohort studies began as perinatal mortality studies with successive sweeps carried out pragmatically to meet a variety of external needs. For this reason the interval between sweeps tends to be irregular and often long, e.g. 10 years between the fourth and fifth sweeps of the NCDS. The NCDS contains income and attitude measures, although the intervals between sweeps are rather long for change in income or attitudes to be an explicit aim of analysis. More usually analysis focuses on an outcome measured in the most recent sweep – for example, occupation at age 33 – and explanatory variables from earlier sweeps are used to model the process which generates that outcome.

Cohort studies need not start at birth, but may begin at much later ages. A series of cohort studies funded by the Medical Research Council and based in the Medical Sociology Unit at Glasgow has sampled cohorts born in 1931, 1951 and 1971 in an area around Glasgow. The US National Longitudinal Study selected two cohorts of men and women aged 30–44 in 1967 and

24–37 in 1978 (Center for Human Resource Research, 1981). In this book, Plewis in Chapter 6 uses data on a cohort of pupils at the end of each of three years of primary schooling, whilst Bynner (Chapter 5) analyzes attitude data at three separate time points for a cohort of young people going through adolescence. In both these examples the data could not have been obtained retrospectively, and only by recording change over several time points is it possible to model *the process of change*. In Plewis's analysis it is change in educational attainment which is of interest, and in Bynner's it is change in attitudes of young people. In both the response variable is a score, recorded at interval level. These studies had a fixed time of a few years. Both identified groups of individuals of a particular age who were experiencing a life process which was the crucial concern of the research.

Panel data   Where data relate to successive intervals for a complete (or, at least, a wider) age distribution, they are often referred to as panel data. Panel data, however, may also be collected for other units such as firms and households.

Some cross-sectional repeated surveys contain a panel element. For example, the British Social Attitudes Survey (Jowell et al., 1992) is repeated annually with a different sample, but, *additionally*, it retains a small panel element where the survey is administered to the *same* individuals. This design enables work on response conditioning effects.

The US Panel Study of Income Dynamics commenced in 1968 with a sample of about 5,000 households and annual interviewing is continuing. A similar panel study began in Britain in 1991: the British Household Panel Study (Rose, 1991). A panel study, however, may collect not only panel data (data recorded for a fixed time point at successive intervals) but also data recorded in continuous time. This latter type of data is discussed in the following section. The precise timing of the first data collection point of a panel study may be fairly arbitrary and fixed to coincide with school terms, holiday periods, or other practical considerations. After the first sweep it is likely – though not inevitable – that further sweeps will be at equal intervals planned to facilitate comparison of the response variable. For example, to compare educational scores, it is appropriate to repeat data collection at the same point in each school year. Similarly, there is value in recording income at similar times of the year as there may often be seasonal variation. With these response variables there is no information available during the time between sweeps.

The OPCS Longitudinal Study (LS) of England and Wales represents a further example of repeated cross-sections of data for the same sample (SSRU, 1991). The LS links data for the same individuals from three successive decennial censuses – 1971, 1981 and 1991. Although these are, in effect, panel data the census is designed as a cross-sectional study and the linkage between a 1 per cent sample of individuals was a later enhancement. The tenure, occupation and marital status (for example) of individuals is recorded at 10-year intervals and therefore represents a snapshot at each time with no information at all about the intervening period. This lack of information about the period between censuses highlights one of the major shortcomings of panel data; it will be addressed in a later section on continuous time data.

Methods of analyzing panel data Panel data may be either categorical or continuous. In Chapters 5 and 6 Bynner and Plewis both use continuous response variables. Often, though, the response variable is categorical and may be represented as binary (e.g. employed or not employed) or multi-category (employed full-time; employed part-time; unemployed; out of the labour force).

Many methods used to analyze repeated measures data are extensions of conventional regression models. At the most basic, linear regression is used with a continuous response variable and the model is given a dynamic component by including measures from earlier periods as explanatory variables. Path analysis uses the causal ordering implicit in such a model to establish the strength of relationships between pathways. Where the response variable is binary, logistic or probit regression may be used; where the response variable is a count, a Poisson regression model may be appropriate; and correspondingly for other non-linear models.

However, repeated measures data violate an important assumption of conventional regression models because, in general, the responses of an individual at different points in time will not be independent of each other. This problem is now routinely overcome by including an additional, individual-specific error term (Chamberlain, 1984; Heckman and Singer, 1986), leading to a number of sophisticated models for panel and cohort data. These models are important because, by allowing explicitly for the intrinsic cluster structure of repeated measures data, they provide an analysis framework within which the effects of omitted variables may be assessed and controlled for, at least in so far as the omitted variables are time-invariant for each individual. As discussed above, this enables the rich potential of longitudinal data to be more fully exploited. Davies in Chapter 2 reports logistic regression analyses of the employment status of married women which illustrate the additional insight obtainable through using models with individual-specific error terms. Plewis in Chapter 6 adopts a similar approach in his linear regression analyses of pupil attainment in mathematics and reading, but there is an additional complication: with pupils grouped in classes and classes grouped in schools, the data already have a clustered, hierarchical structure before their longitudinal characteristics are considered.

Hierarchical data structures are common in educational research. Local education authorities may have quite different policies towards education. Within authorities, schools may differ greatly in the teaching approaches that they use, and, of course, individual teachers may have very different impacts upon the educational attainment of their pupils. More generally, there will often be geographical effects which might, for example, mean that there is clustering on particular characteristics within the local labour market which should be represented in the model. There have been major advances in recent years in multilevel modelling methods for analyzing hierarchical data. Plewis shows how these methods may be used to handle simultaneously both cross-sectional and longitudinal cluster structures.

In structural equation modelling, the analysis objectives are altogether more ambitious and the regression model seeks to represent the causal relationship between 'theoretical' or unobservable latent variables. Empirical progress is made possible by assuming that the latent variables are causally related to a set of observable indicator variables. This modelling approach recognizes that operationalizing theoretical variables is often highly problematic in the social sciences and seeks, in particular, to avoid the systematic underestimation of the correlation between theoretical variables which occurs if they are not measured reliably. It is an approach which has achieved particular favour in psychology. It is extremely flexible and permits far more complex causal models than path analysis; however, as a corollary, effective application is difficult without considerable guidance from substantive theory. With an illustrative analysis of the relationships between delinquency and social life, Bynner in Chapter 5 shows how structural equation modelling may be applied routinely to repeated measures data. Indeed, longitudinal data can simplify the model formulation by limiting the number of causal relationships which are possible.

In an earlier section, we emphasized that interest in longitudinal data analysis often focuses upon state dependence – the dependence of current behaviour upon earlier behaviour. Very often it is adequate just to include previous measures as explanatory variables in regression models. Davies in Chapter 2 provides an example of this approach, adding employment status in the previous period to a longitudinal model of the employment status of married women. It is argued that this provides a parsimonious representation of the stability over time (inertia) in employment histories. However, there is a quite distinct methodological literature concerned with modelling the temporal dependencies in a sequence of outcomes (or 'states'). These discrete-time Markov methods may be appropriate when an understanding of temporal dependence over time is the primary purpose of the analysis. They are reviewed by Langeheine and van de Pol in Chapter 8 and illustrated by applications to data on brand loyalty in purchasing behaviour and to self-assessed measures of work disability. This is a difficult chapter but it is important because it provides a unifying framework for the diverse and complex methodological approaches. Methods which are compared and contrasted in this chapter include both first-order (dependence upon immediately preceding outcome) and higher-order (dependence upon a number of preceding outcomes) Markov chains; heterogeneity with different groups having different patterns of temporal dependence; and latent Markov models in which changes are measured with error and which have evident similarities to structural equation modelling.

Data recorded in continuous time

All the data types discussed so far have been recorded with reference to fixed and predetermined time points. Sometimes, as with voting behaviour at successive elections, discrete time is an intrinsic feature of the process. More often, though, it is an artifact of the data collection method. Thus marital status or voting intention may be recorded at intervals over several years but there may be no information on any changes in the intervening period. Thus we would know that someone had changed from 'single' to 'married' between two sweeps of a survey but we would not know *when* the change occurred or, indeed, whether a number of changes were made between the two time points. Change in categorical variables such as marital state can be recorded much more fully than this. If all changes between marital states were recorded, one would be able to fill in the gaps between the sweeps of a survey. One could obtain an accurate record of the number of times someone had been married or divorced and also record the sequence of marital statuses – for example, whether marriage was followed by separation, then divorce. If, additionally, the date of each change is recorded then the duration in each state may be used in analyses.

It will therefore be evident that, when data are recorded in continuous time, the number and sequence of events *and* the durations between them can all be calculated. Additionally, the relationship of one event to another can be analysed: whether marriage comes before or after child-bearing; whether unemployment precedes or follows divorce. Such information is very powerful when one is concerned with understanding life-course processes and how they interrelate. In particular, it enables the researcher to investigate not only the factors affecting outcomes but also the factors which affect the timing of the outcomes.

Method of data collection   Data recorded in continuous time are often collected retrospectively. In recent years there has been much interest in recording life-course events, and techniques have been developed to collect complete work histories (often employment status and occupation for each month since entry to the labour market) and life-event histories (e.g. births, marriages, divorces) for random samples of the population. Housing histories and geographical mobility histories may also be collected.

Examples from Britain include the Women and Employment Survey – a cross-sectional survey with data collected at one point in time only (Martin and Roberts, 1984) but with work and life histories for each woman since leaving full-time education. The Social Change and Economic Life Initiative (Gallie, 1988), funded by the UK Economic and Social Research Council, collected very detailed retrospective data from over 6,000 respondents with a single interview in each case. This was particularly detailed in terms of jobs held and changes in conditions between jobs. European culture places great store on the dates of birth, death and marriage and these tend to be readily remembered by most people. Other events, such as a change of job or a change of home, may also be well remembered, although the exact dates may be harder to recall. While these data provide very rich material for analysis, they also give rise to a number of measurement issues.

Measurement issues   With retrospective data, decisions have to be made about the point at which data collection should begin. Data collection often begins part way through a process: for example, a longitudinal survey may begin with the current housing of the individual and record all changes from this point. However, because of temporal dependencies, modelling the process over the 'data window' will require information about prior circumstances (Pickles and Davies, 1989). Therefore, when recording data it is important to be aware of the value of recording the 'initial condition' for each event – for example the first job on leaving school, the duration in the current housing – rather than beginning data collection at a pre-defined time point, such as when the respondent was aged 21.

Tuma (Chapter 7) stresses the importance of adopting the appropriate temporal grid for each type of event. If 40 per cent of unemployment lasts less than one month, a considerable amount of information is lost if spells of unemployment of less than one month are not recorded. The problem is not just confined to underreporting but can introduce a variety of biases.

It is often hard to establish the precise timing of an event. Whilst births and deaths are fairly clear-cut, the timing of other events such as leaving home, separation and cohabitation may be much more gradual and much harder to define. Because the importance attached to dates is culturally specific, life and work history information is likely to be less accurate amongst people from cultures where precise dates have no great significance.

Methods of analyzing event data   Modelling event histories not only highlights the regularities in the way in which people live their lives but can also establish the effect of explanatory variables such as parents' social class, or level of education, on the process. The underlying process for event history data recorded in continuous time is typically conceptualized as a hazard model, where the event of interest, such as a birth or obtaining a job, represents the hazard and one is interested in modelling the 'survival' or 'failure' time until that event and the variables that affect the survival time. For example, hazard models can show how different cohorts of women vary in the age of first birth or the timing of second and subsequent births, and can examine the factors such as educational attainment which affect this (see Tuma, Chapter 7). Some of the terminology derives from the biomedical sciences where these methods have been used extensively and where many technical developments have originated or been evaluated (see, for example, Kalbfleisch and Prentice, 1980). The terminology has also been influenced by the use of these methods in reliability studies.

Typically, duration data are collected from living respondents and are therefore censored, in that events may continue to happen after the period for which data are collected. For example, people can go on moving house, changing jobs and changing their marital status until death. Another key characteristic is that explanatory variables are also likely to change values over time. Thus occupation may form an explanatory variable in modelling the risk of dying, but people change their occupations over time. The proportional hazards model, developed by Cox (1972), allows for hazard rates that change with time and also for time-varying explanatory variables. Tuma in Chapter 7 uses Cox's model to estimate the effects of explanatory variables on the hazard rate of first birth of German women.

In principle, hazard models are just non-linear regression models with duration as a response variable. The methodology looks different, and is invariably presented in a different way, partly because of the complexity of censoring and time-varying explanatory variables but also because interpretation is often facilitated by considering how the hazard rate (and sometimes the probability of survival) varies with duration.

Often in the analysis of continuous-time data both the durations between events and the sequence of event outcomes are important. For example, in analyzing residential histories we may be interested in the duration between moves and the housing tenure at each move. Researchers are sometimes tempted to study durations and outcome sequences separately in order to simplify analysis, using hazard models for the former and Markov models (as discussed in the section on recurrent measures) for the latter. There is a well-established tradition of adopting this pragmatic simplification in the consumer behaviour literature, with purchase timing analyzed separately from sequences of brand choice (see, for example, Massy et al., 1970). However, the timing of events may be related to the previous outcome; this is certainly the case for residential mobility, where move rates are quite different for owner-occupiers and renters. It is therefore preferable, in general, to include duration and event outcome data in a single, joint analysis. Markov renewal models provide an appropriate analysis framework and combine the main features of Markov and hazard models. But this takes us beyond the scope of an introductory volume.

Conclusion

We have sought in this chapter to provide a framework within which to locate the chapters which follow. We have tried to present the arguments which will persuade the reader of the necessity to make full use of the longitudinal data now becoming available and of the methods of statistical modelling that can be used.

In the rest of the book each chapter takes a particular type of data and provides an example of analysis which exploits the temporal dimension of those data. The level of statistical complexity varies between chapters and, to assist the non-specialist reader, each chapter has a short editors' introduction which highlights the key points being made in the chapter and explains any non-standard notation which might prove an obstacle to understanding. In some cases, the introduction also suggests sections of the chapter that can be omitted if the reader wishes simply to obtain an overview of the methods discussed.

References

Aitkin, M., Anderson, D., Francis, B. and Hinde, J. (1989) *Statistical Modelling in GLIM*. Milton Keynes: Open University Press.

Banks, M., Bates, I., Breakwell, G., Bynner, J., Emler, N., Jamieson, L. and Roberts, K. (1991) *Careers and Identities*. Milton Keynes: Open University.

Butler, N.R., Golding, J. and Howlett, B. (1986) *From Birth to Five: a Study of the Health and Behaviour of Britain's 5 Year Olds*. Oxford: Oxford University Press.

Center for Human Resource Research (1981) *The National Longitudinal Surveys Handbook*. Columbus: Ohio State University.

Chamberlain, G. (1984) 'Panel Data', in Z. Griliches and M.D. Intriligator (eds), *Handbook of Econometrics*, vol. II. Amsterdam: Elsevier. pp. 1247–318.

Cox, D.R. (1972) 'Regression models and life tables', *Journal of the Royal Statistical Society, Series B*, 34: 187–220.

Davie, R., Butler, N. and Goldstein, H. (1972) *From Birth to Seven*. London: Longman.

Davies, R.B. and Pickles, A.R. (1985) 'Longitudinal versus cross-sectional methods for behavioural research: a first round knockout', *Environment and Planning A*, 17: 1315–29.

Davis, J.A. and Smith, T.W. (1992) *The NORC General Social Survey: a User's Guide*. Newbury Park: Sage.

Dex, S. (1991) *The Reliability of Recall Data: a Literature Review*. Occasional papers of the ESRC Research Centre on Micro-social Change, Paper 6. Colchester: University of Essex.

Festinger, L. (1957) *A Theory of Cognitive Dissonance*. Stanford: Stanford University Press.

Fogelman, K. (1983) *Growing up in Great Britain: collected papers from the National Child Development Study*. London: Macmillan.

Francis, B.J., Green, M. and Payne, C. (1993) *The GLIM Manual*. Oxford: Oxford University Press.

Gallie, D. (1988) *The Social Change and Economic Life Initiative: an Overview*. Economic and Social Research Council, Working Paper 1.

Heckman, J.J. (1979) 'New evidence on the dynamics of female labor supply', in C.B. Lloyd, E. Andrews and C. Gilroy (eds), *Women in the Labor Market*. New York: Columbia University Press.

Heckman, J.J. and Singer, B. (1986) 'Econometric analysis of longitudinal data', in Z. Griliches and M.D. Intriligator (eds), *Handbook of Econometrics*, vol. III. Amsterdam: Elsevier. pp. 1689–786.

Huff, J.O. and Clark, W.A.V. (1978) 'Cumulative stress and cumulative inertia: a behavioural model of the decision to move', *Environment and Planning A*, 10: 1101–19.

Jowell, R., Brooks, L., Prior, G. and Taylor, B. (1992) *British Social Attitudes: the 9th Report*. Aldershot: Dartmouth.

Kalbfleisch, J.D. and Prentice, R.L. (1980) *The Statistical Analysis of Failure Time Data*. New York: Wiley.

Keifer, N. and Neumann, G. (1979) 'An empirical job search model with a test of the constant reservation wage hypothesis', *Journal of Political Economy*, 87: 89–108.

Martin, J. and Roberts, C. (1984) *Women and Employment: a Lifetime Perspective*. London: HMSO.

Massy, W.F., Montgomery, D.M. and Morrison, D.G. (1970) *Stochastic Models of Buying Behaviour*. Cambridge, MA: MIT Press.

McCullagh, P. and Nelder, J.A. (1989) *Generalized Linear Models*, 2nd edn. London: Chapman and Hall.

McGinnis, R. (1968) 'A stochastic model of social mobility', *American Sociological Review*, 23: 712–22.

Morgenstern, R.D. and Barrett, N.S. (1974) 'The retrospective bias in unemployment reporting by sex, race and age', *Journal of the American Statistical Association*, vol. 69: 355–7.

Pickles, A.R. and Davies, R.B. (1989) 'Inferences from cross-sectional and longitudinal data for dynamic behavioural processes' in J. Hauer, W. Timmermans and N. Wrigley (eds), *Contemporary Development in Quantitative Geography*. Dordrecht: D. Reidel. pp. 81–104.

Rose, D. (1991) *Micro-social Change in Britain: an Outline of the Role and Objectives of the British Household Panel Study*, Working Papers of the ESRC Research Centre on Micro-social Change, Paper 1. Colchester: University of Essex.

Short, J.R. (1978) 'Residential mobility', *Progress in Human Geography*, 2: 419–47.

SSRU (1991) *The OPCS Longitudinal Study User Manual*. London: Social Statistics Research Unit, City University.

Wadsworth, M.E.J. (1987) 'Follow-up of the first national birth cohort: findings from the Medical Research Council National Survey of Health and Development', *Paediatric and Perinatal Epidemiology*, 1: 95–117.

2

From Cross-Sectional to Longitudinal Analysis

Richard B. Davies

Paradoxically, cross-sectional analysis provides the main focus of this chapter. This stems from our confident belief that most social scientists courageous enough to confront the complexities of longitudinal data analysis will have already accumulated some experience of cross-sectional analysis. Cross-sectional analysis is consequently a sensible starting point for developing the motivation required to tackle the generally unfamiliar and admittedly often difficult statistical problems presented by longitudinal data.

In this context, a glib claim that longitudinal data analysis is important because it permits insights into the processes of change is inadequate and certainly fails to convince many social science researchers who are concerned with substantive rather than methodological challenges. Cross-sectional analyses, they may argue, are not necessarily uninformative about the dynamics of social change because historical information often collected in cross-sectional surveys is readily incorporated. Questions about place of residence one or more years earlier are common in population censuses and permit comparison between the characteristics of migrants and non-migrants; data on length of unemployment are usually obtained in cross-sectional surveys of the unemployed and may be used as an explanatory variable in studying attitudes, health, or motivation; and even just birth dates of children provide a demographic record which may be used in a cross-sectional study of the employment status of married women.

To develop the necessary motivation, it is therefore appropriate to consider in more detail the limitations of cross-sectional analysis, and this is the first objective of this chapter. We do not attempt a comprehensive assessment of the limitations; not only would this require more space than is available in a single chapter, but it could also defeat its own purpose with the detail tending to obscure the main issues. Our preference is to explain some of the more important limitations which arise in the context of a specific cross-sectional analysis. Hopefully, this practical, empirically based approach makes it easier to understand the relevance of the issues arising and, in helping to convince the reader, more than compensates for the incomplete coverage of the review.

The second objective is to promote positive motivation by demonstrating how some of the limitations of cross-sectional analysis may be overcome in longitudinal studies. The illustrations used are developed from the empirical example and are presented without full technical detail. Our intention is to provide an hors-d'oeuvre for the feast which follows, giving the reader some flavour of the scope and potential of longitudinal data analysis but concentrating on stimulating rather than satisfying a hopefully healthy appetite.

Empirical example: the employment status of married women

In this section we outline a cross-sectional study of the employment status of married women. The data are from a household survey[1] undertaken during the summer of 1986 in Rochdale, England, and cover 621 marriage partnerships with both partners in the age range from 20 to 59, inclusive. The empirical analysis is concerned with identifying and quantifying the household factors which influence whether or not the wife is in paid employment. Asian households are excluded from the study because of the quite different factors which appear to be involved. In the original study (Davies et al., 1992), there was particular interest in the effects of the husband's unemployment and we will return to this issue in a later section.

Although inevitably constrained by available data, the selection of other variables for inclusion in the analysis is strongly influenced by previous discussions in the literature. We do not attempt any detailed justification here and refer the interested reader to the illuminating discussions elsewhere, particularly Joseph (1983) and Joshi (1984). However, it should be noted that the estimated potential wage rate is not included as an explanatory variable. This is an essential component of the orthodox labour supply function analysis but it is also a serious source of statistical problems. It is assumed that qualifications are a proxy for earning potential as well as ease of obtaining a job and 'taste for market work' (McNabb, 1977).

As the response variable is binary with a wife either in employment or not, logistic analysis is used to model the effects of the various household characteristics on employment status. A theoretical derivation of this model is possible using a random utility approach as postulated, for example, by Zabalza (1982). However, it may give a misleadingly rigid theoretical context for the analysis undertaken. The logistic regression model provides a general representation of the relationship between the explanatory variables and the wife's employment status and could be consistent with any number of theoretical perspectives. The results of estimating the parameters of a very simple logistic regression model[2] are shown in Table 2.1. A careful analyst may wish to investigate a more sophisticated formulation including, for example, interaction terms. But these results serve our purpose in quantifying the main

Table 2.1   *Logistic model of wife's employment status*

	Parameter estimate	Standard error	p-value
Constant term	−1.50	1.64	0.36
Husband unemployed[1]	−1.84	0.39	<0.00001
Wife's age	0.27	0.09	0.003
Wife's age squared $\times 10^{-2}$	−0.40	0.11	<0.001
Child less than 5 years old[1]	−0.93	0.31	0.003
Child less than 13 years old[1]	−0.71	0.33	0.033
Family size	−0.37	0.12	0.002
Other household member working[1]	0.50	0.31	0.11
Wife's highest qualification:[2]			
Higher education	1.15	0.49	0.02
Other prof./higher tech.	1.14	0.84	0.18
6th form and equiv.	0.33	0.26	0.21
5th form and equiv.	0.37	0.37	0.32
Husband's highest qualification:[2]			
Higher education	−0.70	0.39	0.07
Other prof./higher tech.	0.42	0.44	0.34
6th form and equiv.	−0.01	0.24	0.96
5th form and equiv.	−0.44	0.43	0.31

[1] Dummy variable.
[2] Block of dummy variables.

relationships of interest and we conclude this section with a brief interpretation of the parameter estimates obtained.

With the parameter estimate for husband's unemployment negative and equal to five times its standard error, there is a clear indication that wives with unemployed husbands are less likely to work than wives with employed husbands. The demographic variables, with the exception of 'other household member working', are also all significant at well in excess of the 5 per cent level, and the parameter estimates have the expected signs. There is evidence that women are less likely to work when they have pre-teenage children and, unsurprisingly, this effect is substantially larger when a child is of pre-school age (note that the total effect for a child less than 5 years old is given by the sum of the parameters for the two children dummy variables; the child is both less than 5 and less than 13). Moreover, the larger the family, the less likely the wife is to work.

The results for the educational qualification variables provide a less clear picture. However, the one parameter significant at the 5 per cent level is consistent with the most highly qualified wives being more likely to work. Age is included in the model as a quadratic: that is, both age and age squared appear as explanatory variables. To aid interpretation, the estimated relationship between age and employment probability is plotted in Figure 2.1. It will be noted that the quadratic formulation permits a non-monotonic

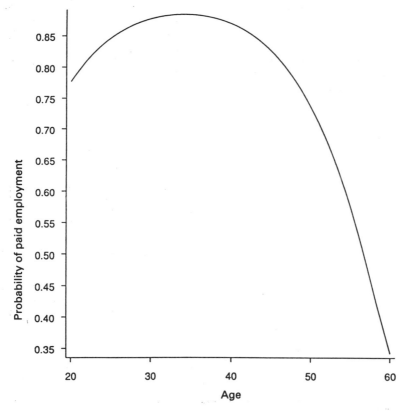

Figure 2.1 *Age effects*

relationship between age and employment probability, with employment probability increasing to a maximum at age 34 and then declining. Apart from family size, assumed to be three, all the other variables were set to zero in constructing this figure, which therefore refers to wives in the reference group for each dummy variable. They will, for example, have no child under 13 years of age and have no formal educational qualifications. Nevertheless, without interaction terms in the model, the general shape of the plot would be the same for wives with other characteristics; the probability of being in paid employment would just be consistently higher or lower, depending upon the other explanatory variables.

It is emphasized that the relationship in Figure 2.1 between employment and age is defined *ceteris paribus*. The estimated trajectories of specific women will move between higher and lower curves depending upon changes in their characteristics over time. In particular, mothers will have greatly reduced employment probabilities for a period following their first child. This accounts for the quite different, bimodal, distribution obtained when the proportion of women working is plotted against age with no controls (see, for example, Martin and Roberts, 1984: 118).

Ageing and cohort effects

Perhaps the best-known limitation of cross-sectional analysis is that ageing and cohort effects are indistinguishable. Davies (1987) gives the example of a survey of car reliability based upon owners' experience over the previous twelve months. Results for a specific model in 1990 may be as follows:

Age of car in years	1	2	3	4	5
Average number of days off the road	4	3	15	16	18

One possibility is that these figures show how reliability changes as a car becomes older and, in particular, the decline in reliability from the second to the third year would indicate a premature ageing effect of some severity. Table 2.2(a) provides hypothetical reliability histories which are consistent with this interpretation. It will be noted that, since the model was introduced in 1986, it has averaged 3 or 4 days off the road in each of the first two years of use but has appreciably poorer reliability when older. However, the survey data are cross-sectional and the reliability figures for each age category are based upon cars manufactured in different years. There is therefore a plausible alternative explanation for the drop in reliability after the second year: it could be due to some of the defects responsible for poor reliability having been successfully eliminated in more recently manufactured cars. In this interpretation, the observed figures are due to cohort rather than ageing effects, as illustrated by the hypothetical reliability histories in Table 2.2(b). The reliability of each cohort of cars does not decline with age in this table but the cars manufactured in the first three years of production, the 1986, 1987, and 1988 cohorts, have consistently poorer reliability than those manufactured subsequently.

Table 2.2　*Hypothetical car reliability histories: average number of days off the road*

(a) Ageing effects dominate

Age of car	1986	1987	Year 1988	1989	1990
5					18
4				15	16
3			17	14	15
2		3	4	4	3
1	4	3	3	3	4

(b) Cohort effects dominate

Age of car	1986	1987	Year 1988	1989	1990	
5					18	1986 cohort
4				15	16	1987 cohort
3			16	17	15	1988 cohort
2		14	18	15	3	1989 cohort
1	17	15	16	4	4	1990 cohort

These two explanations have very different implications for the potential purchaser who would be well advised not to purchase this model if the ageing effect is present. On the other hand, the cohort explanation would indicate that 'teething troubles' have been ironed out and that the model may be an attractive proposition. The important point is that the cross-sectional data are completely uninformative as to which, or what combination, of the explanations is correct. The equivalent social science research situation is being unable to adduce evidence from cross-sectional studies to distinguish between theories suggesting age and cohort effects. The employment status analysis provides a simple example.

Returning to the summary of age effects in Figure 2.1, it is evident that the probability of paid employment declines steeply from middle age onwards. Just as the car reliability results could arise from reliability declining with age, so this pattern may reflect a genuine age effect. Perhaps some wives choose to withdraw from the labour force well before retirement age as financial pressures ease at this stage in the life cycle. Another possibility is that they find it progressively more difficult to obtain employment because of age discrimination by employers. Both mechanisms could generate the decline in employment probabilities shown in Figure 2.1. However, the alternative explanation of the observed pattern as due to cohort effects is also entirely plausible. Perhaps the older wives were inhibited in seeking employment opportunities by attitudes and expectations with respect to paid work which pre-date the major growth in female employment since the 1960s. They may therefore have had low levels of labour force participation throughout their married lives, just as the older cars may have had low reliability since they were manufactured. If this explanation is correct, the decline in employment after middle age could be quite spurious.

Detailed retrospective work and life history data were collected on both husband and wife for 139 of the Rochdale marriage partnerships. The hypothetical car reliability histories in Table 2.2 have demonstrated how longitudinal data may be used to distinguish between ageing and cohort effects and it would be straightforward to construct a similar table for the wives' employment status. However, this approach would have two defects. First, the data would have to be grouped into age ranges with no guarantee that a satisfactory compromise is possible between a coarse grouping to ensure adequate numbers contributing to the 'proportion employed' calculation in each cell of the table, and a fine grouping to reveal possibly complex ageing and cohort effects. Second, there could be no control for the variety of explanatory variables included in the cross-sectional analysis. The important lesson to be drawn from Table 2.2 for more sophisticated analysis is that the two explanatory variables age and calendar time are sufficient to distinguish ageing and cohort effects. Consequently, the defects of the cross-tabulation method may be avoided by the simple expediency of including age and calendar time as explanatory variables in the statistical modelling of longitudinal data.

This approach is illustrated in Figures 2.2 and 2.3 for the Rochdale data.

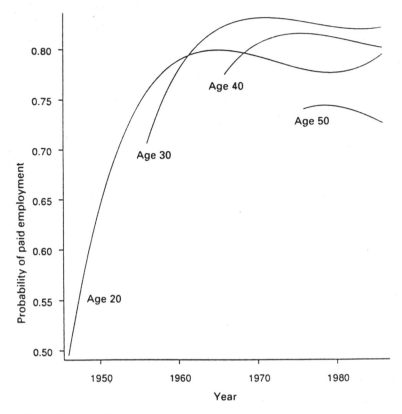

Figure 2.2   *Age-specific variation over time*

The calibrated model is a direct extension of the logistic model used for the cross-sectional analysis and includes a similar set of explanatory variables. Instead of a single outcome, whether or not the wife is in paid employment at the time of the survey in 1986, each partnership contributes a succession of monthly employment status outcomes from marriage to 1986. Technically, this is a 'pooled cross-sectional' analysis (Allison, 1982) because each month's data on a partnership are treated as if they were a separate case. Third-order polynomials with interaction terms are used for the age and time variables; statistical tests indicated that this level of complexity was necessary to adequately characterize the age and cohort variations.

Figure 2.2 shows how the probability of paid employment is estimated to vary over time for specific ages. The plotted lines have been calculated on a similar basis to Figure 2.1 with, in particular, the dummy explanatory variables in Table 2.1 all set to zero (for example, no child under 5). The lines have only been plotted over the age/year ranges for which data were available in this retrospective study. They are equivalent to reading across the rows in Table 2.2 with a different line for each age category, but it is emphasized that the analysis includes control for a number of other variables. Two quite different phases in ageing and cohort effects are suggested by the results. Up to the middle 1960s, there is strong evidence of cohort effects with, for example, employment probabilities for 20-year-old wives increasing from about 0.5 prior to 1950 up to nearly 0.8 by 1965. In more recent years, the age-specific plots are fairly flat, indicating that the importance of cohort effects has been diminishing.

Figure 2.3 tends to support these conclusions. The plotted lines in this figure follow the estimated employment trajectories of individual cohorts and are equivalent to reading along the diagonals of Table 2.2. The 1936, 1946, and 1956 birth cohorts are remarkably similar in their employment status histories. Each displays clear age effects with probability of paid employment increasing to a maximum in the mid-30s and then declining. However, these age effects are mostly within a fairly narrow band. The 1926 birth cohort has a distinctly lower trajectory although the discrepancy with later cohorts does appear to decrease over time. For example, at age 20 the employment probability is about 0.25 lower than that of the 1936 cohort at age 20. By age 40, the gap is reduced to 0.05.

Earlier, we discussed the possible ageing and cohort explanations for the cross-sectional results of Figure 2.1. The longitudinal evidence suggests that

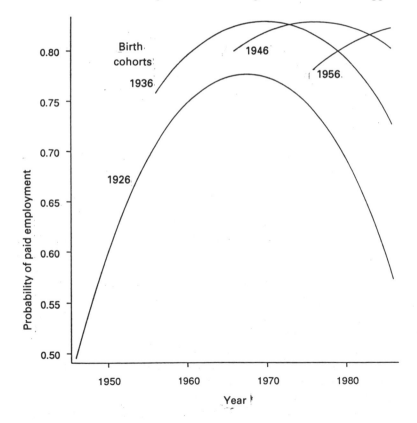

Figure 2.3   *Cohort effects*

both effects are compounded in the observed cross-sectional relationship. The inverted U shape of the relationship between age and employment probability appears to reflect a genuine ageing effect. However, the decline in employment probability after middle age has probably been exaggerated by the cohort effect of lower employment participation by the older wives in the sample.

Direction of causality

Doubts about the direction of causality are common in social science research and, in these circumstances, cross-sectional data are unable to resolve the ambiguity in correlations or other measures of association. Consider, for example, the relationship between unemployment and health mentioned at the beginning of this chapter. There is unequivocal cross-sectional evidence that, overall, the unemployed have poorer physical health than the employed, but this is consistent both with ill-health leading to unemployment and with unemployment leading to ill-health. The basic problem is well known. However, distinguishing empirically between such alternative directions of causality presents more insidious problems than is sometimes appreciated. We would emphasize, in particular, that the 'duration in current state' data often collected in cross-sectional studies are not sufficient to overcome these problems.

This is readily illustrated. Knowing how long each person has been unemployed, we may examine the relationship between level of health and length of unemployment. Typically this will be a negative relationship with general levels of health lower for those who have been unemployed for longer periods. Such a result is obviously consistent with unemployment causing ill-health. Less obviously, it is also consistent with the reverse causality. If ill-health causes unemployment, then those with comparatively modest levels of ill-health will tend to recover relatively quickly and return to employment. Conversely, those with more severe ill-health are likely to remain unemployed for a long time. Thus, with increasing duration of unemployment, those with less severe ill-health will be progressively under-represented while those with more chronic conditions will be progressively over-represented. This 'sample selection bias' could therefore explain the cross-sectional picture of declining health with duration of unemployment.

The logistic regression model used for the analysis of wives' employment status does not permit any ambiguity about the direction of causality: any causality is assumed to run from the explanatory variables to the binary employment status outcome. If this assumption is untenable, then the model is misspecified and the results are impossible to interpret. Educational qualifications generally pre-date employment histories and any causality must be from education to employment. Age is clearly exogenous. But the situation is less clear-cut for some of the other explanatory variables. Causality running from husband's unemployment to wife's economic status implies that the male is the primary wage-earner with the wife having a subordinate and secondary role. This assumption has some empirical justification (Martin and Roberts, 1984) but is far from being a universal rule. Moreover, by including family size in the model and dummy variables for the presence of young children, it is assumed that causality runs from children to mother's employment status. This is a common assumption in sociology and economics, but it is also quite feasible that absence of work opportunities encourages women to start families and reduce birth intervals, suggesting that there may be an element of reciprocity in the relationship.

By definition, a model is a simplification of reality, and a degree of pragmatism in model specification is unavoidable if the social scientist is to make any progress. It is our judgement that the doubts about directions of causality in this particular analysis fall within reasonable pragmatic bounds. Others may disagree. The important point is that, although we do not consider it appropriate to pursue the issue in the context of the empirical study in this chapter, there are longitudinal data analysis methods which researchers may use to address questions about directions of causality. One approach is discussed in Chapter 5.

Omitted explanatory variables

In researching any causal relationship we must, of course, be alert to the fact that empirical associations may be spurious, arising from the dependence of both outcomes upon the same explanatory variable, or set of variables. Randomization methods are used routinely and very effectively to overcome this problem in control experiments. Drug trials provide an important example. However, apart from the notable exception of those working in experimental psychology, few social scientists are in a position to perform control experiments; empirical research has to be based upon observational data. Using observational data to investigate whether one outcome is dependent upon another requires the full burden of control to be assumed by the statistical analysis methodology. The simple textbook will suggest disaggregation by the control variables; the more advanced textbook will suggest incorporating the control variables within a formal statistical modelling approach. But whatever method is adopted to remove the spurious effects of mutual dependence upon control variables, an ultimate problem remains: what about the spurious association due to variables not included in the analysis and whose importance may not even have been suspected by the researcher?

In the original Rochdale analysis of wives' employment status, there was particular interest in measuring the extent to which husbands' unemployment *per se* affects whether or not their wives work. It is a well-replicated result in Britain (e.g. Greenhalgh, 1980; Layard et al., 1980; Martin and Roberts, 1984) that there is an inverse relationship between husbands' unemployment and the labour force participation of married women; the wives of unemployed men are less likely to have paid work than the wives of employed men. The disincentive effect of the unemployment/social benefit system provides a causal explanation for this relationship[3] (see, for example, Dilnot and Kell, 1987). On the other hand, the observed relationship could, at least in part, be due to failure to fully control for appropriate household and labour market characteristics. Husbands and wives may tend to have similar attitudes towards work because of shared experiences and similarities in their social and economic background. Moreover, in areas where labour demand is high, male unemployment will tend to be low and married women will be drawn into the labour market by job opportunities and higher wages; conversely, where labour demand is low, male unemployment will be high and married women will be discouraged by low wages and difficulties in obtaining a job.

With the data confined to a single labour market area, the Rochdale analysis avoided any spurious relationships due to variations between labour markets. The logistic regression modelling was an attempt to control for household characteristics in order to isolate the disincentive effect of the unemployment/social benefit system.

Cross-tabulation of the Rochdale data gives:

Observed frequencies

		Wife in paid employment		
		Yes	No	Total
Husband unemployed	Yes	13 (28%)	33 (72%)	46 (100%)
	No	380 (73%)	142 (27%)	522 (100%)

It is not necessary to carry out a hypothesis test to see that these data display the expected relationship between husband's unemployment and wife's economic status. Only 28 per cent of wives with unemployed husbands are in paid employment compared with 73 per cent of wives with husbands at work. The difference between these two figures, in this case 45 per cent, is a useful measure of the 'employment shortfall' of women with unemployed husbands. It shows the percentage of such women who are not in paid employment but would be if their employment behaviour was the same as other married women.

In discussing the logistic regression results, we have already seen that the effect of husbands' unemployment is not eliminated by controlling for a variety of household characteristics. Further insight is provided by using a sample enumeration method to estimate the combined effect of the control variables. The calibrated model is applied to each wife with an unemployed husband but the dummy variable for husbands' unemployment is set to zero. This gives the estimated probability of each wife working if her husband were not in fact unemployed, and controlling for the other variables in the model. Summing these probabilities allows us to construct an 'expected' frequency table, having eliminated any direct consequences of husbands' unemployment:[4]

Expected frequencies

| | | Wife in paid employment | | |
		Yes	No	Total
Husband unemployed	Yes	25.2 (55%)	20.8 (45%)	46 (100%)
	No	380.0 (73%)	142.0 (27%)	522 (100%)

The lower row is unchanged from the observed table because the husbands are in employment. In the upper row, the percentage of wives working has increased from 28 to 55 per cent, indicating that the control variables have contributed substantially to the observed employment shortfall of 45 per cent. More precisely, 18 percentage points of the shortfall is estimated to be due to control variables, leaving a net shortfall of 27 per cent as a direct consequence of husbands' unemployment. These results are summarized in the first two rows of Table 2.3.

What may we therefore conclude about the true effect of husbands' unemployment? The 27 per cent net shortfall is likely to be an overestimate because, as emphasized earlier in this section, it is inevitable that some relevant control variables have not been included in the analysis and that others will have been operationalized inadequately. For example, the educational qualifications variables were included as proxies for a number of factors and there could be some concern over their limited performance as measured by statistical significance. Strictly speaking, the net shortfall could disappear completely if we were able to include an improved set of control variables in the model; we cannot even conclude that there is a causal relationship,

Table 2.3 *Net employment shortfalls for longitudinal models*

Model	Category	Net employment shortfall (%)
Cross-sectional: no explanatory variables	Wives with unemployed husbands	45.0
Cross-sectional: with explanatory variables	Wives with unemployed husbands	27.0
Longitudinal: with explanatory variables and control for omitted variables	Wives with unemployed husbands	21.5
Longitudinal: with explanatory variables, Markov effect, and control for omitted variables	Wives with unemployed husbands	20.0
	Wives with working husbands	0.8
	All wives	3.1

Number of unemployed husbands in the sample   33
Number of working husbands in the sample   241

let alone quantify it. On the other hand, the control variables incorporated our theoretical knowledge of the main factors likely to be important and yet reduced the observed employment shortfall by less than half; a further reduction of this magnitude due to omitted variables (giving a net shortfall of 9 per cent) is therefore implausible. A more pragmatic conclusion would be that the results provide strong evidence of a causal effect, with the wives' employment shortfall attributable to husbands' unemployment *per se* being less than 27 per cent but probably exceeding 9 per cent. This is clearly less rigorous and more imprecise than one would wish and the question arises as to whether longitudinal data analysis can do better.

The answer is, unequivocally: 'yes!' Indeed, facilitating control for omitted variables is often given as one of the main benefits of longitudinal analysis of micro-level data (e.g. Solon, 1989). The complex methodological issues that arise are beyond the scope of this volume; the interested reader is referred to reviews by Chamberlain (1985) and Heckman and Singer (1985). But the vital feature which makes longitudinal data second best to control experiments is readily understood: inference may be based not only upon variation *between* cases, as in cross-sectional analysis, but also upon variation *within* cases. Thus, using longitudinal data, inference about the effects of husbands' unemployment may take into account the extent to which wives withdraw from paid work after their husbands become unemployed and return when their husbands obtain employment. Longitudinal analysis of the Rochdale data suggests that the true employment shortfall is of the order of 21.5 per cent.

Micro-level dynamics

Some important features of the micro-level dynamics of behaviour are highlighted by problems encountered in transportation planning. For many years, transportation planners have used cross-sectional analyses of the travel-to-work choice between public and private transport ('modal choice') to forecast the effect of policy changes, such as fare increases or shorter waiting times due to a more frequent service. Experience has shown that there is a tendency for these analyses to over-predict change; actual response to changes in policy variables is generally less than the fitted models suggest. In other words, the cross-sectional analyses appear to consistently overestimate the importance of the explanatory variables. The discussion of the previous section anticipates one explanation for this phenomenon, namely that the estimated relationships between policy variables and modal choice are inflated by failure to control fully for other factors. But this is only part of the problem; the over-prediction also arises because cross-sectional analyses cannot characterize the inertial characteristics of behaviour.

Consider individual travel-to-work behaviour over time. Commuters do not regularly reassess the situation and make new modal choice decisions irrespective of their previous practice. On the contrary, once a routine is established, there may be little inclination to consider alternatives. Moreover, other members of the family may adapt their behaviour to the routine, further reducing the chance of subsequent change. Thus, although modal choice may have been made originally after an assessment of the relative merits of public and private transport, fairly dramatic policy changes will now be required to induce a change of behaviour. The forecasting inaccuracy arises because the cross-sectional analyses are not based upon the evolving circumstances which underlie current behaviour; they are concerned with how well explanatory variables such as travel time and travel costs 'explain' the current outcome of those evolving circumstances. Consequently, the results tend to summarize the cumulative influences of explanatory variables in producing the current travel-to-work pattern rather than their actual current influence, attenuated by inertia.

These issues are of general concern for two reasons. First, there are serious implications not just for prediction but also for model interpretation. The basic problem is that it is often unclear how 'cumulative influences' should be interpreted when there is no information about the historical process within which they have operated. Second, the issues are endemic in social research because positive temporal dependence, or inertia, is to be expected of most social behaviour. For example, the theory of cognitive dissonance asserts that, after choosing between alternatives, individuals will align their attitudes to the choice made, upgrading the satisfaction with both positive and negative attributes of the chosen alternative and downgrading those of the rejected alternatives. Becker argues that constraints induce consistency over time: 'What happens is that the individual, as a consequence of actions he has taken in the past or the operation of various institutional routines, finds he must adhere to certain lines of behaviour, because many other activities than the one he is immediately engaged in will be adversely affected if he does not' (1963: 27). Indeed, the empirical evidence together with the logic of ties becoming stronger with the passage of time prompted McGinnis (1968: 716) to propose inertia as an axiom of social behaviour: 'The probability of remaining in any state of nature increases as a strict monotone function of duration of prior residence in that state.'

A priori, a married woman's employment status will be governed by a number of inertial influences. First and foremost in the context of the Rochdale analysis, it could be anticipated that whether or not she is in paid employment in any month is not independent of whether or not she was working in the previous month. This is confirmed by including a Markov component in the longitudinal analysis to provide a parsimonious representation of employment status inertia. The component is simply a dummy variable, taking the value one if the wife was in paid employment during the previous month, and zero otherwise. The result is a massive increase in the log-likelihood;[5] dependence upon previous employment status greatly improves the fit of the model. This is exemplified by the estimated employment probabilities: a 40-year-old wife with the reference category characteristics in 1986 has a 0.992 probability of being in paid employment if she was working in the previous month and a 0.036 probability if she was not working.

The main relationship of interest, that between husbands' unemployment and wives' employment status, is also likely to be subject to inertial effects. Wives who have been working for some time may be less affected in general than wives with shorter spells of employment; the impact of a husband's unemployment may depend upon the wife's previous employment status, with a working wife reluctant to relinquish a job to which return could be difficult but with a non-working wife less reluctant to postpone plans to enter the labour market; and there may be delays both in reacting to the husband's unemployment and in responding to his return to work. All these micro-level dynamics are testable hypotheses within a longitudinal analysis, but our concern in this section is to illustrate how such inertial features constrain interpretation of cross-sectional results even in the unlikely event that control variables are fully effective.

The interpretation of the husbands' unemployment effect was based upon an estimated net employment shortfall of their wives. This was defined as the additional percentage of the wives of unemployed husbands who would be in paid employment if they behaved exactly the same as the wives of working husbands, *ceteris paribus*. It is clearly not a prediction of the type attempted by transportation planners; there is no suggestion that the net shortfall would disappear immediately after removing the social security disincentives. One may be tempted to suggest that it would disappear over time, although a cross-sectional analysis provides no clues as to how long it would take to achieve a new equilibrium. However, any such prediction would be a quite separate issue to that of interpretation. The interpretive significance of the net employment shortfall is as a measure of the accumulated impact of the social security disincentives. Instead of predicting into the future, the concern is with rewriting history and using the model to estimate what the current pattern would be if there had been no disincentives.

It will be evident that there is a fundamental logical flaw in this type of interpretation when the explanatory variable of interest is not time-constant: the full effect of the explanatory variable is represented by its current value whereas, with inertia, previous values will also have an impact. The consequences of this logical flaw will depend upon the implementation of the approach. In this study, the basic problem is that only the wives of currently unemployed men are assumed to be affected by their husbands' unemployment, although the reality of inertia is that the wives of previously unemployed men may also be affected, perhaps because they find it difficult to re-enter the labour market or because their motivation has been reduced by the length of time they have spent without paid work. This invalidates the explicit comparison in the shortfall definition between the disadvantaged wives of unemployed men and the unaffected wives of wage-earning husbands. It also suggests that, by focusing upon the wives of unemployed men, we have an incomplete assessment of the impact of the social security disincentives.

Table 2.3 provides some empirical evidence on the order of magnitude of the resulting errors. The shortfall figures given in the lower part of this table were obtained from the Markov model and therefore include a simple allowance for inertial effects. The 20 per cent employment shortfall for the wives of unemployed men differs only marginally from the figure of 21.5 per cent without the Markov effect. This difference is, in fact, within reasonable sampling variation. The shortfall for the wives of working husbands is estimated at 0.8 per cent: that is, less than 1 per cent of these wives appear to be without paid work as an enduring consequence of their husbands' earlier unemployment. At this level of description, the Markov analysis therefore indicates that inertial effects are quite modest. On the other hand, if these results are aggregated to estimate the total proportion of married women affected by the social security disincentives, the inertial effects are more pronounced. The 0.8 per cent of wives with working husbands corresponds to 0.7 per cent of all wives, while the 20 per cent of wives with unemployed husbands corresponds to 2.4 per cent of all wives. Thus it is estimated that overall 3.1 per cent of wives are not in paid work as a direct result of their husbands' unemployment and that inertial effects account for nearly one-quarter of this total.

Cross-sectional analyses with retrospective questions

In the previous section, we contrasted the snapshot picture provided by cross-sectional analysis with the inference about micro-level dynamics possible from longitudinal data. It is readily seen that strictly cross-sectional data are uninformative about the dynamics of change. Consider, for example, the 40-year-old wives shown in Figure 2.1 as having an estimated 0.85 probability of being in paid work. At one extreme, this is consistent with 85 per cent of such wives pursuing uninterrupted careers and 15 per cent never working. At another extreme, it is consistent with all wives following a similar alternating pattern of 85 days in and 15 days out of work. Common sense, rather than the data, tells us that the truth lies somewhere in between, and that more data are required to characterize empirically the dynamic process which lies behind the cross-sectional snapshot.

However, as intimated earlier in this chapter, cross-sectional data often include responses to retrospective questions and it is less obvious that cross-sectional analyses of such 'pseudo' longitudinal data are uninformative about micro-level change. It is emphasized that the problem is not with retrospective data *per se*; the problem arises when retrospective data are used in cross-sectional rather than longitudinal methodologies. Typically, the data derived from retrospective questions and used in cross-sectional analyses fall into two categories. They may record the outcome in a previous period. For the Rochdale study, this could be whether or not each wife was in paid work a month earlier. Another example, in a study of voting behaviour, would be how individuals voted in the previous election. Alternatively, respondents may have been asked how long ago some previous outcome of interest occurred. Examples include length of time since becoming unemployed, duration of marriage, and so on. The main objective of this section is to demonstrate that including these types of data in cross-sectional analyses does not, in general, permit inference about processes of change. We thereby emphasize an important, and not always acknowledged, limitation of cross-sectional methods. Moreover, because the basic issue is that of distinguishing the effects of micro-level dynamics from the effects of omitted variables, we also tie up some loose ends from earlier discussions.

Figure 2.4 illustrates the fundamental problem which arises when antecedent outcomes or durations are included as explanatory variables in cross-sectional analyses. For simplicity it is assumed that the other explanatory variables do not change over time, but the same logic applies if this assumption is relaxed provided that there is some temporal continuity in their values. The difficulty is caused by the relationship between omitted explanatory variables and the antecedent condition. In the regression model, the observed relationship A between the antecedent condition and the current outcome will therefore reflect both the true dynamic effect and a spurious element because the antecedent outcome or duration also acts as a proxy for the omitted variables. This may be seen as a control problem: inference about the true relationship A requires control for the effects of all the other explanatory variables. It is, however, the most extreme control problem possible because control is necessary for each and every influence upon the outcome of interest. As high levels of explanatory power are not a feature of statistical analysis in the social sciences, this is quite infeasible, even approximately. Estimation of the effects of the other explanatory variables (relationship B in Figure 2.4) is also prejudiced. This is more difficult to

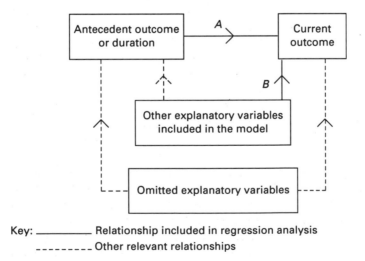

Key: ——————— Relationship included in regression analysis
      — — — — — Other relevant relationships

Figure 2.4   *Cross-sectional analysis with antecedent outcome or duration*

demonstrate but follows from a standard result in regression analysis: correlation between one explanatory variable and the error term can cause biased estimation of all the parameters in the model.

It is recognized that these statistical arguments are not evidence in themselves of a serious practical problem. We have already emphasized that the social scientist must take a pragmatic view of the approximations inherent in any model. This is not without some justification. Many statistical techniques are encouragingly robust to violations of the assumptions upon which they are based. Unfortunately, a wealth of empirical evidence (e.g. Flinn and Heckman, 1982; Davies and Pickles, 1985) suggests that there is no justification for pragmatism in this case; cross-sectional analyses with antecedent outcomes or durations as explanatory variables can generate highly misleading results.

To illustrate the errors that arise, we fitted two models using the Rochdale longitudinal data just for spells in which wives were not in paid work. This allows us to focus on one micro-level dynamic characteristic, namely the effect of the duration of the current spell out of work on the probability of resuming paid employment. This was achieved by including a quadratic in the length in years of the current spell out of work together with the now familiar list of explanatory variables. The first model had a pooled cross-sectional formulation, treating each month's employment status outcome as if it were completely independent of all others. In effect, this is methodologically equivalent to a cross-sectional analysis with an antecedent outcome. The duration-of-stay variable proved to be highly significant (a likelihood ratio test gives a p-value of less than 0.0001) and the estimated relationship with the probability of starting paid work is shown in Figure 2.5 for a 40-year-old wife with the familiar reference group characteristics. The pattern of declining probability of resuming paid work with increasing length of the spell out of employment is clearly consistent with the McGinnis axiom of cumulative inertia. The second model provided a longitudinal analysis with explicit allowance for the effects of omitted variables. The duration of stay is not significant in this analysis (a likelihood ratio test gives a p-value of 0.35) indicating that the cumulative inertia of Figure 2.5 is spurious; there is no evidence that the probability of wives returning to work does actually decline with duration out of employment. In terms of Figure 2.4, the observed relationship A is due to the antecedent duration-of-stay variable acting as proxy for the omitted variables when a cross-sectional methodology is used.

A more intuitive explanation of these different results is that, as duration out of employment increases, so the wives with low probability, *ceteris paribus*, of working are progressively over-represented because those with higher probabilities tend to return to employment. The wives with longer spells out of work therefore have lower rates of returning to employment not because of duration effects *per se*, but because they have always been less likely to take paid work. A full longitudinal analysis is necessary to distinguish these two phenomena; cross-sectional analysis with duration of

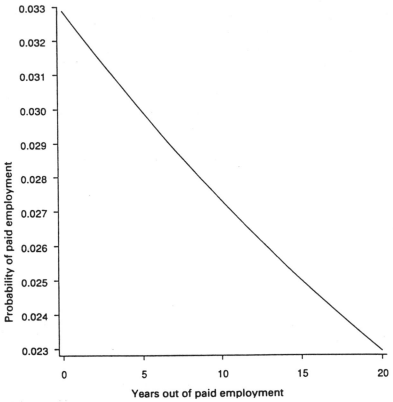

Figure 2.5 *Duration effects*

stay as an explanatory variable is inadequate. The problem of distinguishing between these phenomena has received particular attention in studies of male unemployment (e.g. Jackman and Layard, 1988) because of the different policy consequences. If the probability of obtaining a job declines genuinely with duration of unemployment, then there is some clear justification for training programmes designed specifically for the long-term unemployed, and these programmes should tackle the demoralization and stigma of unemployment. On the other hand, if the decline in the probability of obtaining a job is the spurious consequence of omitted variables, there is less justification for special training programmes and the emphasis should be upon training which improves the skills and morale of the unemployed irrespective of how long they have been unemployed.

Concluding comments

This chapter has introduced some of the main limitations of cross-sectional analysis including the compounding of age and cohort effects, ambiguities in the direction of causality, and the complex ways in which the inevitable omission of unmeasured and possibly unmeasurable variables can generate misleading results, particularly about the dependence of behaviour upon past behaviour. A broad definition is adopted of what constitutes a cross-sectional analysis but this is shown to have surprisingly little impact on the limitations discussed. Hopefully, we have also indicated sufficient of the potential of longitudinal methods to arouse even the sceptical reader's interest. This is not, of course, to repudiate cross-sectional analysis; a cross-sectional analysis will often be quite adequate when interest focuses upon the general propensity of some outcome rather than its dynamic characteristics. On the other hand, for the reasons outlined in this chapter, we consider it inevitable that social scientists will turn increasingly to longitudinal analysis methods as they become more ambitious in the empirical questions they attempt to address with observational data.

Notes

1 The data were collected within the ESRC-funded Social Change and Economic Life Initiative.

2 The logistic regression model may be defined as follows:

linear predictor: $\boldsymbol{\beta}'\mathbf{x}_i = \beta_0 + \beta_1 x_{i1} + \beta_2 x_{i2} + \ldots$

where x_{i1} is 1 if husband in partnership i is unemployed, and 0 otherwise; the x_{i2}, x_{i3}, ... are the values of the other explanatory variables for partnership i; and $\boldsymbol{\beta}$ is a vector of unknown parameters.

link function: $\Pr[y_i = 1] = F(\boldsymbol{\beta}'\mathbf{x}_i) = \exp(\boldsymbol{\beta}'\mathbf{x}_i)/[1 + \exp(\boldsymbol{\beta}'\mathbf{x}_i)]$

where y_i is 1 if wife in partnership i is in paid employment, and 0 otherwise.

3 To simplify exposition, we ignore more speculative causal factors such as wives being reluctant to damage their husbands' self-esteem by becoming the main wage-earners.

4 Let ρ be the proportion of wives with unemployed husbands who would be in paid employment *if there were no direct husband unemployment effect*. The sample enumeration method of estimating ρ is given by

$$\hat{\rho} = \frac{1}{n} \sum_{i \in U} \left[F(\hat{\boldsymbol{\beta}}\mathbf{x}_i) \right]_{x_{i1} = 0}$$

where $\hat{\boldsymbol{\beta}}$ is the vector of parameter estimates, $F(.)$ is the logistic function defined in note 2, U is the set of partnerships with unemployed husbands in the sample, and n is the number of partnerships in set U. Calibration of the logistic model and this calculation is straightforward in GLIM.

5 Roughly speaking, the likelihood is proportional to the probability of the observed outcome occurring if the model is correct.

References

Allison, P.D. (1982) 'Discrete-time methods for the analysis of event histories', in S. Leinhardt (ed.), *Sociological Methodology 1982*. San Francisco: Jossey-Bass. pp. 61–97.

Becker, H. (1963) *Outsiders: Studies in the Sociology of Deviance*. London: Collier-McMillan.

Chamberlain, G. (1985) 'Heterogeneity, omitted variable bias, and duration dependence', in J.J. Heckman and B. Singer (eds), *Longitudinal Analysis of Labour Market Data*. Cambridge: Cambridge University Press. pp. 3–38.

Davies, R.B. (1987) 'The limitations of cross-sectional analysis', in R. Crouchley (ed.), *Longitudinal Data Analysis*. Aldershot: Avebury. pp. 1–15.

Davies, R.B., Elias, P. and Penn, R.D. (1992) 'The relationship between a husband's unemployment and his wife's participation in the labour force', *Oxford Bulletin of Economics and Statistics*, 54: 145–171.

Davies, R.B. and Pickles, A.R. (1985) 'Longitudinal versus cross-sectional methods for behavioural research: a first round knockout', *Environment and Planning A*, 17: 1315–29.

Dilnot, A. and Kell, M. (1987) 'Male unemployment and women's work', *Fiscal Studies*, 8: 1–16.

Flinn, C.J. and Heckman, J.J. (1982) 'Models for the analysis of labour force dynamics', *Advances in Econometrics*, 1: 35–95.

Greenhalgh, C. (1980) 'Participation and hours of work for married women in Great Britain', *Oxford Economic Papers*, 32: 296–318.

Heckman, J.J. and Singer, B. (1985) 'Social science duration analysis', in J.J. Heckman and B. Singer (eds), *Longitudinal Analysis of Labour Market Data*. Cambridge: Cambridge University Press. pp. 39–110.

Jackman, R. and Layard, R. (1988) *Does Long-term Unemployment Reduce a Person's Chance of a Job? A Time Series Test*. Centre for Labour Economics, London School of Economics, Discussion Paper 309.

Joseph, G. (1983) *Women at Work: the British Experience*. Oxford: Philip Allan.

Joshi, H. (1984) *Women's Participation in Paid Work: Further Analysis of the Women and Employment Survey*. Department of Employment, Research Paper 45.

Layard R., Barton, M. and Zabalza, A. (1980) 'Married women's participation and hours', *Econometrica*, 47: 51–72.

McGinnis, R. (1968) 'A stochastic model of social mobility', *American Sociological Review*, 23: 712–22

McNabb, R. (1977) 'The labour force participation of married women', *The Manchester School*, 45: 221–35.

Martin, J. and Roberts, C. (1984) *Women and Employment: a Lifetime Perspective*. London: HMSO.

Solon, G. (1989) 'The value of panel data in economic research', in D. Kasprzyk, G. Duncan, G. Kalton and M.P. Singh (eds), *Panel Surveys*. New York: Wiley. pp. 486–96.

Zabalza, A. (1982) 'The CES utility function, nonlinear budget constraints and labour supply results on female participation and hours', *The Economic Journal*, 93: 312–30.

3

Modelling Trends in Multi-Way Tables

Editors' introduction

This chapter explains the use of logistic and log-linear methods to analyze cross-tabulated data. These are direct, and mostly straightforward, extensions of conventional cross-sectional methods. The basic difference is that one of the variables used to cross-tabulate the data provides an explicit time dimension. The two examples considered are 'year' in a study of youth unemployment, and 'election' in a study of voting behaviour over several general elections in Britain. The data come from cross-sectional surveys with a different sample on each occasion. Similar methods could be used for repeated measures on a single sample but this is not always advisable because, by aggregating such data to create a cross-tabulation, potentially valuable information is lost on the sequence of outcomes for each individual. Moreover, there is no longer independence between individual observations.

Typically, log-linear models are used to investigate the interrelationships between categorical variables where there are no assumed directions of causality. The logistic model is relevant when interest focuses upon the relationship between a set of explanatory variables and a single, binary, response variable. If the response variable has more than two categories, a multinomial logit model may be used. However, logistic and log-linear formulations are mathematically equivalent and the choice between them will usually depend upon the relative ease (or difficulty) of interpreting the results.

The introductory sections to the chapter provide a very clear overview of the log-linear and logistic models and the purposes for which they are suitable. The use of measures based upon 'odds' to facilitate understanding of the different models discussed creates continuity throughout the chapter and ensures that the reader is introduced not just to the characteristics of each model but also to an effective method of interpreting the results. Odds are simply the probability of an outcome occurring, divided by the probability of it not occurring. Nevertheless, log-linear modelling can become very complex. Towards the end of the chapter, the authors discuss several specialized log-linear models for longitudinal data; readers with little experience of log-linear modelling may wish to confine themselves to the earlier, simpler models.

The notation used in this chapter is complicated by the fact that the models have additive and multiplicative formulations. These are entirely equivalent but, as one may be more effective than the other for interpreting the results in any application, both are of interest. In the additive formulations, parameters are denoted by μ; in the multiplicative formulations they are denoted by λ. Each μ is the natural logarithm of the corresponding λ. Note that statisticians tend to use natural logarithms (logarithm to base e), often denoted by 'ℓn' rather than logarithm to base 10. The variable to which each parameter corresponds is indicated by a superscript, while the category of that variable is indicated by a subscript. For example, μ_j^Q or λ_j^Q is the parameter for the jth category of the qualifications variable, whilst μ_{jk}^{QY} or λ_{jk}^{QY} is the (interaction) parameter for the jth category of the qualifications variable and the kth category of the year variable. The constant terms are written as μ or λ.

To illustrate this notation, if the multiplicative model is given by

$$\text{odds} = \lambda \times \lambda_j^Q \times \lambda_k^Y \times \lambda_{jk}^{QY}$$

then the additive model is given by

$$\text{natural logarithm of odds} = \ell n\,(\lambda) + \ell n\,(\lambda_j^Q) + \ell n\,(\lambda_k^Y) + \ell n\,(\lambda_{jk}^{QY})$$

$$= \mu + \mu_j^Q + \mu_k^Y + \mu_{jk}^{QY}$$

Modelling Trends in Multi-Way Tables

Clive Payne, Joan Payne and Anthony Heath

Data on trends often take the form of a multi-way contingency table in which one dimension represents time, and the data for each point in time are based on a fresh sample. Typically these kinds of data are derived from replicated cross-sectional surveys such as the annual Labour Force Survey or General Household Survey in Britain. They could also be obtained in other ways, for example by constructing pseudo-cohorts from a single survey, a standard practice in the analysis of social mobility.

This chapter describes techniques for modelling trends in a multi-way contingency table of this type. Modelling allows us to test whether and how the relationship between variables changes over time. Sometimes we may be interested in whether there is a progressive change in the relationship over time. An example of a hypothesis of this type is the idea of 'class de-alignment' – the contention that in recent years there has been a declining association between social class and allegiance to particular political parties. In other cases time may be viewed as a proxy for underlying social, political, or economic factors whose effects on the relationship between the variables of interest are not necessarily monotonic. An example of a hypothesis of this type is the idea that at times of high unemployment, qualifications are more important as a determinant of who gets jobs than they are at times of low unemployment. The chapter shows how log-linear and logistic models for analyzing multi-way contingency tables can be used to test both types of hypothesis.

The first section gives an elementary description of the logistic model. The aim is to introduce the basic notation and rationale underlying the models, and the section may be skipped by readers already familiar with these. We follow this with a detailed example of the application of the logistic model to trends data. When applied to a contingency table, the logistic model is a special case of the log-linear model which is used to model relationships among a set of categorical variables. We give a brief introduction to the more general log-linear model and go on to illustrate its use in the analysis of trends data.

The final section assesses how useful the logistic and log-linear models are for analyzing trends data and discusses some of the problems involved. Extensions of the basic models are also covered.

The logistic model

Log-linear and logistic models are now standardly used to analyze multi-way tables. A basic description of the models can be found in Gilbert (1993), while the account of Knoke and Burke (1980) is pitched at an intermediate level and those of Fienberg (1980) and Agresti (1990) are more advanced. Almost all major statistical packages include facilities for fitting these models. The GLIM system (Francis et al., 1993) is particularly attractive because of its flexibility, convenient model-fitting language, and interactive facilities. The BMDP system (Dixon, 1983) is also recommended, particularly for the analysis of large tables.

The logistic model is used where one of the variables in a multi-way table has two categories and is treated as a response variable, while the other variables in the table are treated as explanatory variables. In the analysis of trends data we are particularly interested in examining how the relationship between the response variable and the explanatory variables changes with the category or 'level' of the time variable.

Data

The basic model is illustrated by the data given in Table 3.1. These data are extracts from the employment and education records of young men and women aged 16–19 interviewed in the annual General Household Survey in Great Britain. We have data for eight years, from 1974 to 1981. The table is confined to young people who were economically active, that is, they were either in work or unemployed seeking work. They are classified by their economic activity status (unemployed or employed), whether they have any qualifications (none or some), and the year in which they were interviewed.

The binary response variable in this case is whether or not the respondent was unemployed (or, equivalently, employed), and we want to model how this depends on qualifications and year. Thus we can organize the data in Table 3.1 to give the percentage of young people who were unemployed in each cell of the cross-tabulation of qualifications by year. We can inter-

Table 3.1   *Ratio of unemployed to employed young people (age 16–19) by qualifications, Great Britain, 1974–81*

Year	No qualifications	Some qualifications
1974	39/468	20/424
1975	66/435	46/571
1976	98/377	57/629
1977	87/282	60/654
1978	82/272	67/692
1979	72/299	58/661
1980	90/241	96/722
1981	135/215	125/668

pret these percentages as observed probabilities or rates of unemployment. They show that although overall unemployment rates varied from year to year, unqualified young people had a consistently higher unemployment rate than those with qualifications.

These data are sample estimates only. We need to test whether the differences in the observed unemployment rates reflect real relationships with qualifications and year, or whether they could have arisen by chance as a result of sampling fluctuations. We could, of course, use separate tests of association between economic activity status and each explanatory variable in turn, but statistical modelling allows us to test the joint effects of all the explanatory variables simultaneously. It gives us smoothed estimates, conditional on the model fitted, of the probability of unemployment for each combination of qualifications and year.

In our illustrative data there are several questions of interest. The first is whether unqualified young people are significantly more likely to be unemployed than qualified ones. Second, we want to test whether there is a systematic trend in young people's unemployment rates over time, and if so, whether these rates are related to underlying changes in labour market conditions for which the time variable is a proxy. Third, we want to explore whether the effect of qualifications on the probability of unemployment varies in any systematic way over time; whether, in other words, there are some periods when qualifications are relatively more important or less important as a determinant of a young person's chances of being unemployed. All these questions can be answered by statistical modelling.

Why the logistic?

We can represent Table 3.1 in the standard data matrix form where each row represents a cell in the multi-way table, and columns contain the values of the response variable (the observed rate of unemployment) and the explanatory variables (qualifications and year) corresponding to each cell. This is done in columns 1–3 in Table 3.2. The data are now arranged in a standard regression structure where the response variable is a proportion (or rate) and the explanatory variables are all categorical, analogous to regression with dummy explanatory variables.

One possible statistical model for the analysis of a table of proportions is the analysis of variance, with weights for each cell equal to the frequency upon which the proportion is based. This is equivalent to a multiple regression with dummy explanatory variables defined for each level of the explanatory categorical variables, and is known as the linear probability model. This model uses the ordinary least squares (OLS) estimation procedure, a basic assumption of which is that the variance of the response variable is constant, no matter what the value of the variable is. This assumption is violated when the response variable is a proportion: the variance of a proportion p is $p(1 - p)$, and this figure clearly varies with the value of p. Furthermore, with OLS one may obtain fitted values of a proportion which are negative or

Table 3.2   *Data matrix structure for Table 3.1*

Qualifications	Year	Proportion unemployed	Odds of unemployment	Odds of employment
1	1	0.077	0.083	12.00
2	1	0.045	0.047	21.02
1	2	0.132	0.152	6.59
2	2	0.075	0.081	12.41
1	3	0.206	0.260	3.85
2	3	0.083	0.091	11.04
1	4	0.236	0.309	3.24
2	4	0.084	0.092	10.09
1	5	0.232	0.301	3.32
2	5	0.088	0.097	10.33
1	6	0.194	0.241	4.15
2	6	0.081	0.088	11.40
1	7	0.272	0.373	2.68
2	7	0.117	0.133	7.52
1	8	0.386	0.628	1.59
2	8	0.158	0.187	5.34

greater than one. However, for values of p in the range 0.2–0.8 the variance of p is approximately constant, and the linear probability model is reasonably satisfactory in this case.

These problems in modelling proportions can be overcome by using the logit transformation for the response variable, defined as the natural logarithm of $p/(1 - p)$. Various authors, such as Fienberg (1980), have demonstrated that this variance-stabilizing transformation has many desirable properties for modelling proportions across the whole range 0–1. Other transformations, such as the probit, have also been used. The probit gives very similar results to the logit, but the logistic model is rather easier to interpret.

Definitions

We now introduce some notation and give formal definitions of the quantities of interest in the illustrative data.

f_{ijk} is the observed frequency in cell (ijk) of the three-way table of economic activity status (subscript i) by qualifications (subscript j) by year (subscript k).

F_{ijk} is the fitted frequency for cell (ijk) obtained by calibrating a model. In other words, this is the expected frequency if the model is correct.

Denoting unemployment by $i = 1$ and employment by $i = 2$, the observed proportion unemployed in each cell (jk) of Table 3.1 is then

$$P_{jk} = f_{1jk}/(f_{1jk} + f_{2jk}) \tag{3.1}$$

i.e. the ratio of the number of young people unemployed to the total number of young people in each cell.

The logit for cell (*jk*) is defined as

$$L_{jk} = \ell n[P_{jk}/(1 - P_{jk})] \tag{3.2}$$

where ℓn refers to the natural logarithm.

If we substitute for P_{jk} from equation (3.1) in equation (3.2) we get an alternative definition of the logit as

$$L_{jk} = \ell n(f_{1jk}/f_{2jk}) \tag{3.3}$$

This quantity is the logarithm of the odds $O_{jk} = f_{1jk}/f_{2jk}$ that a respondent is unemployed rather than employed.

Odds are simply a ratio of two frequencies and an alternative way of expressing probabilities, from which they can be derived by the formula $O = p/(1 - p)$. In a sample of 100 people where 75 were employed and 25 were unemployed, the probability of unemployment would be 0.25 or 25 per cent, and the odds of unemployment rather than employment would be 25/75, or 0.33:1. This can be expressed by saying that sample members are one-third as likely to be unemployed as employed. Conversely, the odds of employment rather than unemployment would be 75/25, or 3:1: sample members are three times more likely to be employed than unemployed. Column 4 of Table 3.2 gives the observed odds of unemployment in our data; column 5 gives the observed odds of employment. Odds (and ratios of odds) provide a very convenient way of interpreting both logistic and log-linear models.

Models

Returning to the substantive questions raised by our illustrative data, we can now formulate a range of basic models which can be fitted to the data. The simplest model specifies that the log odds of unemployment are constant; they do not vary with either qualifications or year. This is equivalent to the null hypothesis of no association. Formally this model is given by

$$\ell n(O_{jk}) = \ell n(F_{1jk}/F_{2jk}) = \text{constant} \tag{model A}$$

In the sample as a whole the observed odds of unemployment rather than employment are 1188/8808 = 0.135. If model A were correct, we could replace our separate estimates of the odds of unemployment in each cell of the table with this single value.

The fitted frequencies in the original three-way table, F_{ijk}, can be constructed from the fitted log odds. In order to test the hypothesis that a given model fits the observed data we use the likelihood ratio test statistic. This is defined as

$$G^2 = 2\Sigma f_{ijk} \, \ell n(f_{ijk}/F_{ijk}) \tag{3.4}$$

This measure is also known as the 'deviance' and our aim is to achieve a model with the lowest possible deviance relative to the degrees of freedom used by the model. It has an approximate chi-square distribution with degrees of freedom equal to the number of cells in the table minus the number of independent parameters estimated. When model A is fitted to our illustrative data, the deviance is 416.4 with 15 DF, which according to the distribution of chi-square gives a *p*-value of <0.0001. The *p*-value is interpreted as the probability that differences at least as large as those between the observed and fitted values could have arisen by chance, given that the model is correct. Model A therefore fits the data very badly indeed, and we can infer that the log odds of unemployment are not constant.

The next step is to test whether the log odds of unemployment vary only with qualifications. To do this we introduce another term into the model, which becomes

$$\ell n(O_{jk}) = \text{constant} + \text{qualifications}(j) \qquad \text{(model B)}$$

where the term qualifications(j) represents the effect on the logit of being in category j of the qualifications variable.

There are two parameters in this additional term, one for each level of the variable (no qualifications and some qualifications), but their values cannot be determined unless constraints are introduced. This can be done in various ways, and each statistical package has its own particular method. A convenient way, used by the GLIM system, is to constrain the parameter for the first level of the variable to zero, so that the parameter for the second is interpreted as the effect on the log odds of being at the second level of the variable rather than the first. This is directly analogous to regression with dummy variables. Model B thus has two independent parameters to estimate, the constant and the effect for qualification level 2. With this model G^2 is 212.35 with 14 DF, giving a *p*-value of <0.0001. Thus this model still fits the data very badly, but we have achieved a large reduction in deviance compared with model A.

The G^2 statistic is also used to test whether the addition of a term to the model significantly improves its fit. The difference in deviance between two models has an approximate chi-square distribution with degrees of freedom equal to the difference in the degrees of freedom between the two models, provided that the second model includes all the terms in the first model in addition to the extra terms. Compared with model A, model B reduces the deviance by 204.07, while using up one more degree of freedom. According to the distribution of chi-square, this gives a *p*-value of less than 0.001. In this case the *p*-value is interpreted in the usual way: we want a large reduction in deviance relative to the degrees of freedom used, and hence a small *p*-value. In our illustrative data we can infer that the odds of unemployment vary with qualifications, for model B achieves a highly significant reduction in deviance over the constant model A.

The next hypothesis to test is whether the log odds of unemployment vary with year. To do this we fit the model

$$\ell n(O_{jk}) = \text{constant} + \text{year}(k) \qquad\qquad \text{(model C)}$$

The term year(k) represents a set of parameters measuring the effect on the log odds of being in each of the eight years. Thus model C estimates seven independent effects for this term (number of levels of year minus one) plus the constant, giving 16–8=8 degrees of freedom. As before, the effect for year(1) is constrained to be zero. Model C also gives a significant reduction in deviance from the constant model ($G^2 = 146.05$ on 7 DF, p-value < 0.0001) but again does not fit the data at all well.

Model C is known as the minimal model for these data, for it contains the smallest set of parameters permissible. The minimal model must include the terms which correspond to any margins in the table which are fixed by the sampling scheme for the data. In our illustrative data, the figures for each year are obtained from a separate survey, so the minimal model must include the term year(k).

The next model includes both the year and the qualifications terms:

$$\ell n(O_{jk}) = \text{constant} + \text{qualifications}(j) + \text{year}(k) \qquad\qquad \text{(model D)}$$

This model implies that the log odds vary with both qualifications and year, and that each explanatory variable has an independent effect on the log odds. It is directly analogous to a main effects model in the analysis of variance. This model has nine independent parameters (the constant plus one of the qualifications term, plus seven for the year term) giving $16 - 9 = 7$ DF. This model fits well, with $G^2 = 9.15$ and p-value $= 0.24$, and would be accepted on conventional statistical criteria.

The final model we consider extends model D by adding a term to test for the effect of interaction between the two explanatory variables on the log odds, giving

$$\ell n(O_{jk}) = \text{constant} + \text{qualifications}(j) + \text{year}(k)$$
$$+ \text{qualifications}(j) \times \text{year}(k) \qquad\qquad \text{(model E)}$$

The additional term represents a set of parameters which estimate the effect on the log odds of the particular combination of year and qualifications, over and above the separate main effects of the two variables. If the values of the parameters in this set as a whole are significantly different from zero then we conclude that the effect of qualifications on the log odds differs in different years, and vice versa.

The number of independent parameters in an interaction term is calculated by subtracting one from the number of levels of each separate term, and then forming the product of these numbers. In this case, qualifications has two levels and year has eight, so the number of parameters in the interaction term for qualifications and year is $(2 - 1) \times (8 - 1) = 7$.

Model E is known as the saturated model, for it fits the data perfectly and uses up all the degrees of freedom. It implies that we need to know each particular combination of qualifications and year in order to predict the log odds of unemployment. However, it is not a substantively interesting model because it implies that there is no underlying pattern over time in the effects of qualifications on unemployment chances.

Using standard statistical notation, the saturated model E for our illustrative data may be rewritten as

$$\ell n(F_{1jk}/F_{2jk}) = \ell n(O_{jk}) = \mu + \mu_j^Q + \mu_k^Y + \mu_{jk}^{QY} \qquad \text{(model E)}$$

with $i = 1, ..., I$ ($I=2$, economic activity status: 1 unemployed, 2 employed), $j = 1, ..., J$ ($J=2$, qualifications: 1 no qualifications, 2 some) and $k = 1, ..., K$ ($K=8$, year: 1 is 1974, ..., 8 is 1981). The terms on the right-hand side of the equation represent the sets of parameters to be estimated by the model, as shown in Table 3.3.

Models A to E are summarized in Table 3.4. How do we decide which is the best model for our data? In modelling the task is to achieve an acceptable model somewhere between the minimal and the saturated models. It should be substantively meaningful, its parameters should be statistically significant, and it should fit the data well. Complex models involving large numbers of parameters will usually fit the data better than simpler models, but simpler ones are generally preferred on grounds of parsimony and ease of interpretation. The choice of which terms to include should be guided by substantive hypotheses, and the likelihood ratio test should be used to help decide between models. On these criteria the best model we have so far is model D, but this can be improved on, as we shall show later.

Interpretation

Model E is an additive model, that is the log odds of unemployment are a linear function of the terms included in the model. It can be reformulated as a multiplicative model for the odds O_{jk} with

$$F_{1jk}/F_{2jk} = O_{jk} = \lambda \times \lambda_j^Q \times \lambda_k^Y \times \lambda_{jk}^{QY} \qquad \text{(model Em)}$$

Table 3.3   *Parameters of the saturated model E*

Term	Parameters	Number of independent parameters
constant	μ	1
qualifications(*j*)	μ_j^Q	$J-1$
year(*k*)	μ_k^Y	$K-1$
qualifications(*j*) $\times$ year(*k*)	μ_{jk}^{QY}	$(J-1) \times (K-1)$

Table 3.4 *Logistic models for Table 3.1*

Model	Terms	Deviance	DF	Probability
A	constant	416.42	15	<0.0001
B	constant + qualifications(j)	212.35	14	<0.0001
C	constant + year(k)	270.37	8	<0.0001
D	constant + qualifications(j) + year(k)	9.15	7	0.24
E	constant + qualifications(j) + year(k) + qualifications(j) $\times$ year(k)	0.0	0	–

where the λs are simply the exponentials of the equivalent μs (that is, $\lambda =$ exp μ). In this formulation we test whether sets of parameters differ from the value 1 (since exp $0=1$) and constrain the parameter for the effect at the first level of each explanatory factor to have the value 1. The point of reformulating the model in this way is that the parameters now have a clearer interpretation.

Table 3.5 gives the parameter estimates for model D in both the additive and multiplicative formulations. In the latter each parameter estimate refers to a multiplicative effect on the odds of unemployment corresponding to the specified level of the explanatory variable. In the GLIM system the multiplicative effects corresponding to the first level are constrained to the value 1, and the effects of being at a different level of the explanatory variable are interpreted relative to the base categories. The parameter for the constant term represents the fitted odds for sample members in the base (or reference) categories of all the explanatory variables included in the model. Thus

Table 3.5 *Parameter estimates for model D*

Parameter	Description	Additive model		Multiplicative model	
		Symbol	Estimate	Symbol	Estimate
constant		μ	−2.342	λ	0.096
qualifications(1)	none	μ_1^Q	0.000	λ_1^Q	1.00
qualifications(2)	some	μ_2^Q	−1.042	λ_2^Q	0.35
year(1)	1974	μ_1^Y	0.000	λ_1^Y	1.00
year(2)	1975	μ_2^Y	0.615	λ_2^Y	1.85
year(3)	1976	μ_3^Y	0.991	λ_3^Y	2.69
year(4)	1977	μ_4^Y	1.087	λ_4^Y	2.97
year(5)	1978	μ_5^Y	1.097	λ_5^Y	3.00
year(6)	1979	μ_6^Y	0.934	λ_6^Y	2.55
year(7)	1980	μ_7^Y	1.363	λ_7^Y	3.91
year(8)	1981	μ_8^Y	1.781	λ_8^Y	5.94

with model D, the fitted odds of unemployment for young people with no qualifications in 1974 are 0.096 (0.096 × 1.0 × 1.0). The effect of having some qualifications is to reduce these odds by a multiplicative factor 0.35; in other words, the odds of unemployment for young people with qualifications are about a third of the odds for unqualified young people. Compared with 1974, the odds of unemployment in 1981 were increased by a factor of 5.94 – that is, they were nearly six times greater.

The values of the parameters of a logistic model depend on the particular parameterization used in the computer package. Some packages such as BMDP and SPSS constrain the sum of the parameter values for a term to be zero, and these give rather different estimates to those obtained with the GLIM system. Thus care must be taken when interpreting parameter estimates. However Scott Long (1984) shows that, depending on the type of model fitted, certain functions of the parameters are the same, no matter what the method of parameterization. In particular, he shows that for an additive model with no interaction terms (such as model D) the differences between parameter values within a term are invariant to the method of parameterization; in the multiplicative formulation, ratios of parameter estimates are invariant.

The odds ratio

The odds ratio is a basic quantity in the analysis of contingency tables. It is defined as the ratio of two odds, the choice of which is determined by our substantive interests in fitting the model.

Consider the odds ratio

$$R^Q(k) = \frac{F_{11k}/F_{21k}}{F_{12k}/F_{22k}} \tag{3.5}$$

where $R^Q(k)$ is defined as the odds ratio comparing the odds of unemployment for each qualification level (j) which varies with year (k). The numerator is the odds that a young person with no qualifications is unemployed rather than employed in year k; the denominator is the equivalent odds for a young person with qualifications. According to Table 3.1, the observed value of this ratio in 1981 was (135/215) / (125/668) = 0.623/0.187 = 3.46.

The odds ratio is a measure of association between two variables, in our example economic activity status and qualifications. A ratio greater than the value 1, as in this case, indicates that the odds of unemployment are much greater for an unqualified young person than someone with qualifications; a ratio of less than 1 would indicate that the reverse was true. If the ratio had the value of 1, then the two variables would be independent of each other.

We can use odds ratios to measure trends over time. Here we are interested in whether there is any pattern in the degree of association between qualification and economic activity status across different years. In 1974 the value of the observed odds ratio $R^Q(k)$ was (39/468) / (20/424) = 0.083/0.094

= 0.883. This is much smaller than the corresponding ratio in 1981, and so the data suggest that the difference between the unemployment chances of qualified and unqualified young people increased considerably between 1974 and 1981. If the odds ratio in 1974 were identical to the odds ratio in 1981, the relative chances of unemployment for unqualified and qualified young people would not have changed between those two dates.

So far we have talked only about odds ratios calculated from the observed data, but we can also calculate odds ratios from the parameter estimates we obtain when we fit the logistic model (or, equivalently, from the fitted frequencies). Model D implies that the odds ratios $R^Q(k)$ are independent of year. Substituting the multiplicative version of model D into equation (3.5) gives

$$\frac{F_{11k}/F_{21k}}{F_{12k}/F_{22k}} = \frac{\lambda \times \lambda_1^Q \times \lambda_k^Y}{\lambda \times \lambda_2^Q \times \lambda_k^Y} = \frac{\lambda_1^Q}{\lambda_2^Q} = \frac{1.000}{0.353} = 2.83$$

Thus if model D is correct, the odds of unemployment for unqualified young people in each year are 2.83 times greater than for young people with qualifications. The model fits reasonably well, although, as we have seen above, the observed odds ratios vary quite a lot.

For all the models fitted in this chapter, the fitted odds ratios are invariant to the model parameterization.

Modelling trends in youth unemployment

The previous section has explained the basic ideas behind the logistic model, using simplified data taken from a real research problem. We now wish to show how the logistic model can be used to analyze trends over time, and to do this we present a detailed analysis of the full data set. This is the four-way table given as Table 3.6, in which there is an additional explanatory variable, age. The analysis was first published by Payne and Payne (1985).

Table 3.6 *Ratio of unemployed to employed young people by qualifications and age, Great Britain, 1974–81*

| | Age 16 | | Age 17–19 | |
Year	No qualifications	Some qualifications	No qualifications	Some qualifications
1974	13/68	4/62	26/400	16/362
1975	22/73	18/110	44/362	28/461
1976	39/81	17/101	59/296	40/528
1977	38/56	23/77	49/226	37/577
1978	39/62	12/91	43/210	55/601
1979	27/71	13/63	45/228	45/598
1980	26/46	18/80	64/195	78/642
1981	44/44	16/64	91/171	109/604

Between 1974 and 1981 there was an enormous growth in youth unemployment in Great Britain, though the rate of growth was not constant. Youth unemployment rates rose between 1974 and 1976, remained steady between 1976 and 1978, fell slightly between 1978 and 1979, and rose very steeply between 1979 and 1981. In response to this problem, in 1978 the government introduced the Youth Opportunities Programme, a training scheme which eventually became very large and was aimed particularly at 16-year-olds who were entering the labour market for the first time. Also over the period 1974 to 1981 there were various changes in the educational system which led to a fall in the proportion of young people leaving school with no formal qualifications.

We were interested in the impact of all these developments on the employment chances of young people. In particular, we believed that the low demand for youth labour combined with the rise in the proportion of young people who possessed qualifications would make the employment chances of unqualified young people deteriorate relative to the chances of young people with qualifications – a version of the hypothesis that there is a 'tightening bond' between qualifications and employment. We also felt that, as government training programmes were directed towards young school leavers, their introduction might, through various mechanisms, jeopardize the employment chances of older teenagers. These are the particular hypotheses that the modelling is designed to test.

The quantity that we model is the log odds that a respondent is unemployed rather than employed. The saturated model for the table is

$$\ell n(F_{1ijk}/F_{2ijk}) = \mu + \mu_i^Q + \mu_j^A + \mu_k^Y + \mu_{ij}^{QA} + \mu_{ik}^{QY} + \mu_{jk}^{AY} + \mu_{ijk}^{QAY} \quad \text{(model F)}$$

where F_{1ijk} is the number unemployed, F_{2ijk} the number employed in cell (ijk) in the three-way table of qualifications (Q) by age (A) by year (Y), with subscripts now defined as $i = 1, ..., I$ $(I = 2$, qualifications: none, some), $j = 1, ..., J$ $(J = 2$, age: 16, 17–19) and $k = 1, ..., K$ $(K = 8$, year: 1974, ..., 1981). Note that $F_{1ijk}/F_{2ijk} = P_{ijk}/(1 - P_{ijk})$ where P_{ijk} is the proportion unemployed of the total $(F_{1ijk}+F_{2ijk})$ in the cell (ijk) of the three-way table of proportions unemployed for qualifications by age by year.

The multiplicative formulation of the saturated model is

$$F_{1ijk}/F_{2ijk} = \lambda \times \lambda_i^Q \times \lambda_j^A \times \lambda_k^Y \times \lambda_{ij}^{QA} \times \lambda_{ik}^{QY} \times \lambda_{jk}^{AY} \times \lambda_{ijk}^{QAY} \quad \text{(model Fm)}$$

where the λ parameters are the exponentials of the equivalent μ parameters. The terms in this model are defined in Table 3.7.

We want to formulate models which use a subset of the terms in the saturated model and test the hypotheses described above. We then need to establish how well the models fit the data, and whether the parameters which make up the individual terms are significantly different from zero. The series of models we fit is set out in Table 3.8. The first model (model G) fits the constant term only and tests the hypothesis that the odds of employment do not vary with age, qualifications, or year.

Table 3.7 *Terms in the saturated logistic model for Table 3.6*

Parameter	Term	Meaning
λ	constant	Odds of unemployment are constant and do not vary with age, qualifications, or year
One-way terms		
λ_i^Q	qualifications(i)	Odds vary with qualifications
λ_j^A	age(j)	Odds vary with age
λ_k^Y	year(k)	Odds vary with year
Two-way terms		
λ_{ij}^{QA}	qualifications(i) $\times$ age(j)	Difference in odds between the two levels of qualifications is different in each level of age
λ_{ik}^{QY}	qualifications(i) $\times$ year(k)	Difference in odds between the two levels of qualifications is different in each year
λ_{jk}^{AY}	age(j) $\times$ year(k)	Difference in odds between the two levels of age is different in each year
Three-way term		
λ_{ijk}^{QAY}	qualifications(i) $\times$ age(j) $\times$ year(k)	The differential pattern of odds for combinations of age and qualifications differs between years

The first model of substantive interest is model H, which fits the constant plus all the one-way terms. This is called the 'independence model' as all the explanatory variables have an independent effect on the response, there being no interaction terms in the model. It fits the data reasonably well, with a *p*-value of 0.36, and the change in fit between it and the constant model is highly significant statistically ($p < 0.001$). In order to test whether each individual term in the model is significantly different from zero, we calculate the reduction in deviance when each is introduced into the model successively. We do not give these calculations here, but they show that the introduction

Table 3.8 *Logistic models for the odds of unemployment*

Model	Terms	Overall model G^2	DF	p	Change of fit G^2	DF	p
G	constant	551.60	31	<0.0001	–	–	–
H	constant + qualifications(i) + age(j) + year(k)	23.76	22	0.36	527.84	9	<0.001
I	constant + qualifications(i) + age(j) + year(k) + age(j) $\times$ intervention(l) + qualifications(i) $\times$ unemployment(m)	11.88	19	0.89	11.88	3	<0.01

of each one-way term achieves a significant reduction in deviance (in whichever order they are introduced) and we can conclude, not surprisingly, that the chances of unemployment for young people are significantly related to their age, qualifications, and the year in question.

In its multiplicative form, model H is written as

$$F_{1ijk}/F_{2ijk} = \lambda \times \lambda_i^Q \times \lambda_j^A \times \lambda_k^Y \qquad \text{(model Hm)}$$

So far, so good; but the independence model implies that the odds ratios of unemployment for unqualified compared with qualified young people are constant across years, and that the odds ratios for 16-year-olds compared with 17–19-year-olds are also constant across years. We have not yet tested the hypothesis that the relative chances of employment for unqualified respondents worsened as unemployment rose, or that the relative chances of employment for older teenagers deteriorated following the launching of government programmes targeted specifically at recent school leavers. Model I is designed to do this.

In order to test the first hypothesis we divide the years 1974–81 into two periods according to the level of youth unemployment. This gives us a new variable 'unemployment' which has the value 1 for the years 1974–5, a period of relatively low unemployment, and the value 2 for the years 1976–81, a period of high unemployment. To test the second hypothesis we define a new variable 'intervention' which takes its value according to the degree of government intervention in the youth labour market. Thus the years 1974–7 are allocated to a period of minimal intervention before a large-scale youth training programme was launched, 1978 and 1979 to a period of moderate intervention when the programme was getting under way, and 1980 and 1981 to a period of high government intervention when the number of young people involved was very large.

Model I includes all the terms that were included in model Hm, plus two additional terms. The term qualifications(i) $\times$ unemployment(m) (or, equivalently, λ_{im}^{QU}) specifies that the effect of qualifications is the same within each of the two unemployment periods, but may differ between periods. Similarly the model term age (j) $\times$ intervention(ℓ) (or, equivalently, $\lambda_{j\ell}^{AI}$) specifies that the effect of age is the same within each of the three intervention periods, but may differ between them. This model has a p-value of 0.89, showing that it fits the data considerably better than the independence model. The change in fit between model H and model I is statistically significant ($p < 0.01$), and the introduction of each additional interaction term separately achieves a reduction in deviance significant beyond the 0.05 level. We therefore accept model I as our final model in preference to model H.

In formal notation, the multiplicative version of the model we have accepted is

$$F_{1ijk}/F_{2ijk} = \lambda \times \lambda_i^Q \times \lambda_j^A \times \lambda_k^Y \times \lambda_{im}^{QU} \times \lambda_{j\ell}^{AI} \qquad \text{(model Im)}$$

Table 3.9 *Multiplicative parameter estimates for model I*

Term	Description	Estimate
constant		0.19
age(2)	Age 17–19	0.36
qualifications(2)	Some qualifications	0.53
year(2)	1975	1.70
year(3)	1976	1.92
year(4)	1977	2.17
year(5)	1978	2.32
year(6)	1979	2.01
year(7)	1980	3.34
year(8)	1981	5.09
age(1) × intervention(2)	Age 16 with moderate government intervention	0.80
age(1) × intervention(3)	Age 16 with high government intervention	0.63
qualifications(1) × unemployment(2)	No qualifications with high unemployment	1.48

Table 3.9 gives the multiplicative parameter estimates we obtain by fitting this model to the data in Table 3.6.

We can interpret this model in terms of odds ratios. Consider the effect of qualifications. The relevant odds ratio, $R^Q(jk)$, is

$$R^Q(jk) = \frac{F_{11jk}/F_{21jk}}{F_{12jk}/F_{22jk}} \tag{3.6}$$

where the numerator is the odds of unemployment rather than employment for unqualified young people ($i=1$) at level j of age and k of year, and the denominator is the equivalent odds for young people with qualifications ($i=2$). Substituting model Im in this equation with i set to 1 in the numerator and to 2 in the denominator gives

$$R^Q(jk) = \frac{\lambda \times \lambda_1^Q \times \lambda_j^A \times \lambda_k^Y \times \lambda_{1m}^{QU} \times \lambda_{j\ell}^{AI}}{\lambda \times \lambda_2^Q \times \lambda_j^A \times \lambda_k^Y \times \lambda_{2m}^{QU} \times \lambda_{j\ell}^{AI}}$$

$$= \frac{\lambda_1^Q \times \lambda_{1m}^{QU}}{\lambda_2^Q \times \lambda_{2m}^{QU}} \tag{3.7}$$

since all terms not involving Q cancel out. Thus this odds ratio is independent of age(j) and only depends on year(k) through the new variable unemployment(m) which groups year into two periods.

As a result, there are just two fitted odds ratios for the effect of qualifications and these arise because the interaction term λ_{im}^{QU} has permitted qualifications to have a different effect in the two unemployment periods. During the period of low youth unemployment the ratio of the fitted odds of unemployment for a young person with no qualifications relative to the odds for a young person with qualifications is given by

$$R^Q(jk) = \frac{1.00 \times 1.00}{0.53 \times 1.00} = 1.89$$

where the 1.00s are reference category values. In the period of high unemployment the corresponding ratio is given by

$$R^Q(jk) = \frac{1.00 \times 1.48}{0.53 \times 1.00} = 2.79$$

This can be interpreted to mean that the relative disadvantage conferred by having no qualifications was greater when unemployment was high, and clearly supports our first hypothesis.

In the same way we can examine how the effect of age varies with the degree of government intervention in the youth labour market. As model H showed, 16-year-olds have a higher unemployment rate in general than 17–19-year-olds, presumably because they have only recently entered the labour market. Under model I, during the period of minimal government intervention the fitted odds of unemployment for 16-year-olds were 2.78 times the corresponding odds for 17–19-year-olds. (This is calculated from Table 3.9 as $(1.00 \times 1.00) / (0.36 \times 1.00)$ where, once again, the 1.00 values refer to the reference categories.) In the period of moderate government intervention this ratio fell to 2.22 (=$(1.00 \times 0.80) / (0.36 \times 1.00)$), and in the period of high government intervention it fell still further, to 1.75 (=$(1.00 \times 0.63) / (0.36 \times 1.00)$). Thus our second hypothesis is also supported by the data; as government programmes targeted at 16-year-olds grew in size, the relative advantage of older teenagers over 16-year-olds diminished.

Table 3.10 shows another way to present the results for model I, which is to calculate odds ratios for particular pairs of years. Comparing 1981 with 1974, we find that the odds of unemployment increased for all young people. However, the group whose odds of unemployment increased the most were 17–19-year-olds with no qualifications (odds ratio 7.53), while the group whose odds of unemployment increased the least were 16-year-olds with some qualifications (odds ratio 3.21).

Now compare 1974 with 1977, when there was rising unemployment but only minimal government intervention. Model I constrains the effect of age on unemployment to be constant in this period, as the two years fall within the same period for government intervention. Hence the change in the odds of unemployment is the same for 16-year-olds as it is for 17–19-year-olds. According to the model, the odds of unemployment for an unqualified young person increased by a factor of 3.21 between these years, while the odds for a qualified person increased by a somewhat smaller factor.

The final comparison is between 1977 and 1980. In these two years youth unemployment stood at similar levels, but there had been a conspicuous growth in government intervention by 1980. Model I constrains the relationship between qualifications and unemployment to remain constant in

Table 3.10   *Odds ratios fitted under model I for selected pairs of years*

	Odds ratio
1981 compared with 1974:	
age 17–19, no qualifications	7.53
age 17–19, some qualifications	5.09
age 16, no qualifications	4.74
age 16, some qualifications	3.21
1977 compared with 1974:	
age 17–19, no qualifications	3.21
age 17–19, some qualifications	2.17
age 16, no qualifications	3.21
age 16, some qualifications	2.17
1980 compared with 1977:	
age 17–19, no qualifications ⎫	
age 17–19, some qualifications ⎭	1.54
age 16, no qualifications ⎫	
age 16, some qualifications ⎭	0.97

these two years as they both fall within the same period for our level of unemployment variable. According to the model, the odds of a 16-year-old being unemployed fell slightly between 1977 and 1980 (odds ratio 0.97), while the odds of a 17–19-year-old being unemployed rose by a factor of 1.54.

The youth unemployment data show how it is possible to use the logistic model to test hypotheses about how the relationships between variables change over time. Associations between explanatory and response variables are measured by odds ratios, and the changes in odds ratios are modelled. The same way of operationalizing the process of hypothesis testing applies to the log-linear model, to which we now turn.

The log-linear model

In the youth unemployment data the response variable, economic activity status, has two categories, employed and unemployed. Sometimes, however, our interest lies in a response variable with more than two categories, such as the political party that people support. Where these categories are unordered, the main modelling technique is the standard log-linear model. The log-linear model can also be used for examining the mutual relationships between the variables defining a table when there is no clear response variable.

The log-linear model is very similar in formulation to the logistic model and similar notation can be used. The essential difference is that with the log-linear model we model not the log odds but the log frequency in each cell (the natural logarithm of the observed cell frequency), and examine how this depends on the combination of levels of the categorical variables which define each cell, taking account of sampling variation. The logistic model is in fact a special case of the log-linear model, and the log-linear model can also be applied to tables with a binary response variable. In this case the log-linear model is equivalent to fitting simultaneously separate logistic models for each pairwise comparison of levels of the response variables, for example (citing the main three British political parties in the late 1960s and 1970s) the odds of supporting the Conservative Party rather than the Labour Party, of supporting the Conservative Party rather than the Liberal Party, and of supporting the Labour Party rather than the Liberal Party. However the parameters of the logistic model are rather easier to interpret than the parameters of the log-linear model, so the logistic is preferred when the response variable is binary.

When a log-linear model has been fitted, the likelihood ratio test statistic G^2, with degrees of freedom equal to the number of cells minus the number of independent parameters fitted, is used to calculate the probability that the differences between the observed and the fitted frequencies may have arisen by chance, given that the model under consideration is correct. A good descriptive measure of fit is provided by the 'proportion misclassified', which is defined as

$$\text{proportion misclassified} = 0.5 \, \Sigma \, (|F_{ijk} - f_{ijk}|) \, / \, f_{..} \tag{3.8}$$

where F_{ijk} are the fitted frequencies under the model, f_{ijk} are the observed frequencies, and $f_{..}$ is the total sample size. This measure gives the proportion of cases which have to be reallocated to other cells for the fitted values to exactly match the observed frequencies.

Modelling trends in the class and party relationship

The changing relationship between class and party in Britain has been the subject of considerable interest and debate. It has been suggested that the social classes have been changing their character over time, losing their social cohesion and ideological distinctiveness and thus becoming more similar to each other. In turn, it has been argued that these changes in the social classes will have led their voting patterns to become more similar. On this hypothesis, the observed relationship between class and vote will have become weaker. Furthermore, since the argument concerns long-run processes of social change, it can be hypothesized that this trend will have been a gradual and continuous one.

An alternative line of argument is that the relationship between class and vote will depend on political factors such as the electoral strategies of the parties and the policies they espouse, or on the extent to which they satisfy their supporters' aspirations when in office. If this argument is correct, changes in the relation between class and vote may be discontinuous, reflecting discrete political periods such as a government's period in office.

These questions can be pursued using the series of British Election Surveys which have been conducted after every General Election since 1964. We use data from the eight surveys between 1964 and 1987. They are representative probability samples of the electorate, analogous in many respects to the General Household Survey which we used for modelling trends in youth unemployment.

The data which we shall be modelling are presented in Table 3.11. A detailed analysis of these data is given in Evans et al. (1991). The table shows how respondents in each class voted in each of the eight election samples. We have excluded non-voters and voters for 'minor' parties, leaving us with three categories of vote – Conservative, Labour and Liberal (including the Social Democratic Party (SDP) in 1983 and 1987). In allocating respondents to social classes, we have used the following procedure: respondents who were working, unemployed seeking work or retired have been allocated to a class on the basis of their own occupation (and economic status); other respondents have been allocated on the basis of their spouse's occupation

Table 3.11   *Three-way table of election by vote by social class (frequencies)*

| General Election | Party voted for[1] | Social class | | | | |
		Salariat SAL	Routine non-manual RNM	Petit bourgeoisie PB	Foremen and technicians FT	Working class WC
1964	CON	167	115	76	45	175
	LAB	52	51	14	54	469
	LIB	49	31	12	18	47
1966	CON	170	106	68	38	169
	LAB	69	88	19	68	500
	LIB	41	22	15	5	38
1970	CON	178	95	77	43	196
	LAB	84	76	21	62	370
	LIB	26	16	12	6	37
Feb. 1974	CON	221	147	111	41	199
	LAB	91	97	31	42	510
	LIB	98	85	22	23	139
Oct. 1974	CON	208	136	97	40	165
	LAB	91	98	18	59	501
	LIB	100	73	22	15	119
1979	CON	231	108	100	68	193
	LAB	83	66	17	65	331
	LIB	64	35	13	17	80
1983	CON	439	287	162	80	341
	LAB	105	110	27	51	547
	LIB	249	150	38	52	239
1987	CON	467	297	158	69	319
	LAB	130	148	39	64	492
	LIB	242	131	48	43	213

[1] CON, Conservative; LAB, Labour; LIB, Liberal (including the Social Democratic Party in 1983 and 1987).

(and economic status), providing that they had a spouse who was working, unemployed seeking work, or retired. The five classes which we distinguish can be described briefly as follows (for further details see Heath et al. 1985).

I   the salariat (managers, professionals, administrative staff and non-manual supervisors) (SAL)
II routine non-manual workers (clerks and sales workers) (RNM)
III the petty bourgeoisie (employers and own account workers, including farmers and smallholders) (PB)
IV foremen and technicians (FT)
V   the working class (rank and file employees in industry, services and agriculture) (WC).

Table 3.11 is thus a three-way table of observed frequencies f_{ijk}, showing party (P) by class (C) by election (E). The saturated log-linear model for this table is given by

$$\ell n(F_{ijk}) = \mu + \mu_i^P + \mu_j^C + \mu_k^E + \mu_{ij}^{PC} + \mu_{ik}^{PE} + \mu_{jk}^{CE} + \mu_{ijk}^{PCE} \qquad \text{(model J)}$$

where F_{ijk} is the expected frequency in cell (ijk) with $i = 1, ..., I$ (I=3, parties: CON, LAB, LIB), $j = 1, ..., J$ ($J = 5$, classes: SAL, RNM, PB, FT, WC) and $k = 1, ..., K$ (K=8, elections: 1964, ..., 1987).

The terms on the right-hand side of the model represent parameters to be estimated. Constraints have to be imposed so that the parameters can be estimated. Again we use the GLIM method which sets all parameters involving the first category to zero in each term. This formulation is directly analogous to the analysis of variance for factorial arrangements, but in the log-linear model the dependent variable is the cell log frequency. The parameters for this saturated model are listed in Table 3.12. The constant term represents the fitted log frequency for the cell where all three variables which define Table 3.11 are at level 1, the base category.

Model J is a linear model in the log frequencies. It can be re-expressed as a multiplicative model for frequencies with

$$F_{ijk} = \lambda \times \lambda_i^P \times \lambda_j^C \times \lambda_k^E \times \lambda_{ij}^{PC} \times \lambda_{ik}^{PE} \times \lambda_{jk}^{CE} \times \lambda_{ijk}^{PCE} \qquad \text{(model Jm)}$$

where the λs are the exponentials of the equivalent μs. In the multiplicative formulation of the model all parameters involving the base category of a variable are set to the value one.

Just like the logistic model, the log-linear model is operationalized in terms of odds ratios. In the present example our interest lies in whether and how the relationship between party and class has changed over time, and all the models we fit imply statements about how the odds ratios involving party and class vary across elections. Odds ratios can be calculated for all combinations of pairs of parties and pairs of classes. They are defined as follows. For an arbitrary pair of parties (i, i') and an arbitrary pair of classes (j, j') we define the odds ratio for election k as

Table 3.12   *Parameters of the saturated model for Table 3.11*

Term	Parameters	Number of independent parameters
constant	μ	1
party(i)	μ_i^P	$I-1$
class(j)	μ_j^C	$J-1$
election(k)	μ_k^E	$K-1$
party(i) $\times$ class(j)	μ_{ij}^{PC}	$(I-1) \times (J-1)$
party(i) $\times$ election(k)	μ_{ik}^{PE}	$(I-1) \times (K-1)$
class(j) $\times$ election(k)	μ_{jk}^{CE}	$(J-1) \times (K-1)$
party(i) $\times$ class(j) $\times$ election(k)	μ_{ijk}^{PCE}	$(I-1) \times (J-1) \times (K-1)$

$$R^k(i, i' : j, j') = \frac{F_{ijk}/F_{i'jk}}{F_{ij'k}/F_{i'j'k}} = \frac{F_{ijk} \times F_{i'j'k}}{F_{i'jk} \times F_{ij'k}} \tag{3.9}$$

This is the ratio of the odds that people in class j vote for party i rather than party i' at election k to the corresponding odds for people in class j'. Odds ratios can be formed for each of the $I \times (I-1)/2$ pairs of parties in combination with each of the $J \times (J-1)/2$ pairs of classes.

The procedure can be clarified by an example using the observed data in Table 3.11. The ratio of the odds for a member of the salariat voting Conservative rather than Labour in 1964 to the corresponding odds for members of the working class is $(167/52) / (175/469) = 3.21/0.37 = 8.61$. This means that in 1964 members of the salariat were 8.61 times more likely than members of the working class to vote Conservative rather than Labour. In the 1987 election this odds radio is $(467/130) / (319/492) = 3.59/0.648 = 5.54$.

We can now introduce the relative odds ratio, a quantity which has a fundamental role to play in the analysis of trends in the association between class and party. For an arbitrary pair of parties i and i', an arbitrary pair of classes j and j', and an arbitrary pair of elections k and k', this is defined as

$$V(k,k') = \frac{R^k(i, i' : j, j')}{R^{k'}(i, i' : j, j')} \tag{3.10}$$

In terms of the example above, the ratio of the odds ratio for 1987 and the odds ratio for 1964 gives the relative odds ratio. This is calculated to be $5.54/8.61 = 0.643$. Thus the relative odds ratio from the observed data suggests that the odds for a member of the salariat voting Conservative rather than Labour relative to the corresponding odds for members of the working class were smaller in 1987 than they had been in 1964.

We can specify a range of models for the data in Table 3.11, and each one implies particular relationships between the response variable, party, and the explanatory variables, class and election. In effect, each model sets particular terms in the saturated model, model J, to zero (or, equivalently, sets them to one in the multiplicative formulation of the model). Each model implies particular structures for the odds ratios and relative odds ratios, and we illustrate this with the particular odds ratio R^k(CON,LAB:SAL,WC), which compares the odds that a member of the salariat votes Conservative rather than Labour with the corresponding odds for a member of the working class, for each year (k).

No-trends model

$$\ell n(F_{ijk}) = \text{constant} + \text{party}(i) + \text{class}(j) + \text{election}(k) + \text{party}(i)$$
$$\times \text{class}(j) + \text{party}(i) \times \text{election}(k) + \text{class}(j) \times \text{election}(k) \quad (\text{model K})$$

The no-trends model for Table 3.11 implies that the association between party and class does not vary with election. The one-way terms, party, class and election simply control for the variations in the numbers of respondents in the different categories of each variable. The two-way term party × class implies that party associated with class; party × election controls for variations in the popularity of parties in different elections; and class × election controls for variations in the numbers in each class in different elections consequent upon changes in the class structure.

The no-trends model sets all the parameters λ_{ijk}^{PCE} to one in the term party × class × election in the multiplicative version of the saturated model (model Jm). This implies that the association between party and class does not vary with election. The model has $G^2 = 84.75$, DF = 56, p-value < 0.01, indicating that it does not fit well. The proportion misclassified is nevertheless only 0.026.

Substituting model Jm, with λ_{ijk}^{PCE} all set to one, in equation (3.9) gives

$$R^k(i, i': j, j') = \frac{\lambda_{ij}^{PC} \times \lambda_{i'j'}^{PC}}{\lambda_{i'j}^{PC} \times \lambda_{ij'}^{PC}} \quad (3.11)$$

So according to the no-trends model, the ratio of the odds that a member of a particular social class votes for a particular party rather than for another party, to the corresponding odds for a member of another social class, does not vary with the levels of election (k). Its value depends only on which combination of pairs of classes and parties is being considered. The particular odds ratio R^k (CON, LAB: SAL, WC) = 6.07, and under the no-trends model it has this value for every election.

As the odds ratios are the same for each election, the no-trends model implies that all relative odds ratios are constant and are equal to one. Formally,

$$V(k, k') = \frac{R^k(i, i': j, j')}{R^{k'}(i, i': j, j')} = 1 \tag{3.12}$$

since $R^k(i, i': j, j') = R^{k'}(i, i': j, j')$ for all k and k'. We shall see that all trends models can be described in terms of the change in the relative odds ratios for particular party/class pairs as we go from election to election.

We simplify the notation by defining $R(k)$ as the odds ratio for a particular party/class combination at election k, and we consider the relationship between the odds ratios at successive elections, $R(k)$ and $R(k + 1)$. With the no-trends model this relationship is

$$R(k) = R(k + 1) \quad \text{or equivalently} \quad V(k, k + 1) = 1 \tag{3.13}$$

Across all eight elections the relationship between the odds ratios is therefore

$$R(1) = R(2) = R(3) = \ldots = R(8) \tag{3.14}$$

With more complex models we can model relationships of the form

$$\begin{aligned}
R(2) &= R(1) \times X_{12} \\
R(3) &= R(2) \times X_{23} \\
R(4) &= R(3) \times X_{34} \quad \text{etc.}
\end{aligned} \tag{3.15}$$

where the Xs are scaling factors as we go from election to election whose value may be allowed to differ according to the particular party/class combination. With the no-trends model we set all the Xs to one, implying that there is no trend in the relative odds ratio, and this applies to all possible party/class odds ratios.

Saturated model

The saturated model (model J) is formed by adding the three-way term party $\times$ class $\times$ election to the no-trends model. In the multiplicative version it corresponds to setting all the independent λ^{PCE}_{ijk} parameters to be different from the value 1. This model fits the data exactly with fitted values equal to the observed values. G^2 is reduced from 84.75 under the no-trends model to zero, using 56 DF, a significant improvement in fit ($p < 0.01$).

The saturated model is not substantively interesting in the analysis of trends because it implies that there are no systematic trends in the party/class relationship, rather that this relationship is different in every election. In terms of odds ratios it implies that there is a different odds ratio for each party/class combination which differs for each election. The fitted odds ratios are identical to the observed odds ratios for each party/class/election combination. Under the saturated model the scaling factors in equation (3.15) vary with both the particular party/class combination and with the particular elections compared:

$$R(k) = \frac{\lambda_{ij}^{PC} \times \lambda_{i'j'}^{PC}}{\lambda_{i'j}^{PC} \times \lambda_{ij'}^{PC}} \times \frac{\lambda_{ijk}^{PCE} \times \lambda_{i'j'k}^{PCE}}{\lambda_{i'jk}^{PCE} \times \lambda_{ij'k}^{PCE}} \qquad (3.16)$$

Thus in using the log-linear model to model trends we are looking for a well-fitting model intermediate between the no-trends and the saturated models, which imposes some structure on the scaling factors as we go from one time point to the next.

Constant-trend model

The log-linear models considered so far treat all the variables defining the multi-way table as nominal and unordered. Recently, a number of special log-linear models have been proposed for contingency tables where one or more of the variables is treated as ordinal (Agresti, 1990; Goodman, 1979). These models incorporate additional parameters which specify that the associations between the nominal variables depend in a systematic way on the ordinal variables.

In the present example, election can be treated as an ordinal variable, and party and class as nominal variables. For this situation the following model has been proposed:

$$F_{ijk} = \lambda \times \lambda_i^P \times \lambda_j^C \times \lambda_k^E \times \lambda_{ij}^{PC} \times \lambda_{ik}^{PE} \times \lambda_{jk}^{CE} \times (\beta_{ij}^{PC})^{W_k} \qquad \text{(model L)}$$

This is a 'constant-trend' model which specifies that the change in the odds ratios for each party/class combination is the same for all successive pairs of elections. It is equivalent to the no-trends model (model K) with an extra term, $(\beta_{ij}^{PC})^{W_k}$. The W_k are scores assigned to the levels of the election variable. A natural scoring system to adopt is the linear sequence 0, 1, 2, 3, 4, 5, 6, 7. In GLIM this represents the additional term party × class × score with $(I–1) \times (J–1) = 8$ extra parameters, coded as party(i) × class(j) × score where score = $k–1$ for election k.

$R(k)$ for this model is obtained by substituting model L in equation (3.9), giving

$$R(k) = \frac{\lambda_{ij}^{PC} \times \lambda_{i'j'}^{PC}}{\lambda_{i'j}^{PC} \times \lambda_{ij'}^{PC}} \times \left[\frac{\beta_{ij}^{PC} \times \beta_{i'j'}^{PC}}{\beta_{i'j}^{PC} \times \beta_{ij'}^{PC}} \right]^{W_k} \qquad (3.17)$$

and the relative odds ratio is therefore given by

$$V(k,k') = \left[\frac{\beta_{ij}^{PC} \times \beta_{i'j'}^{PC}}{\beta_{i'j}^{PC} \times \beta_{ij'}^{PC}} \right]^{W_k - W_{k'}} \qquad (3.18)$$

When model L is fitted to our data we get $G^2 = 70.47$ on 48 DF with a p-value of 0.02. This represents a reduction in deviance of 14.28 from the no-trends model, using 8 additional DF, which is not quite significant at the 0.05 level. So it is not a particularly good model, although it gives a slightly better fit than the no-trends model.

The scoring used above implies an equal spacing of elections in time. It is perhaps more appropriate to use a scoring system which sets W_k to the number of days (or alternatively, months) since the 1964 election, so that the scoring represents real time. However this change produces very little difference in the fit of the model ($G^2 = 69.62$, DF = 48, p-value = 0.022).

Substituting the estimated parameter values in equation (3.9), we get the following fitted odds ratio for R^k(CON,LAB:SAL,WC) in the 1970 election (election 3)

$$R(3) = \frac{1.0 \times 6.74}{1.0 \times 1.0} \times \left[\frac{1.02 \times 1.0}{1.05 \times 1.0}\right]^2 = 6.74 \times (0.97)^2$$

The first component of this is the ratio of the fitted odds in the 1964 election (election 1) that a member of the salariat votes Conservative rather than Labour to the corresponding odds for a member of the working class. The second component is a constant factor, 0.97, by which these odds are multiplied as we go from election to election. The W_k acts as a 'power function' for this factor with the power determined by the number of the election in the time sequence. The fitted values for this odds ratio in each election under model L are given in Table 3.13. In contrast to the no-trends model (model K) which constrains the odds ratios to be the same in each election, they show a constant, but small, relative decline as we move from election to election. More precisely, we have

$R(1) = 6.74$
$R(2) = 6.74 \times 0.97$
$R(3) = 6.74 \times (0.97)^2$
$R(4) = 6.74 \times (0.97)^3$ etc.

Clearly, the scaling factors of equation (3.15) are all equal for any particular party/class pair under this model and, correspondingly, the relative odds ratio $V(k,k+1)$ for successive elections is a constant (here 0.97). Note that the model does not constrain all the odds ratios to change in the same direction; some may increase and others may decrease. A strict test of the 'class-de-alignment' hypothesis would require that those particular odds ratios which are initially larger than the value 1 should decrease while those initially smaller than 1 should increase.

Log-multiplicative model

The log-multiplicative model was originally proposed by Goodman (1979). Its formulation follows that of the constant-trend model (model L), except that the scores W_k are estimated from the data to give minimum deviance

Table 3.13   *Fitted odds ratios (CON,LAB:SAL,WC) under various trend models for Table 3.11*

	Observed odds ratio	Fitted odds ratio under model:			
Election		K No trends	L Constant trend	M Log-multiplicative	N Disaggregated
1964	8.61	6.07	6.74	9.25	7.47
1966	7.29	6.07	6.57	6.36	5.56
1970	4.00	6.07	6.39	4.23	5.56
Feb. 1974	6.22	6.07	6.22	6.37	7.47
Oct. 1974	6.94	6.07	6.06	6.52	5.56
1979	4.77	6.07	5.90	5.02	5.56
1983	6.71	6.07	5.75	6.92	5.96
1987	5.54	6.07	5.59	5.34	5.96
G^2	–	84.75	70.47	43.42	75.04
DF		56	48	41	54
p-value		0.008	0.02	0.40	0.03
Proportion misclassified	–	0.026	0.024	0.015	0.024

G^2. Thus the model fits a different scaling factor for each election, and these factors are not constrained to be in any monotonically increasing (or decreasing) order. As with the constant-trend model, the same W_k apply to each of the possible relative odds ratios we can calculate. Thus the interest lies in whether the estimated W_k do in fact have a monotonic order.

The log-multiplicative model for our data is

$$F_{ijk} = \lambda \times \lambda_i^P \times \lambda_j^C \times \lambda_k^E \times \lambda_{ij}^{PC} \times \lambda_{ik}^{PE} \times \lambda_{jk}^{CE} \times (\beta_{ij}^{PC})^{D \times W_k} \qquad \text{(model M)}$$

It is equivalent to the no-trends model with an extra term $(\beta_{ij}^{PC})^{D \times W_k}$, with $(I–1) \times (J–1) + K–1 = 15$ extra parameters. In this model the W_k and the scaling constant D are parameters to be estimated. The actual values that are estimated for the W_k are arbitrary; only the ratios of the differences in the scores between elections are meaningful. Thus the W_k can be scaled to give scores in the range 0 to 1, and if this is done, $\exp(D)$ gives the scaling factor comparing the two elections, where W_k is set to 1 and 0 respectively.

Fitting this model involves a two-stage iterative fitting process. At the first stage, model M is fitted to estimate the W_k. At the second stage, model M is fitted again but using the W_k obtained from the first stage which are now treated as known. Initially W_k is set to 1,2, ..., 8 and the whole process is repeated until the estimates of W_k stabilize. This process converges and gives unique estimates of the W_k and a final model with minimum deviance. Breen (1985) gives a GLIM macro to fit this model to a two-way table where both variables are ordinal. This has been modified to suit the data structure we have in our example, namely a three-way table where one of the variables (election) is ordinal.

The odds ratios $R(k)$ obtained by substituting model M in equation (3.9) are given by

$$R(k) = \frac{\lambda_{ij}^{PC} \times \lambda_{i'j'}^{PC}}{\lambda_{i'j}^{PC} \times \lambda_{ij'}^{PC}} \times \left[\frac{\beta_{ij}^{PC} \times \beta_{i'j'}^{PC}}{\beta_{i'j}^{PC} \times \beta_{ij'}^{PC}} \right]^{D \times W_k} \tag{3.19}$$

This differs from the equivalent formula for the constant-trend model given in equation (3.17) in two ways: the W_k are estimated, and there is a scaling constant D. The relative odds ratios are given by the formula

$$V(k,k') = \left[\frac{\beta_{ij}^{PC} \times \beta_{i'j'}^{PC}}{\beta_{i'j}^{PC} \times \beta_{ij'}^{PC}} \right]^{D \times (W_k - W_{k'})} \tag{3.20}$$

The log-multiplicative model fits our data very well: G^2 is 43.42 on 41 DF (p-value = 0.40). The reduction in G^2 on the no-trends model is 41.33 using 15 DF, which is highly significant ($p < 0.001$). The estimates of the W_k parameters for the calculation of fitted odds ratios are given in Table 3.14. The scaling constant D is estimated as 0.5716. Note that these estimated 'optimum' scores do not form a monotonic trend; they increase between 1964 and 1970, but thereafter fluctuate considerably.

The fitted odds ratio for R^k(CON,LAB:SAL,WC) at the 1970 election is given by

$$R(3) = \frac{1.0 \times 9.25}{1.0 \times 1.0} \times \left[\frac{1.0 \times 0.25}{1.0 \times 1.0} \right]^{0.5716 \times 1.0}$$

$$= 9.25 \times (0.25)^{0.5716} = 4.23$$

The first component is the corresponding odds ratio for election 1 (1964). The second component is a factor, different for each odds ratio, which is raised to the power of a scaling factor $D \times W_k$ which is constant for election k.

The relative odds ratio for elections k and k' is a constant, dependent on the particular odds ratio considered, which is raised to the power of $D \times (W_k - W_{k'})$. Under the model this power function is the same for all the odds ratios based on all pairwise combinations of class and party.

Table 3.13 gives the fitted odds ratios for R^k(CON,LAB:SAL,WC) in each election under model M. There is a decline between 1964 and 1970, with Labour also doing badly in 1979 and 1987.

Disaggregated three-way interaction models

An alternative approach to modelling trends in the relationship between class and party across elections is to disaggregate the three-way interaction term party × class × election. This involves models which allow particular odds ratios for particular party/class combinations to vary with election. The formulation of such models should be guided by *a priori* hypotheses.

Table 3.14 *Parameter estimates for scores W_k for model M*

Election	k	W_k
1964	1	0.00
1966	2	0.48
1970	3	1.00
Feb. 1974	4	0.48
Oct. 1974	5	0.45
1979	6	0.78
1983	7	0.37
1987	8	0.70

In such models we may treat election not as an ordinal variable, but as a proxy for underlying social, political or economic factors which we hypothesize to affect the relationship between class and party in a systematic way. In this case we would define certain periods according to our hypotheses; in our data these periods would be defined as groups of elections, not necessarily successive ones. The model would imply that the odds ratios for particular class/party pairs were constant within these periods, but differed between periods. Our hypothesis may also predict the nature of the differences between periods. This type of model is analogous to the logistic model I for the youth unemployment data. There is a very large number of possible disaggregated models which we could fit to the data. We shall not attempt a definitive analysis of this class of models, but will use an example to illustrate what can be done.

Let us hypothesize that the critical element in the relationship between class and party is the relationship between the working class and the Labour Party. According to this hypothesis, the relative propensity of members of the working class (compared with the members of other classes in general) to vote Labour rather than Conservative or Liberal varies from election to election. For example, it has been argued that the Labour administrations in the 1960s and the 1970s particularly alienated the working class since they failed to achieve full employment and rising standards of living. Again, it has been argued that Labour's policy of unilateral nuclear disarmament and fear of the 'loony left' may have alienated working-class voters in the 1980s.

Model N allows us to test these hypotheses. On the right-hand side it includes all the terms in the no-trends model (model K) plus an additional term Labour × working × electype. 'Labour' is scored 2 for Labour voters and 1 for people who vote for the Conservative Party or the Liberals, i.e. it contrasts Labour voters with voters for other parties. 'Working' is scored 2 for members of the working class and 1 for members of all other social classes, i.e. it contrasts members of the working class with members of other social classes. 'Electype' recodes election into one of three types:

1   pre-eighties election, Conservative Party in power at the time of the election (1964 and February 1974 elections)

2   pre-eighties election, Labour Party in power at the time of the election (1966, 1970, October 1974 and 1979 elections)

3   eighties elections, Conservative Party in power (1983 and 1987 elections).

Note that this model assumes that odds ratios for other class/party pairs (those not involving the Labour Party and the working class) fit a no-trends model. The fit is about the same as the fit of the constant-trend model (model L) with $G^2 = 75.04$ on 54 DF (p-value $= 0.03$). There is a significant reduction in deviance from the no-trends model of 9.71 using 2 DF (p-value < 0.01).

In formal terms, model N is the no-trends model (model K) with the addition of two extra independent parameters to give

$$F_{ijk} = \lambda \times \lambda_i^P \times \lambda_j^C \times \lambda_k^E \times \lambda_{ij}^{PC} \times \lambda_{ik}^{PE} \times \lambda_{jk}^{CE} \times a_m \qquad \text{(model N)}$$

where a_m structures the three-way term λ_{ijk}^{PCE} as follows:
$a_m = a_1$ if Labour (i) is 2, working (j) is 2, and electype (k) belongs to type 2;
$a_m = a_2$ if Labour (i) is 2, working (j) is 2, and electype (k) belongs to type 3; and $a_m = 1.0$ otherwise.

The odds ratios for this model, obtained by substituting model N in equation (3.9), are

$$R(k) = \frac{\lambda_{ij}^{PC} \times \lambda_{i'j}^{PC}}{\lambda_{i'j}^{PC} \times \lambda_{ij}^{PC}} \times \frac{\lambda_{ijk}^{PCE} \times \lambda_{i'j'k}^{PCE}}{\lambda_{i'jk}^{PCE} \times \lambda_{ij'k}^{PCE}} \qquad (3.21)$$

where the parameters in the second component are either a_1, a_2, or 1.0 as set out above.

In the GLIM system the model yields parameter estimates $a_1 = 0.744$ and $a_2 = 0.798$. The estimated odds ratio $R^k(\text{CON,LAB:SAL,WC})$ for an election of type 2 is given by

$$\frac{1.0 \times 7.47}{1.0 \times 1.0} \times \frac{1.0 \times 0.744}{1.0 \times 1.0} = 7.47 \times 0.744 = 5.56$$

The first component gives the odds ratio for elections of type 1; the second gives the adjustment required for type 2 elections. Similarly to calculate the odds for elections of type 3 we multiply the odds for type 1 elections by 0.79, giving fitted odds of $7.47 \times 0.79 = 5.96$. Thus the extra parameters a_1 and a_2 are scaling factors as we go from election to election. Model N is in fact an example of a model where the scaling factors differ according to the particular odds ratio and election under consideration. Thus $V(k,k') = 0.74$ if the odds ratio involves Labour or the working class, k refers to an election of type 1 and k' refers to an election of type 2.

Table 3.13 gives the odds ratios fitted under model N for (CON,LAB: SAL,WC), which are, as we have seen, constrained to be the same for elections of the same type. The model indicates that in type 2 elections (pre-1983 elections where the Labour Party was in power at the time of the election) the working class was relatively less likely to vote Labour compared with members of the other social classes than they were in type 1 elections, when the Conservative Party was in power. They were also relatively less likely to vote Labour in type 3 elections (elections where the Conservative Party was in power but which took place in the eighties) than they were in pre-eighties elections where the Conservative Party was in power.

Monotonic changes in odds ratios

The model that provides the best test of the hypothesis of class de-alignment specifies that the scaling factors change in the same direction across elections, either consistently down or up, but are not constrained to change at any particular rate. Odds ratios which are initially greater than 1 should reduce monotonically; odds ratios initially less than 1 should increase montonically. Erikson and Goldthorpe (1992) and Xie (1992) have recently developed such a model.

In terms of the relative odds ratios the monotonic changes model implies that $X_{12}, X_{23}, \ldots > 1$ when $R(1) < 1$ and $X_{12}, X_{23}, \ldots < 1$ when $R(1) > 1$.

Choosing between models

It is not an entirely straightforward matter to choose between the various models which we have described. The standard test for comparing models requires that they be 'nested', but the constant-trend, log-multiplicative and disaggregated models are not in fact nested except with respect to the no-trends model. In other words, we can state whether any one of the three is a significant improvement on the no-trends model, but we have to be more circumspect in comparing the three models with each other.

In practice, as Table 3.13 shows, of the models that we have been able to fit, the log-multiplicative model (model M) has the highest probability that any differences between the observed and the fitted values have arisen by chance and gives the lowest proportion of cases misclassified under the model. This is probably the model that we should accept. However, it is quite possible that further explorations with disaggregated models might yield fits that were as good or nearly as good. In theory, there is no reason to expect a unique, best-fitting model. It is quite possible to have different models which fit the data equally well. Nonetheless, it is fairly clear that we must reject the no-trends model. The relationship between class and party does seem to have varied from election to election, and in particular the log-multiplicative model suggests that de-alignment was clearest between 1964 and 1970.

Conclusions

This chapter has shown how log-linear and logistic models may be used for modelling trends in relationships between categorical variables. These models are specifically designed to take account of the categorical nature of the variables and they enable us to formulate and test specific hypotheses concerning the mutual relationships between variables, taking account of sampling variability. One of their particular strengths is that they allow us to control for variations observed over time in the marginal distributions of variables so that changes in relationships can be assessed net of these variations. This feature has been particularly important in the analysis of trends in social mobility (see, for example, Goldthorpe et al., 1987) where log-linear models are now used routinely. These models provide a powerful scheme for the analysis of multi-way tables and represent a major improvement over traditional techniques such as the method of elaboration (Davis, 1971) which is restricted to a particular type of hypothesis subsumed in the log-linear model.

However, log-linear and logistic models can present various problems when applied to real data and there has not been space for a full discussion of these difficulties here. For more information the reader is referred to the main texts on modelling categorical data, such as Agresti (1990). Problems include the sensitivity of significance tests to sample size, the choice of measures of fit, the effect of a clustered sample design (common to much survey data) on inferences, and the presence of cells with very small or zero frequencies. Provided that cell sizes are adequate, log-linear and logistic models can readily be fitted to tables with many dimensions, but it can be very difficult to interpret higher-order interactions between variables. A further problem is that the global tests for the parameters that make up an interaction term may mask individual changes involving particular combinations of categories of variables. Thus in some cases it may be necessary to fit the rather complex disaggregated models described in the later part of the chapter. The specification of such models should be guided by substantive hypotheses, but it may sometimes be difficult to choose between competing models.

The account given in this chapter of how log-linear models are applied to the analysis of multi-way tables is introductory only. A full treatment would include the analysis of tables where some or all of the variables defining the table have ordered categories (see Agresti, 1990), fitting categorical data models in a path analysis framework (see Goodman, 1973), and the development of both graphical models to investigate tables with many dimensions (see Whittaker, 1990) and multilevel models to analyze data with a hierarchical structure (Goldstein, 1987). Finally good modelling practice prescribes that diagnostic tests be carried out to examine the effect of deviant cells on the inferences drawn and the validity of the assumptions underlying the models; these topics are beyond our scope here.

Note

This chapter was written with the support of the ESRC (grant no. Y303253002), which is gratefully acknowledged.

References

Agresti, A. (1990) *Categorical Data Analysis.* New York: Wiley.

Breen, R. (1985) 'Log-multiplicative models for contingency tables using GLIM', *GLIM Newsletter*, 10: 14–19.

Davis, J. (1971) *Elementary Survey Analysis.* Englewood Cliffs, NJ: Prentice-Hall.

Dixon, W. (ed.) (1983) *BMDP Statistical Software.* Berkeley: University of California Press.

Erikson, R. and Goldthorpe, J.H. (1992) *The Constant Flux: a Study of Class Mobility in Industrial Societies.* Oxford: Clarendon Press.

Evans, G., Heath, A. and Payne, C. (1991) 'Modelling trends in the class/party relationship 1964–1987', *Electoral Studies*, 10: 99–117.

Fienberg, S. (1980) *The Analysis of Cross-Classified Data*, 2nd edn. Cambridge: MIT Press.

Francis, B.J., Green, M. and Payne, C. (1993) *The GLIM Manual.* Oxford: Oxford University Press.

Gilbert, G. N. (1993) *Analyzing Tabular Data.* London: University College London Press.

Goldstein, H. (1987) *Multilevel Models in Educational and Social Research.* New York: Oxford University Press.

Goldthorpe, J. (in collaboration with Llewelyn, C. and Payne, C.) (1987) *Social Mobility and Class Structure in Modern Britain*, 2nd edn. Oxford: Oxford University Press.

Goodman, L. (1973) 'The analysis of multiway tables when some variables are posterior to others', *Biometrika*, 60: 179–92.

Goodman, L. (1979) 'Simple models for the analysis of association in cross-classifications having ordered categories', *Journal of the American Statistical Association*, 74: 537–52.

Heath, A., Curtice, J. and Jowell, R. (1985) *How Britain Votes.* Oxford: Pergamon.

Knoke, D. and Burke, J. (1980) *Log-Linear Models.* Beverly Hills and London: Sage.

Payne, J. and Payne, C. (1985) 'Youth unemployment 1974–81: the changing importance of age and qualifications', *The Quarterly Journal of Social Affairs*, 1(3): 177–92.

Scott Long, J. (1984) 'Estimable functions in log-linear models', *Sociological Methods and Research*, 12(4): 399–431.

Whittaker, J. (1990) *Graphical Models in Applied Multivariate Statistics.* Chichester: Wiley.

Xie, Y. (1992) 'The log-multiplicative layer effect model for comparing mobility tables', *American Sociological Review*, 57: 380–95.

4

The Analysis of Pooled Cross-Sectional Data

Editors' introduction

An important theme in the previous chapter is the pooling and simultaneous analysis of data from a number of comparable cross-section surveys. Micklewright develops this theme further, focusing upon individual-level modelling rather than data aggregated into a cross-tabulation. In particular, this allows continuous explanatory variables to be included in the analysis; variables such as age and income do not have to be divided into categories to enable cross-tabulation of the data.

In the first section of this chapter, Micklewright provides a very general perspective on pooled cross-sectional approaches, reviewing their advantages and disadvantages and comparing them with alternatives. The example in the second section is concerned with the factors which influence staying on at school beyond the statutory minimum leaving age. The method used is very similar to the first example in Chapter 3. The response variable is binary and the longitudinal dimension is represented by including time as an explanatory variable in a model usually associated with cross-sectional analysis. However, the Micklewright example has some distinctive characteristics. We would draw the reader's attention to two which are closely related.

First, the example demonstrates the rigour which economists typically apply to model formulation; they have a healthy tradition of deriving models from first principles rather than selecting a model 'off the shelf'.

Second, the example indicates some of the flexibility of the statistical modelling approach. As so often happens in practice, the problem addressed has a number of non-standard characteristics which require an additional level of sophistication in model formulation and model fitting. In particular, some of the sample of 16-year-olds do not have the right to leave school. The model is therefore complicated by the need to allow for some respondents to be constrained while others are able to choose. This is termed the double-hurdle model – the first hurdle being the statutory right to leave school and the second the decision whether or not to leave.

Some technical notes are in order for this chapter. It is sometimes possible to estimate population (or process) characteristics without making any probability distribution assumptions. Such estimates are referred to as being *non-parametric*. In contrast the more common parametric approach requires assumptions about probability distributions (the probability model). Technically, probability distributions may be defined in a variety of entirely equivalent ways. For example, $\epsilon \sim N(\mu, \sigma^2)$ indicates that e is normally distributed with mean μ and variance σ^2. The probability density function specifies the shape of a continuous probability distribution, and the notation $\phi(\epsilon)$ is often used for the probability density function of the standard normal distribution (i.e. the normal distribution with zero mean and unit variance). The cumulative probability density (or distribution) function specifies the probability of each value not being exceeded and must increase from zero to one. The notation $\Phi(\epsilon)$ is often used for the distribution function of the standard normal (see Figure 4.1).

In modelling binary outcomes it is necessary to adopt an S-shaped transformation for relating the probability of outcome to a linear predictor which summarizes the effects of the explanatory variables. The basic problem is that a linear predictor can vary anywhere between plus and minus infinity

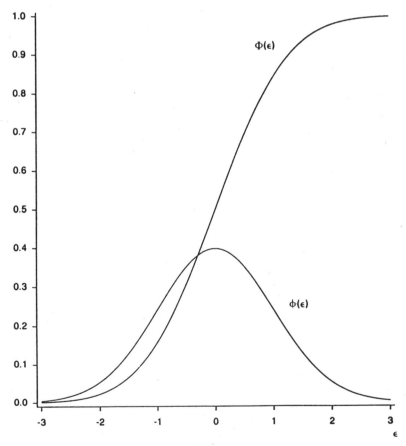

Figure 4.1 *Probability density $\phi(\epsilon)$ and distribution $\Phi(\epsilon)$ functions for the standard normal distribution*

while probabilities are necessarily constrained to the interval between 0 and 1 inclusive (see Figure 4.2). In Chapter 2 (Davies) and Chapter 3 (Payne et al.) a logistic (or logit) transformation is used, whereas Micklewright chooses a probit transformation. The S shape in the probit transformation is that of the standard normal distribution function. As it happens, the logistic and probit transformations have very similar shapes and selecting between them is relatively unimportant.

The likelihood is the basis of most model-fitting procedures. Roughly speaking, it is the probability (or probability density) of obtaining the outcomes actually observed *if the model is correct*. It is a function of (that is, it varies depending on) parameters whose values are unknown. The maximum likelihood parameter estimates are those values which maximize the likelihood function; they are the values for which the observed outcomes were the most likely outcomes to occur, assuming, of course, that the model is correct. Mathematically, it is usually more convenient to maximize the logarithm of the likelihood function but this does not affect the results.

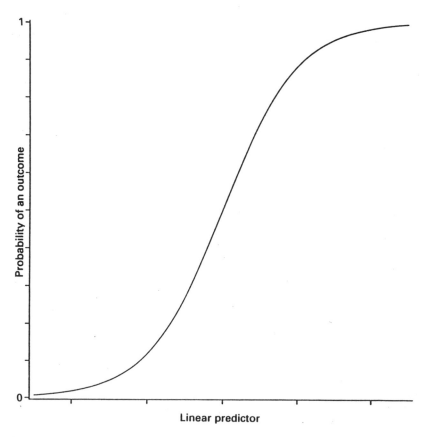

Figure 4.2   *S-shaped transformation from a linear predictor summarizing the effects of explanatory variables to an outcome probability*

The Analysis of Pooled Cross-Sectional Data: Early School Leaving

John Micklewright

This chapter considers the use of *pooled cross-sectional data*.[1] This term is used to describe the pooling of successive cross-sections of different observational units. The effect of this pooling is to produce a large cross-section, with time of observation as one attribute which varies across units. Examples might be the combination of several years of the UK Family Expenditure Survey or the General Household Survey, both annual cross-sections of several thousand households. An example from the US would be the use of a number of years of micro-data from the Current Population Survey.

The first section considers the reasons for using pooled cross-sectional data. What can a pooled cross-section offer the researcher which a simple cross-section or a pure time series of aggregate data cannot? How may such data be used to address important research questions? The attractions of a pooled cross-section are considerable, but at the same time this type of source has several problems of which the researcher should be aware when contemplating use. These are discussed in the second half of the section. Both the attractions and the problems of pooled cross-section survey information are illustrated by reference to various studies which have been based on this type of data.

The second section provides a practical example of the use of a time series of cross-sections. Individual-level data on 16-year-olds and their families, drawn from seven consecutive years of the UK Family Expenditure Survey (FES), are used to analyze the probability of leaving school at the first legal opportunity. The statistical technique which is used can be viewed as a development of the binary model presented in Chapter 2, a development which was required because the FES does not record the precise date of each respondent's birth. While this problem of the FES data is not peculiar to its use in a pooled cross-section study, the technique of a 'double-hurdle' model (defined below) is one which researchers have increasingly realized as having general applicability to cross-section data. The first part of the section describes the data used in the analysis, highlighting their strengths and weaknesses, while the second part presents the double-hurdle model and results.

As a final prefatory remark, the reader is warned that although mention will be made of particular data sets, and of some of their quirks, it is not the aim of this chapter to provide a comprehensive guide to cross-section surveys that could be pooled. For this, the reader must consult available sources for the relevant country.[2]

The use of pooled cross-sectional data

Many countries have cross-section surveys which are carried out on a regular basis, thus offering the possibility of pooling the data for different years. The Labour Force Surveys of the European Community countries (with a core of common questions: see Eurostat, 1985), those of other OECD countries, and the US Current Population Survey (CPS) are all examples. To make things simple, in what follows I assume the existence of an *annual national household survey*, that is a national cross-section survey of a representative sample of households and the individuals contained in them. I also assume the availability to the researcher of the *micro-data* from the survey. Such a situation does exist in the UK (where the Family Expenditure Survey (FES) and General Household Survey (GHS) both have long histories and are available for secondary analysis) but it should be noted that much of what is said below is applicable to countries where the survey in question may not be annual, carried out on households, or even national.

Unless one is satisfied with the published tabulations in the official survey reports (which may not take a constant format), access to the micro-data from each year's survey is essential if *descriptive* analysis of a variety of topics is to be carried out. For example, pooled data have been used to describe unemployment rates by skill (Micklewright, 1984) and change in the youth labour market (Payne, 1985). When assessing the benefits of pooling cross-sections, I concentrate, however, on the advantages for *multivariate* analysis (using linear regression, logit or probit models, or some other statistical technique).

Table 4.1 provides examples both of studies which have undertaken descriptive analysis and of those which have applied statistical techniques to pooled cross-section data. That almost all these studies refer to Britain or the UK is not important; it does however reflect the fact that the availability of regular high-quality cross-sections, together with a relative paucity of panel data, has led to pooled cross-section data being widely used in Britain. The subjects analyzed in the studies in the table are not necessarily representative of the type of research which pooled cross-sections can support; what does matter are the benefits derived from pooling which are suggested in the final column.

Benefits of pooling

Sample size Perhaps the most obvious advantage of the existence of a number of surveys carried out on the same basis is that by combining surveys for different years, a major increase in sample size may be achieved. The information obtained by general-purpose cross-section surveys may be suitable for a whole range of highly specialized research topics but progress with

Table 4.1   *Examples of pooled cross-section studies*

Author	Data	Subject analyzed	Benefits from pooling
Micklewright (1985)	FES 1972–80	Unemployment benefit	Sample size
Payne (1987)	GHS 1980–81	Unemployment in the family	Sample size
Atkinson et al. (1984)	FES 1972–77	Unemployment duration	Sample size Varying labour market conditions
Payne and Payne (1985)	GHS 1974–81	Youth unemployment	Varying labour market conditions
Breen (1986)	ISL 1980–82	Youth labour market	Varying labour market conditions
Atkinson et al. (1990)	FES 1971–83	Spending on alcohol	Price variation
Browning et al. (1985)	FES 1971–77	Male labour supply and consumption	Pseudo-panel
Baker et al. (1989)	FES 1972–83	Ownership of central heating	Cohort effects
Gomulka and Stern (1990)	FES 1970–83	Married women's work	Growth accounting
Blank and Card (1989)	CPS 1968–87	Unemployment insurance	Growth accounting

FES   UK Family Expenditure Survey   GHS   UK General Household Survey
ISL   Irish School Leavers Survey   CPS   US Current Population Census.

a single year's data may in practice be impossible owing to a very small number of observations. In this situation, pooling may be essential in order to achieve a sample which will allow any analysis to take place. This applied to the study by Micklewright (1985) of the receipt of earnings-related unemployment insurance amongst short-term unemployed men. Even when data from nine years of the Family Expenditure Survey were used, the resulting sample contained only 512 observations of the particular type required. Similarly, studies by Ermisch and Wright (1989) and by Walker (1989) of lone parents' labour force participation would have been very difficult to undertake on a single year's data of the surveys concerned.

Even if the subject under study involves a large proportion of the cases in a single year, an increase in sample size will always be desirable, other things equal, since it will result in an increase in the precision of statistical analysis. Assuming random sampling, standard errors should be proportional to the square root of the sample size. On this basis, a quadrupling in sample size achieved by pooling four years of data would be expected to result in a halving of confidence intervals, allowing more precise conclusions to be drawn. On the other hand the *ceteris paribus* nature of this benefit of pooling must be emphasized. If the true parameters of the model being estimated change over time then precision may not increase (this point is returned to below).

Temporal Change   The opportunity to inject substantial temporal variation into explanatory variables used in statistical modelling represents a major attraction of pooling. Examples may clarify the issues involved.

Individuals' behaviour in the labour market (and arguably in other markets) can in general be expected to be a function of labour market conditions. For example, a higher unemployment rate may induce a 'discouraged worker' effect on labour force participation, something which a complete model of participation should take into account. Although a single year's cross-section will contain some geographical variation in labour market conditions, major temporal variation will typically be lacking (some temporal variation will be present if interviews are spread through the year as in the Family Expenditure and General Household Surveys).

And yet it is temporal variation in which one is most interested. If the labour market worsens, will fewer married women participate? Will the period spent out of work by the unemployed lengthen? It is unsatisfactory to hope for the job to be done by geographical variation in an unemployment rate (say) attached to the data set. This is particularly true if one wishes to introduce dummy variables for different areas (e.g. regions) into the estimated equations. A full set of regional dummy variables would be perfectly collinear with a time-invariant regional unemployment rate, whereas in the absence of the former the latter may partly proxy regional effects which have nothing to do with unemployment. Pooling cross-sections for a number of years produces genuine temporal variation. In the study by Atkinson et al. (1984) which used six years of cross-section data, a much bigger impact of labour demand proxies on the length of spells of unemployment was found than by Nickell (1979) who used a single year of data to study the same subject.

In the above example, I looked at a single year of cross-section data and asked what is the benefit of using extra years of micro-data. Another way of arriving at a pooled cross-section is to imagine one is using aggregate time-series data and to ask what is the advantage of introducing individual-level variation in each of the years in question by pooling annual micro-data.

Statistical analysis of aggregate time series is often dogged by problems of multicollinearity. Income, social class indicators, education levels and prices may all move together over time, making it hard to pin down their independent effects. By using a time series of cross-sections, individual-level effects coming from income, social class and education will be identified using the enormous variation present in micro-data. The effects of prices, for example, can be identified by the temporal variation introduced by pooling, thus avoiding the problems of collinearity present in aggregate time series. This is one of the benefits of pooling exploited in the research by Atkinson et al. (1990) and Baker et al. (1989) who include analysis of the effect of changing prices on household expenditure on alcohol and energy respectively.[3]

Pseudo-panel data and cohort effects   The difficulties of distinguishing age or life-cycle effects from cohort effects in cross-sectional data are well known. For example, if one observes with a 1980 survey that the labour market participation rate of women aged 41–50 is *x* per cent lower than that of women aged 31–40, one cannot tell how much (if at all) this is due to the life cycle (age, fertility etc) and how much to birth cohort. It may be the case, for example, that women born in 1930–9 (aged 41–50 in 1980) received less education on average than those born in 1940–9 and that (perhaps via lower wages) this is an explanation for their lower participation rate.

The major attraction of using panel data is the ability to track the behaviour or experiences of the same people over time. Panel data (whether collected through recall or through regular surveying) allow one to separate out the effects of cohort from life cycle. Successive observations on individuals from both the 1930–9 and 1940–9 birth cohorts will show whether the former always participate less or whether the difference observed in their participation rates at a single time is entirely due to the life cycle. A more detailed example is given in Chapter 2.

It is wrong to think of pooled cross-section data as being a poor cousin of panel data, but a series of cross-sections can be used to create a 'pseudo-panel'. A series of cross-sections cannot be used to monitor exactly the same people over time but it can be used to track samples from fixed subpopulations, in particular birth cohorts. A cross-section drawn in 1970 could be used to obtain information on samples of people aged 31–40, born during 1930–9, and 21–30, born in 1940–9. A 1971 cross-section provides information on the behaviour in the next year of another two samples from these two birth cohorts. The 1971 samples will be composed of sets of individuals which differ from those in the 1970 samples, but, with the exception of deaths and migration, sampling will be from a fixed population of 1930–9 and 1940–9 births. In this way, the changing behaviour of the two birth cohorts could be tracked up to 1980, so allowing light to be shed on the problem posed earlier. The data set which results from this sort of exercise consists of repeated observations over time of samples from the same birth cohorts; it may be termed a pseudo-panel.

The fact that the samples from any birth cohort are different in each year means that summary statistics relating to the cohort, for example the proportion of married women in work, will be subject to considerable fluctuation as a result of sampling variation. The smaller one makes the birth cohort, e.g. five instead of ten years, the more this will be a problem. Any change in the determinants of survey response may cause spurious change in the summary statistic. The same is true of course of genuine panel studies which rely on continued response of the same individuals. Moreover, as Deaton (1985) points out, genuine panels have the additional problem of cumulative non-response, or 'attrition', something that will not occur with pseudo-panels.[4]

Pseudo-panels may be used for descriptive analysis or they may be used for the estimation of multivariate statistical models. Deaton (1985) considers the conditions under which such models estimated with pseudo-panels will produce results which are equivalent to those obtained with genuine panels. Browning et al. (1985) provide an example of the use of a pseudo-panel to estimate a model of male labour supply.

It may not always be necessary to create pseudo-panels from pooled cross-sections to proxy some of the attributes of genuine panels. For example, although year of birth and age are perfectly correlated in a single year's cross-section (leading to the problem of interpretation discussed earlier) this will not be the case in a sample of pooled cross-section micro-data. Thus year of birth and age can be entered as separate variables in statistical models estimated on pooled cross-sections and in this way the advantages of large sample size and micro-level variation, which are lost in a pseudo-panel, are retained. For an example see Baker et al. (1989).

Growth accounting   Between 1970 and 1977 the proportion of married women in employment in the UK rose from 50 to 60 per cent (Gomulka and Stern, 1990). Between 1977 and 1987 the proportion of eligible unem-ployed persons who claimed unemployment insurance benefit in the US is estimated to have fallen from 75 to 66 per cent (Blank and Card, 1989). Were these changes due to a change in behaviour over the periods in ques-tion of a population with fixed characteristics, or were they due to a change in the characteristics of a population whose behaviour was fixed? Pooled cross-section data, used in both the studies referred to, can help shed light on this.

A suitable methodology is very clearly described by Gomulka and Stern and their paper represents an important contribution to the literature on the use of pooled cross-section data. In essence, the technique involves estimat-ing the same statistical model *separately* for each year of data. The coeffi-cients obtained from estimation with one year are then applied to the explanatory variables in the data from other years, and each time a summary aggregate measure of the predicted value of the response variable can be obtained. In the case of Gomulka and Stern, this is the proportion of married women in employment. A matrix is built up of values of the overall partici-pation rate obtained with year *i*'s data and year *j*'s coefficients etc. In this way we can see firstly how the overall participation rate is predicted to change over time for a fixed sample, as successive years' coefficients are applied. This will measure the effect of changes in behaviour for a fixed set of popu-lation characteristics. Secondly, we can see how participation is predicted to change if we apply a single year's set of coefficients to successive years of data. This will show the effect of demographic and other change in explana-tory variables on participation, when behaviour is fixed. In this way, cross-section data from different years can be used to decompose the causes of aggregate change.

Mutually exclusive benefits?   The discussion of growth accounting should have alerted the reader to the fact that it is not possible to realize all the benefits of pooling simultaneously. It is worth repeating that the methodol-ogy for growth accounting described by Gomulka and Stern involves the estimation of a statistical model separately for each year of data. This represents a very different approach to pooling to that discussed earlier under the headings 'Sample size' and 'Temporal change'. Those benefits of pooling require that the statistical model be estimated on the entire pooled sample. Pooling to increase sample size may be undertaken because estimation with individual years – necessary for growth accounting – is impossible. By estimating models using separate years, temporal variation in, for example, labour market conditions is removed and the equations estimated by Gomulka and Stern contain no variable to pick up aggregate labour market effects.

It is clear that if sample sizes in individual years (or groups of years) are sufficient, then estimation should in any case be undertaken on the individual years to check the stability of the estimated model. Using the results from the same model estimated on both pooled data and the separate years, standard statistical tests can be used to check the hypothesis of parameter stability. In the research by Gomulka and Stern, the hypothesis of stability of coefficients across the entire 14-year period (necessary for pooling) was decisively rejected by the data and was frequently rejected at the 5 per cent level even if stability was checked on only three consecutive years. The authors note that their result put into perspective those obtained from a single year's data and the ability to check the representativeness of estimates from a single cross-section is certainly a major attraction of pooling.

Problems

Some of the problems of pooling cross-section data have already been touched on in the discussion above. The reader will find further consideration in papers which have explicitly considered methodology in this area, e.g. Deaton (1985) and Gomulka and Stern (1990). Here I will discuss a few practical points.

Changing definitions   The main structure of an annual cross-section may change little over time or may change in a way that is 'invisible' to the user, such as a switch in sampling frame (as occurred in the case of the UK General Household Survey in 1984, from electoral registers to postcodes). However, there may often be detailed changes which can be of major consequence to researchers wishing to pool surveys from a number of years. By way of illustration, I give a number of examples from the UK Family Expenditure and General Household Surveys (FES and GHS).[5] Readers interested in different surveys should not skip ahead; the examples serve as a warning of the type of changes which may occur in any survey in any country. (Anyone thinking of using FES or GHS should also note that these examples are far from a complete list.)

Firstly, there are those variables which are only present for a few years. The existence of a variable in one year should not be taken as implying that it will be there in earlier or later years. Age of completing full-time education was first introduced in the FES in 1978; any analysis of the impact of length of education using pooled FES data can only begin in that year. Changes like this are easy enough to spot but it is of course necessary to check in advance that variables crucial to a particular research project are present in each year.

Secondly, there are variables which may always be present but which may change definition. The income section of GHS underwent a radical revision in 1979. The survey had collected income information from the outset but the scale of the changes made in 1979 (described in OPCS, 1981, Chapter 9) means that any researcher using GHS income data from both the 1970s and the 1980s needs to proceed with caution. Great care is needed with changes which may be less dramatic than this and hard to spot without detailed study of codebooks. The variable indicating employment status in FES changed in 1972. Prior to this year the relevant variable did not distinguish between the unemployed seeking work and the unemployed who, owing to temporary illness or injury, were not (the distinction being an important one as far as the numbers in the two categories were concerned: see Atkinson and Micklewright, 1980). Moreover, although other categories had (with one exception) the same definition, the actual coded values in some cases differed from those in later years. More recently, the treatment of those on government training schemes has changed, reflecting the increasing importance of such labour market programmes. It cannot be stressed too much (and this advice comes from bitter experience) that one must use codebooks and questionnaires to check, check and check again to see if variables have consistent definitions across the period of interest. Remember, the survey was not specifically designed for use on a pooled basis.

The general nature of poolable sources The type of survey suitable for pooling will typically be a general-purpose household or labour force survey. In choosing this type of source in order to derive some of the advantages of pooling, e.g. temporal change, it should of course be recognized that the level of detail on particular subjects may well not be as great as that present in a one-off *ad hoc* survey designed specifically to throw light on the issue the researcher is interested in. For example, the 1978 DHSS Cohort Study of the Unemployed, used by Narendranathan et al. (1985) to look at the disincentive effects of unemployment benefits in Britain, contained much more detail on benefit receipt and the duration of unemployment than did the pooled FES data used by Atkinson et al. (1984). On the other hand, labour demand effects had to be identified by Narendranathan et al. by using largely geographical variation, whereas the use of pooled FES data allowed temporal variation to be exploited. There may therefore be a trade-off between the use of pooled general surveys and more detailed one-off data sources. They each have their attractions and it is clearly wrong to see a pooled cross-section as the ideal data set for all purposes.

Effort required including computing power Any research using large micro-data sets requires a lot of effort and computing power. The analysis of pooled cross-section data is no exception and anyone thinking of embarking on a research project that would use this type of data needs to consider the manpower and computing requirements carefully. Does one's computer centre have a mainframe machine which could handle a data set which might have 100,000 observations or more, each with several hundred variables? While estimation of statistical models may eventually take place using much smaller samples (and may occur on a microcomputer), the preparatory task of extracting data, computing intermediate variables etc. will typically require a combination of decent mainframe and software package. The work reported in the second section illustrates this. The data were first assembled on a mainframe and then brought down on to a microcomputer for model fitting.

Early school leaving: evidence from the Family Expenditure Survey

The second half of this chapter illustrates the use of pooled cross-section data to estimate a model explaining the probability of leaving full-time education at the first legal opportunity. The analysis concerns Britain where individuals may leave full-time education when they are 16. The data which are used are observations on 2,177 16-year-olds taken from the Family Expenditure Survey (FES) for the seven years 1978–84.

A poorly educated and trained workforce is seen by many as a major weakness of the British labour market (e.g. Prais, 1981; and the collection of papers in the autumn 1988 issue of the *Oxford Review of Economic Policy*). One aspect of the debate is post-compulsory education. The proportion of teenagers who remain in full-time education in Britain beyond the minimum legal leaving age of 16 is far lower than in many other OECD countries.[6] While is is true that the proportion of 16-year-olds remaining in education has increased substantially since the mid 1970s, the staying-on rate in Britain is still relatively low.

The Family Expenditure Survey data

Three aspects of the FES data need to be discussed. Firstly, why use this source? Secondly, why pool the data for different years? Thirdly, what problems arise?

Why use FES data? Existing theoretical and applied work by sociologists and economists suggests that a variety of factors will influence school leaving decisions, e.g. Halsey et al. (1980), Pissarides (1981), Behrman and Taubman (1986), Gambetta (1987) and Kodde (1988). There is not space to review these here but it is worth noting a few key variables which one would ideally wish to observe. These are summarized in Table 4.2 together with an indication as to whether they are present in the FES.

The FES contains somewhat limited information on parental social class and on education. Broad socio-economic group is recorded together with the age at which the parents themselves completed full-time education. The data record the number of other children present in the household and their relationship to the head of household. Siblings who have left the home are not recorded. Wages of those who leave school at 16 are known, provided work has been obtained (current or last job), but since the survey is not a panel there is no information on later earnings as exploited in the models of school leaving estimated with panel data by Willis and Rosen (1979) for the US and Micklewright (1988) for the UK. There is no information at all on individual ability as measured by achievement tests or exam success. This is in marked contrast to the National Child Development Study (NCDS) data which show that if one is able to control for ability the effect of parental class and education is reduced, suggesting both a direct and an indirect effect from family background (Micklewright, 1989).

On the other hand, there is very good information on family income and this represents a major attraction of the FES as a source for the study of school leaving.[7] Many writers have speculated on the effect of family income on school leaving decisions or have produced evidence from case studies, but high-quality income data are hard to come by. For example, the Oxford Mobility Study used in the seminal work on educational demand by Halsey et al. (1980) contained no income data on the family during the child's schooling, while the data on family income in the NCDS used by Micklewright (1989) are very weak.

Why pool?   There are two reasons for pooling: to increase sample size and to introduce temporal variation in labour market conditions. As far as the former is concerned, a single year of FES data produces around 300 16-year-olds, hardly enough to estimate with precision the parameters of interest. As for the latter reason, a single year's data contain mainly regional variation in labour market conditions, as the FES has no area identifier at a finer level than this (there are 11 standard British regions). The survey interviews are spread out evenly through the year which results in some temporal variation, but this is greatly increased by pooling the data for a number of years.

Table 4.2 *Subjects relating to schooling in the FES*

Subject	FES contains information?
Family class	Yes
Siblings	Partial
Parental education	Yes
Family income	Yes
Wages	Partial
Individual ability	No
School type	No

Contrary to what is sometimes suggested, the qualitative impact of changing levels of unemployment (as a summary of labour market conditions) on school leaving decisions is far from clear-cut (Kodde, 1988; Micklewright et al., 1989b; 1990). By pooling data for 1978–84, substantial temporal variation is introduced into the sample, the national unemployment rate climbing from about 4 per cent at the beginning of the period to over 10 per cent at the end. The seasonally adjusted unemployment rate in the quarter, and region of interview, was attached to each individual in the data set. In addition, the FES contains information on parental unemployment (discussed further below) and this is exploited in the model estimated here.

Problems   The use of the 1978–84 pooled FES sample on 16-year-olds illustrates some of the attractions and problems of pooled cross-section data. By pooling the sample, temporal variation is introduced but it is clear that the data do not contain all the variables one would like. FES data prior to 1978 do not contain information on parental education; hence it was not possible to extend the data set further back in time, given the desire to observe this important information. The information on parental unemployment also illustrates the changes that can take place in subjects covered by an annual cross-section. The model estimated below contains an explanatory variable measuring the proportion of the previous year that the head of household had spent unemployed, but it is only for three of the years between 1978 and 1984 that the FES recorded weeks of unemployment in the previous 12 months. However, weeks of receipt of National Insurance unemployment benefit (unemployment insurance) and of Supplementary Benefit (means-tested welfare payments) are recorded throughout the period, and a variable based on these measures was used instead (details given in Micklewright et al., 1989b: 22). This had a correlation of 0.85 with reported weeks of unemployment for those years (1981–3) where the latter was available.

A major problem with using the FES to study school leaving at 16 is caused by the absence of the actual date of birth from the survey. This is illustrated by Figure 4.3 which shows the proportion of the FES sample in full-time education at 16, and also the stay-on rate past the first legal leaving age indicated by administrative data. The movements in the two series are reasonably similar over time – which is encouraging – but it is striking how in every year the FES figure is considerably above the stay-on rate shown in the official statistics. At first sight, this might suggest that the FES sample must be very unrepresentative owing, for example, to some problem of differential non-response. However, the reason is much simpler.

An individual is not legally able to leave school in Britain on the day he or she is 16. The date at which leaving may take place depends on the month in which the 16th birthday falls. In England and Wales, leaving may occur at Easter if the 16th birthday falls in the previous September–January (inclusive) but is not permitted until June if the birthday is in February–August (an individual who is 16 in the last three of these months may thus leave education when still aged 15).[8] The administrative data refer to the propor-

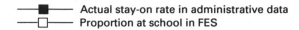

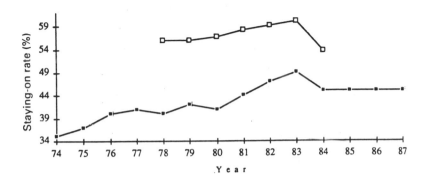

Figure 4.3   *Sixteen-year-olds' staying-on rates in education (administrative data from Employment Gazette, September 1987, p. 460)*

tion of those legally able to leave who remain in education, while the FES includes individuals constrained to be still at school. FES interviews are spread evenly through the year and thus some 16-year-olds in each year's sample are interviewed prior to the time at which they could leave. For example, a person in England and Wales who had a 16th birthday in February and who was interviewed in March would be constrained to remain at school until June.

If, in addition to the month of interview recorded in the FES, one observed each individual's month of birth, then those not legally entitled to leave could simply be excluded from the sample (the months of birth and interview being sufficient to allow calculation of whether a 16-year-old is legally constrained to be at school or not). However, given that the birth date is not observed, both constrained and unconstrained individuals must be included in the analysis.

Modelling the probability of leaving school at 16

It is well known that if there are no institutional constraints on choice and no rationing of the object of choice, the logistic regression model examined in Chapter 2 can be interpreted as a model explaining *choice* between two alternatives, rather than simply a statistical technique appropriate for binary data (e.g. Amemiya, 1981: 1490). In modelling the probability of leaving school at 16, the natural wish is to be able to interpret the parameter estimates as those relating to a model which explains choice. However, we have seen that there are constrained individuals in the sample and the binary logit model (or the probit model) is therefore not appropriate if we wish to interpret the results in terms of choice. In what follows, the separate probabilities of constraint and of choosing to leave are explicitly allowed for in the statistical model.

To observe an individual in the labour market, two conditions need to be satisfied. First, the individual must be in a position to choose whether or not to remain at school. For this to occur the individual must have been interviewed *after* the point at which he or she was legally able to leave school. Second, he or she must have exercised the choice to leave school.[9] In this situation a 'double-hurdle' model is applicable. This model has attracted increasing interest in the econometrics literature in recent years (see Blundell and Meghir, 1987 for a discussion of the relationship of this model to other micro-econometric models). Given the data set, both the hurdle of being legally able to leave and that of choosing to leave must be crossed before an individual can be observed in the labour market.

We observe a binary variable y_i such that $y_i=1$ if an individual has left school and 0 if not. Assume that there is an unobserved continuous index D_i^* which measures the desire to leave:

$$D_i^* = \beta' x_i + \varepsilon_i \qquad (4.1)$$

where x_i is a vector of observable characteristics affecting the desire to leave, β is a vector of parameters which we wish to estimate, and ε_i summarizes the influences not observed in the FES data.

Defining n_i as the probability that an individual is *not* constrained to be at school, we can write down the probabilities of observing y_i equal to 1 or 0 in the FES data. I assume independence between the probabilities of desiring and being able to leave (a not unreasonable restriction unless one believes that conception is timed to exploit the rules some 16 years later).

$$P(y_i = 1) = n_i \, P(D_i^* > 0) \qquad (4.2)$$

$$P(y_i = 0) = 1 - n_i \, P(D_i^* > 0)$$
$$= (1 - n_i) \, P(D_i^* > 0) + (1 - P(D_i^* > 0)) \qquad (4.3)$$

The probability of being observed in the labour market is the product of the probabilities of no constraint and a positive desire to leave index. An individual may be observed in education either because he or she does not want to leave or because there is the desire but not the ability to enter the labour market.

In a typical application of a double-hurdle model, both hurdles are parameterized as a function of data and unobservable influences (e.g. Atkinson et al., 1984; Blundell et al., 1987). However, we are able in this instance to provide an excellent and very simple non-parametric estimator for the first hurdle, n_i. For each month of interview observed in the data, I apply the leaving rules for each possible month of birth and see which months would imply a binding constraint. Assuming that the distribution of births through the year is uniform, the proportion of unconstrained months can be taken as an estimate of the probability of not being constrained. For a 16-year-old interviewed in January in England and Wales this procedure yields an estimated probability of 15/24 that he or she is not constrained.[10] I label these estimates n_i. Finally, I assume the unobservable influences on the desire to leave to be normally distributed with mean zero and variance one, i.e. that $\varepsilon_i \sim N(0, 1)$.[11] With this assumption the parameters of interest in the desire to leave index, β, can be estimated by maximizing the following like-lihood function with respect to β, where $j = 1, ..., J$ is the set of leavers ($y_i=i$) and $k = 1, ..., K$ is the set of those in education ($y_i=0$).

$$L = \prod_{j}^{J} \hat{n}_j \; \Phi \left(\beta' x_j \right) \prod_{k}^{K} \left[1 - \hat{n}_k \; \Phi \left(\beta' x_k \right) \right] \qquad (4.4)$$

Equation (4.4) may look rather daunting but all it represents is the probability (the 'likelihood') of simultaneously observing all the individuals in the sample doing what they are doing, i.e. having left school or still at school.

Note that if n_i were to equal one for all individuals, the expression in equation (4.4) would reduce to the likelihood function for a binary probit model. In this case, the only difference from the model of logistic regression described in Chapter 2 would be in the functional form of the distribution function of the unobservable influences, ε_i, which results from the assumption of a normal as opposed to a logistic distribution. Note also that any time a logistic regression package is applied to individual-level data, a like-lihood function of the type just described will be maximized by the computer.[12] The likelihood function in equation (4.4) is, however, non-standard, implying that it has to be programmed by the researcher. For the function just described, GAUSS, a very flexible and powerful microcomputer package, was used. This is reviewed by Dolton (1988) who notes that until recently anyone wishing to estimate a non-standard likelihood function had recourse only to a high-level language like FORTRAN, involving a substantial amount of programming experience. Estimation with GAUSS is very simple. For the double-hurdle model described above it involved little more than typing equation (4.4) into a template provided in the package. (It is worth noting that GAUSS also contains standard logit, probit and tobit models.)[13]

Results

In presenting results, I concentrate on those that illustrate the use of pooled cross-section data and which indicate the advantages of allowing for legal constraints in the manner just described. Full details of results, together with information on the construction of sample and variables, are given in Micklewright et al. (1989b; 1990).

Two sets of estimates are reported in Table 4.3. When interpreting the signs of estimated coefficients it should be remembered that the model is explaining the probability of *leaving* school and not the converse. The first column gives the results of a simple probit of whether the 16-year-olds in the FES data have left full-time education. This model is obtained if the probabilities of not being constrained are set to one in equations (4.2)–(4.4). There is a substantial improvement in the log-likelihood when this restriction is relaxed for the estimation of the double-hurdle model in column 2. While this latter model produces a better 'fit' to the data, there is no formal test between the two sets of results given that exactly the same number of parameters are estimated parametrically.[14]

In general, the move between probit and double-hurdle models leads to an increase in the absolute size of the estimated coefficients, something that occurs even when probit parameters are quite well determined, e.g. the coefficients on the owner-occupier dummy. A notable change occurs to the coefficients on the Scotland dummy. The probit results suggest that there is no difference in the leaving probability in Scotland, whereas in the double-hurdle model the relevant coefficient is significant at the 1 per cent level and indicates that early leaving is, other things equal, less likely compared with the excluded regions. This pattern of results is the result of the Scotland dummy in the probit proxying two offsetting effects. On the one hand the desire to leave, as revealed by the double-hurdle results, is lower. (This may be associated with the single extra year required to obtain Scottish high-school qualifications, or 'highers', by comparison with England and Wales where two years are typically required.) On the other hand, the differences in the institutional framework in Scotland imply that the probability of not

Table 4.3 *Parameter estimates[1] of school leaving model*

Variable	1 Probit Coefficient	t	2 Double hurdle Coefficient	t
Constant	1.179	3.6	1.565	3.7
Child is female	−0.256	4.5	−0.300	4.2
Head of household (HoH) non-manual	−0.316	4.5	−0.395	4.6
HoH years of extra education	−0.151	6.1	−0.178	7.2
Number of children in household (log)[2]	0.101	1.8	0.161	2.2
Owner-occupier household	−0.356	5.5	−0.475	5.7
Income per adult (log)[2]	−0.205	3.0	−0.201	2.3
Scotland	−0.007	0.1	−0.300	2.5
HoH proportion last year unemployed	0.359	2.3	0.548	2.4
Regional unemployment rate (%)	0.007	1.0	0.008	0.9
Log-likelihood	−1,329.8		−1,279.85	
$\phi(\beta x_i)$ for assumed[3] x_i	0.385		0.309	

[1] Estimates obtained with a sample of 2,177 16-year-olds in the Family Expenditure Surveys 1978–84. Sample details given in Micklewright et al. (1989b).
[2] Variables entered in logarithms are in natural logarithms.
[3] Characteristics x_i, assumed in the calculation of $\phi(\beta' x_i)$ as follows: child is male; manual head of household with no post-compulsory education and no unemployment in previous 12 months; not an owner-occupier household; one other child in household; England or Wales; 5 per cent unemployment rate; mean household income.

being constrained – the ability to leave – will be higher (see notes 8 and 10); the average estimated probability of being able to leave school $[\hat{n}_i]$ in Scotland is 0.94 compared with 0.79 in England and Wales. Once the latter effect is allowed for in the first hurdle, the former is revealed.[15]

As an aid to judging the implication of coefficient size, note that the derivative of the probability P of observing an individual in the labour market, with respect to the mth element of the x vector, is

$$dP / dx_m = \beta_m \phi (\beta'x) n \qquad (4.5)$$

where the subscript i has been omitted for simplicity. In other words, the effect of a change in any explanatory variable on the probability of leaving is a non-linear function both of that variable's coefficient and of the values of all the explanatory variables (and their coefficients) of the person for whom the calculation is made. The probability density function ϕ for a person with a hypothetical set of characteristics (described at the bottom of Table 4.3) is given below each column of results. To calculate the effect of a marginal change in an explanatory variable on the probability of leaving for someone with these characteristics and who is legally able to leave school, the figure beneath the relevant column of results should be multiplied by the estimated coefficient. For example, using the results in column 2 we see that the effect of 'switching' to a non-manual head of household would be to decrease the probability of leaving by over 10 per cent (0.395 times 0.309). A similar sized effect is associated with the household head having had two years of post-compulsory education (0.178 times 0.309 times 2).

Note that the t-statistic for the coefficient on the variable indicating parental education is quite large, reflecting the advantage of pooling so as to increase sample size and precision of estimates. On the other hand, despite pooling, the effects of other children in the household and of income are not very well determined, although it should be noted that a data set of 2,000 cases is still very small compared with some that could be produced by pooling. As well as being of only marginal significance, the estimated impact of income is also rather small: a 10 per cent rise in income is estimated to result in only a 1 per cent fall in the leaving probability for someone with the characteristics described at the bottom of Table 4.3.[16]

The other reason for pooling in the research reported here was to introduce substantial temporal variation in labour market conditions. We see that the coefficient of the regional unemployment rate in column 2 is negligible and is quite insignificant. However, the impact is being estimated under two strong assumptions. First, with the exception of the allowance for Scotland, the specification assumes that there are no regional effects other than those coming through unemployment or other variables in the model. Secondly, no allowance is being made for any exogenous changes in stay-on rate that may have occurred over the period owing, for example, to the introduction of YTS or other special employment measures. Temporal change is being forced largely through the unemployment rate. Results of experimenting with further dummies are reported in detail in Micklewright et al. (1989b; 1990), where we conclude that the pooled FES data set for 1978–84 does *not* suggest that the substantial increase in unemployment during the period was responsible for the rise that occurred in the staying-on rate. The lack of any robust evidence from the empirical work reflects the ambiguous predictions of economic theory in this area.

Conclusions

This chapter has reviewed the attractions and problems of using pooled cross-section data, defined here as the data obtained by combining individual-level data from different years of a regular cross-section survey. An empirical example was provided in the second half of the chapter: the analysis of the probability of leaving school in Britain at the first legal opportunity. Besides illustrating the use of pooled cross-sections, the empirical analysis provided an example of the sort of statistical model which is being increasingly applied to individual-level data, this being an extension of the binary probit model. The empirical example exploited the benefits offered by pooling of increased sample size and temporal variation but, as the review of the attractions of this type of source made clear, there are other reasons for pooling, including pseudo-panels, cohort effects, and growth accounting.

Notes

The author thanks Mark Pearson and Stephen Smith of the Institute for Fiscal Studies, London, for their permission to draw on joint work reported in the second section, and the editors and Joan Payne for helpful comments.

1 This term is sometimes used to describe repeated observations over time for the same cross-section of observational units, but a better description of these is 'panel' data.

2 For the UK see Hakim (1982), who also briefly describes some non-UK cross-section sources.

3 As well as producing temporal variation in prices and labour market conditions, pooling will also result in varying institutional parameters of tax and benefit schemes. Atkinson et al. (1984) exploit this.

4 It should be noted that for the interpretation of the data as pseudo-panel to be acceptable, the subpopulation has to be one that is reasonably fixed. If one were to look at the changing income, for example, of owner-occupiers over 20 years, this would certainly not be the case owing to the large movements into and out of home ownership during the period.

5 The consequences of such a switch should not, of course, be ignored. The General Household Survey is in fact restricted to Britain but for convenience I refer to both this survey and the Family Expenditure Survey (which includes Northern Ireland) as UK surveys.

6 In the USA and Japan some 85–90 per cent of 16-year-olds are in full-time education, and in many European countries the figure is over 75 per cent (see Micklewright et al., 1989a). Note that I use the phrase 'school leaving' in this chapter to mean leaving full-time education. Many 16-year-olds do in fact leave school but continue in full-time education in sixth-form colleges, tertiary colleges and colleges of further education. These are included in my references to 'school'.

7 The quality of the FES data on earnings and on all forms of income is assessed by comparison with other sources by Atkinson et al. (1989) and Atkinson and Micklewright (1983) respectively. Both these papers pool the FES data and consider the comparison for a number of years.

8 Leaving may take place in Scotland at the end of December if the 16th birthday is in September–February.

9 Although the text implies that the 'choice' is always exercised by the 16-year-old, one would expect that parents have a large say in the matter (for some rather dated Italian data on this question, see Gambetta, 1987). For the purposes of the model in this chapter, the distinction is not important.

10 I assume that if they occur in the same month, interview follows birthday in 50 per cent of cases. For the example in the text, the legal constraint certainly binds if birth is in September –December and with a 50 per cent chance if birth is in January. Differences in rules in Scotland are taken into account where the average probability of constraint is thus considerably lower. The assumption of a uniform distribution of births is not a bad one. Information from the *Monthly Digest of Statistics* shows that the variation of births by quarter is very small, and when data from the relevant years (1961–8) are used to estimate the n_i there is only a tiny improvement in log-likelihood.

11 The assumption that the error variance is equal to one is not important and is made entirely for ease of exposition. Without this assumption estimated coefficients of the model would be interpreted as ratios of the parameter estimates divided by the standard deviation of ε_i (for further discussion see Maddala, 1983: 23).

12 It may be useful to think of the procedure as being analogous to that for estimation of the coefficients in an ordinary least squares regression, where an expression involving a sum of squared deviations from the mean is minimized (whereas here a product of individual probabilities is maximized).

13 Another option would be the GLIM package.

14 However, the following argument in favour of the double-hurdle model is compelling. The results in column 2 do not represent full information maximum likelihood (FIML) since the likelihood function in equation (4.4) is conditional on the estimates of n_i. Were these probabilities to be estimated parametrically with a full set of month of interview dummies (implying a FIML model), the likelihood would therefore be at least as good as that achieved in column 2. The probit in column 1 would be nested in this model with 12 degrees of freedom and would clearly be inferior on a likelihood ratio test. I am grateful to Andrew Chesher of Bristol University for this observation.

15 The generally higher parameter estimates for the double-hurdle model may, at least in part, be due to a lower value of the variance of the unobserved influences when some of the variation is taken up by the $\hat{n}_i$. I am grateful to Richard Davies for this comment.

16 Note that one cannot draw any conclusions from these results concerning the likely effect of 'educational maintenance allowances', i.e. payments to the individual or his or her family *conditional* on post-compulsory education. This is because the model contains no variables measuring the separate income streams in the two options, leaving and staying on.

References

Amemiya, T. (1981) 'Qualitative response models: a survey', *Journal of Economic Literature*, 14(4): 1483–536.

Atkinson, A.B., Gomulka, J., Micklewright, J. and Rau, N.R. (1984) 'Unemployment benefit, duration and incentives in Britain: how robust is the evidence?', *Journal of Public Economics*, 23(1/2): 3–26.

Atkinson, A.B., Gomulka, J. and Stern, N. (1984) *Household Expenditure on Tobacco 1970–80*. ESRC Programme on Taxation, Incentives and the Distribution of Income, London School of Economics, Discussion Paper 57.

Atkinson, A.B., Gomulka, J. and Stern, N. (1990) 'Spending on alcohol: evidence from the Family Expenditure Survey 1970–1983', *Economic Journal*, 100 (402) : 808–27.

Atkinson, A.B. and Micklewright, J. (1980) *Unemployment: the FES Sample 1972–75*. ESRC Programme on Taxation, Incentives and the Distribution of Income, London School of Economics, Unemployment Project Working Note 1.

Atkinson, A.B. and Micklewright, J. (1983) 'On the reliability of income data in the Family Expenditure Survey 1970–77', *Journal of the Royal Statistical Society, Series A*, 146(1): 33–61.

Atkinson, A.B., Micklewright, J. and Stern, N.H. (1989) 'Comparison of the FES and New Earnings Survey 1971–1977', in A.B. Atkinson and Holly Sutherland (eds), *Tax–Benefit Models*. London School of Economics, STICERD Occasional Paper 10.

Baker, P. Blundell, R.W. and Micklewright, J. (1989) 'Modelling household energy expenditures using micro-data', *Economic Journal*, 99(397): 720–38.

Behrman, J.R. and Taubman, P. (1986) 'Birth order, schooling and earnings', *Journal of Labour Economics*, 4(3): S121–45.

Blank, R. and Card, D. (1989) *Recent Trends in Insured and Uninsured Employment: is There an Explanation?*. National Bureau of Economic Research, Working Paper 2871.

Blundell, R.W., Ham, J. and Meghir, C. (1987) 'Unemployment and female labour supply', *Economic Journal*, 97(Conference 1987): 44–64.

Blundell, R.W. and Meghir, C. (1987) 'Bivariate alternatives to the tobit model', *Journal of Econometrics*, 34 (Annals 1987–1): 179–200.

Breen, R. (1986) 'Does experience of work help school leavers to get jobs?', *Sociology*, 20(2): 207–27.

Browning, M., Deaton, A. and Irish, M. (1985) 'A profitable approach to labour supply and commodity demands over the life-cycle', *Econometrica*, 53(3): 503–44.

Deaton, Angus (1985) 'Panel data from time-series of cross-section', *Journal of Econometrics*, 30: 109–26.

Dolton, P. (1988) 'A new breed of software? GAUSS, MATLAB and PC-ISP, a comparative review', *Journal of Economic Surveys*, 2(1): 77–96.

Ermisch, J. and Wright, R. (1989) *Welfare Benefits and Lone Parents' Employment in Great Britain*. Department of Economics, Birkbeck College, University of London, unpublished paper.

Eurostat (1985) *Labour Force Sample Survey: Methods and Definitions*. Luxembourg: European Community.

Gambetta, D. (1987) *Were They Pushed or Did They Jump?* Cambridge: Cambridge University Press.

Gomulka, J. and Stern, N. (1990) 'The employment of married women in the UK: 1970–1983, *Economica*, 57(226): 171–200. (A longer version circulates as Discussion Paper 98 of the ESRC Programme on Taxation, Incentives and the Distribution of Income, London School of Economics.)

Hakim, C. (1982) *Secondary Analysis in Social Research*. London: George Allen and Unwin.

Halsey, A.H., Heath, A.F. and Ridge, S.M. (1980) *Origins and Destinations*. Oxford: Oxford University Press.

Kodde, D.A. (1988) 'Unemployment expectations and human capital formation', *European Economic Review*, 32: 1645–60.

Maddala, G.S. (1983) *Limited-Dependent and Qualitative Variables in Econometrics*. Cambridge: Cambridge University Press.

Micklewright, J. (1984) 'Male unemployment and the Family Expenditure Survey 1972–80', *Oxford Bulletin of Economics and Statistics*, 46(1): 31–54.

Micklewright, J. (1985) 'On earnings related unemployment benefits and their relation to earnings', *Economic Journal*, 95(377): 133–45.

Micklewright, J. (1988) *Schooling Choice, Educational Maintenance Allowances and Panel Attrition*. Department of Economics, Queen Mary and Westfield College, University of London, Discussion Paper 185.

Micklewright, J. (1989) 'Choice at Sixteen', *Economica*, 56(221): 25–39.

Micklewright, J., Pearson, M. and Smith, S. (1989a) 'Has Britain an early school leaving problem?', *Fiscal Studies*, 10(1): 1–16.

Micklewright, J., Pearson, M. and Smith, S. (1989b) *Unemployment and Early School Leaving: evidence from the Family Expenditure Survey 1978–84*. Department of Economics, Queen Mary and Westfield College, University of London, Discussion Paper 185.

Micklewright, J., Pearson, M. and Smith, S. (1990) 'Unemployment and early school leaving', *Economic Journal*, 99 (Conference 1990).

Narendranathan, W., Nickell, S.J. and Stern, J. (1985) 'Unemployment benefits revisited', *Economic Journal*, 95: 307–29.

Nickell, S.J. (1979) 'The effect of unemployment and related benefits on the duration of unemployment', *Economic Journal*, 89: 34–49.

OPCS (1981) *General Household Survey 1979*. London: HMSO.

Payne, J. (1985) 'Changes in the youth labour market 1974 to 1981', *Oxford Review of Education*, 11(2): 167–79.

Payne, J. (1987) 'Does unemployment run in families? Some findings from the general household survey', *Sociology*, 21(2): 199–214.

Payne, J. and Payne, C. (1985) 'Youth unemployment 1974–1981: the changing importance of age and qualifications', *The Quarterly Journal of Social Affairs*, 1(3): 177–92.

Pissarides, C.A. (1981) 'Staying on at school in England and Wales', *Economica*, 48: 345–63.

Prais, S.J. (1981) 'Vocational qualifications of the labour force in Britain and Germany', *National Institute Economic Review*, 98: 47–59.

Walker, I. (1989) *The Determinants of Labour Force Participation of Lone Mothers: evidence from the 1979–1984 Family Expenditure Surveys*. Institute for Fiscal Studies, London, Working Paper 89/17.

Willis, R.J. and Rosen, S. (1979) 'Education and self-selection', *Journal of Political Economy*, 87(5) Part 2: S7–S36.

5

Analyzing Change over Time Using LISREL

Editors' introduction

This chapter is relatively self-contained, explaining how a distinct method-ological approach – structural equation modelling – may be applied to longi-tudinal data. Structural equation modelling has been used mainly, but not solely, in psychology. Bynner provides a useful historical perspective which explains the genesis of the approach in both factor analysis and linear regres-sion. The basic feature of the method is that the causal relationships of inter-est are conceptualized as occurring between latent or theoretical variables. These variables are usually hypothetical constructs which cannot be measured directly. However, variables which are, in principle, measurable are sometimes treated as latent variables to avoid inordinate data collection costs. Empirical progress in quantifying the causal relationships is made possible by postulating that each latent variable may be measured with error by means of one or more indicator (or manifest) variables. The crucial assumption here is that of *conditional independence* – that the correlation between indicator variables is due solely to their common dependence on the latent variable. In the example given, the theoretical variable 'delin-quency' is measured by three indicator variables while the other theoretical variables – social life, parental control, and parental punitiveness – are each measured by a single indicator variable.

Using a simplified notation, Bynner introduces the complexities of struc-tural equation modelling through the well-established software package LISREL. A structural model is set up to test a variety of hypotheses in which explanatory variables are causally and linearly related to a response vari-able. By introducing or removing causal pathways it is possible to specify and test hypotheses about the relationships within the data.

In explaining how to formulate structural models with an explicit longi-tudinal dimension, Bynner distinguishes between exogenous and endogenous variables. The former affect but are not affected by the process of interest, while the latter affect the process but are themselves related to earlier outcomes. He also emphasizes that identifiability is an important issue in structural equation modelling: it is easy to formulate models which are too complex for the data available and, as a result, to find that some of the postulated relationships cannot be distinguished from each other.

Analyzing Change over Time Using LISREL: Social Life and Delinquency

John Bynner

Social Science Theory and Structural Equation Models

To test a social science theory we have to solve two problems: how to operationalize the theoretical variables or concepts to which the theory relates, and how to estimate the structural relations among the variables. The latter relations can be among variables measured at a particular point in time or across time as in a longitudinal study.

Thus if we wish to test a theory to elucidate the role of family social class in educational attainment, we need to operationalize the concept of class and the concept of educational attainment and find a means of estimating the structural relationship between them. In the case of class we may derive a single indicator from a classification of father's occupation, or use a number of correlated indicators such as father's and mother's occupation and education, the family's housing tenure and so on. Similarly with educational attainment we may have a single measure obtained from a teacher's overall assessment or a number of scores based on measured attainment in different areas of the curriculum. In either case we believe that the separate indicators share something in common which can be measured. Traditionally, factor analysis has been used to test this assumption, and the resulting factor or factors can be treated as measured variables representing the construct or constructs. The factor loadings in such a *measurement model* express the strength of the relationships between the indicators and the factors hypothesized to underlie them.

Factor analysis is a branch of data analysis concerned with 'interdependence'. Other multivariate methods based on linear relationships, such as multiple regression analysis, analysis of variance and discriminant analysis, are concerned with the analysis of 'dependence' and provide solutions to the second problem. They provide estimates of the strength of the relationships between measures of educational attainment and social class in terms of a *structural model*. The estimate of the regression of educational attainment on social class, for example, expresses the size of the structural relationship; the square of the product moment correlation coefficient between them expresses the proportion of variation in educational attainment accounted for or 'explained' by social class within the structural model.

The common feature of both types of model, measurement models and structural models, is that they model the form and assess the strength of *linear* relationships. In the early 1970s, with the advent of greatly enhanced computing power, there was interest in the development of a single computer-based data analysis system in which the testing and estimation of each model using the classical multivariate statistical procedures would be special cases.

Structural equation modelling is the means of achieving this aim. It embraces the estimation and testing of measurement relations between theoretical variables and their indicators (the measurement model) and the estimation and testing of the theoretical variables' structural relations (the structural model): see Duncan (1975) for a comprehensive introduction. It is this combination of two major methodologies that has appealed to researchers across the social sciences. Inclusion of the measurement relations in the model alongside structural relations adjusts the model, in effect, for errors of measurement in the observed variables. Consequently the reliability of the variables in the 'internal consistency' sense (Wheaton et al., 1977) is taken into account; in other words, all structural parameter estimates are corrected for attenuation. In particular, the size of regression coefficients and the multiple correlation coefficient in a multiple regression analysis are typically underestimated when errors of measurement are not taken into account. Structural equation modelling thus leads to a better appraisal of empirical relations postulated from theory. We can, for example, see what part of the 'unexplained' variation in the dependent variable can be attributed to measurement error as opposed to omitted variables.

Basic data for structural equation models comprise covariances or correlations among a set of variables; mean values can also be included and their relations modelled. In all cases, the aim of the model is to arrive at a set of parameters (e.g. factor loadings, regression coefficients) from which the original correlations or covariances can be recovered. The extent to which the two sets of correlations – estimated and observed – correspond represents the 'goodness of fit' of the model to the data. An overall chi-square goodness-of-fit test is routinely provided as are other indices of fit such as the goodness-of-fit index (a form of correlation measure) and average and maximum residual correlations.

A number of structural equation modelling programs have been developed: LISREL (Joreskog and Sorbom, 1979), EQS (Bentler, 1980) and COFAM (McDonald, 1978). These differ from each other in the range of facilities they provide the investigator for specifying the model, diagnosing faults in it and testing its goodness of fit to the data. The first one to be made available was LISREL which is now in its eighth version and is a supplementary procedure in SPSSX. It has been widely used across the range of disciplines in social science, especially in the USA. In this chapter we shall use LISREL to demonstrate structural equation modelling in an analysis of longitudinal data on the relation between teenage social life and delinquency. The program is described in Joreskog and Sorbom (1981). For a non-technical introduction see Bynner and Romney (1985), and for a basic textbook see Saris and Stronkhorst (1984).

In what follows, to simplify the exposition, roman alphabetic notation is used throughout rather than the Greek notation in which the (population) parameters estimated and the theoretical variables in LISREL are customarily expressed. As the program documentation uses Greek notation for parameter specifications. (phi, psi and so on), a translation from Roman to Greek is given in Table 5.1. All variables are expressed in deviation units – that is the means are zero throughout. Bold type is used to symbolize vectors (row/column matrices) and matrices.

LISREL models

As noted previously, the basic elements of a structural equation model are measurement models and structural models. The distinction between them in LISREL is best illustrated diagrammatically.

Measurement model

Figure 5.1 shows a latent variable or factor measured by a set of observed variables, y_1, y_2, y_3. Note that the direction of the arrows reflects the causal nature of the model. It is postulated that observed correlations among the y can be explained or are caused by a single f variable which is considered to underlie them. In other words the variances of each y can be attributed entirely to f and a random error component e unrelated to f. The extent to which f accounts for each y is given by a factor loading b. Providing all the y have a loading from just the one factor f, partialling out f from the correlations among the y will reduce them to zero. Looking at this another way, the y are the means of measuring a general factor or latent variable f such as in the social class and educational attainment example considered earlier.

Table 5.1   *Translation of symbols used in paper to LISREL notation*

Our notation	LISREL notation	LISREL parameter specification[1]	Definition
x	x	–	An observed exogenous variable
y	y	–	An observed endogenous variable
f	η	eta	An endogenous latent variable
F	ξ	ksi	An exogenous latent variable
z	ζ	zeta	A residual of f
e	ϵ	epsilon	A residual measurement error component of y
d	δ	delta	A residual measurement error component of x
b	λ_y	lambda y (LY)	A factor loading of f on y
a	λ_x	lambda x (LX)	A factor loading of F on x
V_e	Θ_ϵ	theta epsilon (TE)	Dispersion matrix of e
V_d	Θ_δ	theta delta (TD)	Dispersion matrix of d
h	β	beta (BE)	Matrix of path coefficients between f
g	γ	gamma (GA)	Matrix of path coefficients from F to f
V_z	Ψ	psi (PS)	Dispersion matrix of z
V_F	Φ	phi (PH)	Dispersion matrix of F

[1] The parameter specifications in LISREL are referred to by the capital letters in parentheses, e.g. to specify that a value of beta should be fixed at zero we specify the value of 0 for BE.

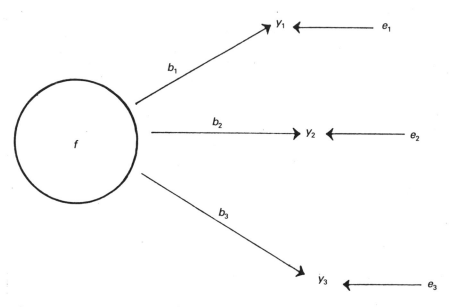

Figure 5.1   *Measurement model*

This is the classical factor model (Spearman, 1904) with the one exception that e embraces both the independent components of y which are specific to it and the independent (random) measurement error. In the classical factor model the specific and the measurement error components of y are considered conceptually distinct though, for the purposes of estimation, the former is typically ignored. The simplest form of the model is thus expressed in the following set of equations:

$$y_1 = b_1 f + e_1$$
$$y_2 = b_2 f + e_2$$
$$y_3 = b_3 f + e_3$$

or

$$\mathbf{y} = \mathbf{b}\, f + \mathbf{e}$$

where $\mathbf{b}$ comprises loadings for the common factor components and $\mathbf{e}$ contains the specific error components. As the separate components of $\mathbf{y}$ are independent, i.e. uncorrelated with each other, the variances of $\mathbf{y}$, $\mathbf{V}_y$, can be partitioned as follows:

$$V_{y1} = b_1^2 + V_{e1}$$
$$V_{y2} = b_2^2 + V_{e2}$$
$$V_{y3} = b_3^2 + V_{e3}$$

Structural model

The logic of the factor model extends to the structural relations among the latent variables. Figure 5.2 represents a typical postulated 'causal system' for such variables. This time we have three latent variables, the first of which, F_1, is considered antecedent or 'exogenous' to the others, f_1 and f_2, which are 'endogenous'. Each endogenous f is considered functionally dependent on the latent variables preceding it in the causal system. Thus f_2 is dependent on f_1 and F_1; f_1 is dependent on F_1 alone. This is the classic path analysis model (Wright, 1921) which is expressed in the following set of 'recursive' simultaneous equations, i.e. equations in which each variable is dependent on other variables in a prior sequence and there is no reciprocal dependency:

$$f_2 = g_{21}F_1 + h_{21}f_1 + z_2$$
$$f_1 = g_{11}F_1 + z_1$$

or

$$\mathbf{f} = \mathbf{h}\mathbf{f} + \mathbf{g}\mathbf{F} + \mathbf{z}$$

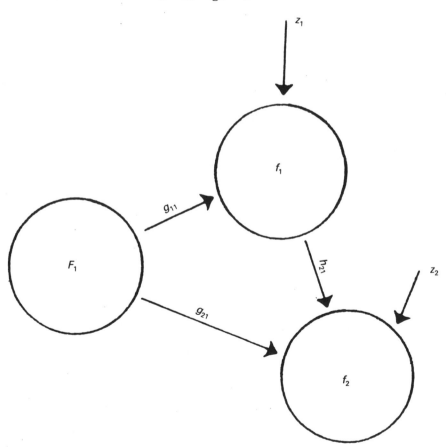

Figure 5.2   *Structural model*

where **g** and **h** comprise standardized partial regression coefficients and **z** comprises residual components of the endogenous **f**. (Note that **g** represents the paths from exogenous to endogenous constructs and that **h** represents the paths between endogenous constructs.) Again, if **z**, **f** and **F** are independent then the variances of f_2 and f_1 can be partitioned as follows:

$$V_{f2} = g_{21}^2 + h_{21}^2 + Vz_2$$
$$V_{f1} = g_{11}^2 + Vz_1$$

Combined model

A structural equation model brings these two separate models into a single model as shown in Figure 5.3. Nine observed variables **x** and **y** are used to operationalize three theoretical variables F_1, f_1 and f_2 which are related in terms of the causal pattern shown in Figure 5.3. Conventionally the *x* represent the observed indicators of the exogenous variables *F* and the *y*

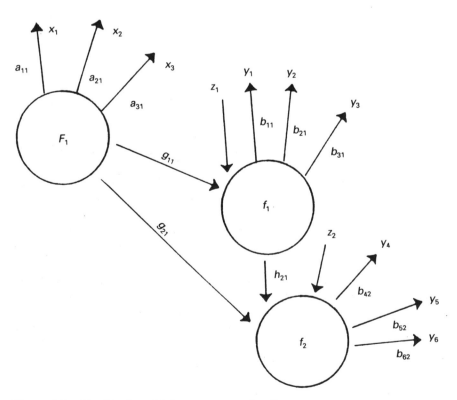

Figure 5.3   *Combined model (error terms omitted)*

represent the observed indicators of the endogenous variables f. The full set of matrix equations for the model is as follows:

$$\mathbf{y} = \mathbf{bf} + \mathbf{e}$$
$$\mathbf{x} = \mathbf{aF} + \mathbf{d}$$
$$\mathbf{f} = \mathbf{hf} + \mathbf{gF} + \mathbf{z}$$

where $\mathbf{a}$ are the factor loadings for $\mathbf{F}$ on $\mathbf{x}$ and $\mathbf{d}$ is the vector of random measurement error components of $\mathbf{x}$. Note that for each endogenous f there is a residual component z; for each indicator y there is a residual error term e; and for each indicator x there is a residual error term d. In more familiar terminology, including the $\mathbf{d}$ and $\mathbf{e}$ in the model corrects the structural parameters $\mathbf{g}$ and $\mathbf{h}$ for attenuation; for simplicity the error terms are not shown in Figure 5.3. The variances of the $\mathbf{z}$ in the model indicate that part of the variance of each latent endogenous variable which cannot be explained by the exogenous or endogenous variables preceding it in the causal chain.

Two additional features of the model should be mentioned. Although a basic assumption is that within each structural equation model the residual term and the error term for each variable are uncorrelated with each other and with the variable itself, this restriction does not apply between such residuals and errors in the same variable measured at different times. Unlike path analysis, in structural equation modelling error components can be correlated. For example, the measurement error in an opinion variable measured at two time points can be hypothesized as correlated to represent a systematic memory effect (or bias). Including such a correlation in the model corrects the model for the bias and provides another means of improving the estimates of the structural (causal) parameters with which the theory is concerned.

The other important feature of the model is that it applies regardless of how many observed variables are considered necessary to measure the F or f. In the simplest case of only one observed variable x, the F is no more than x corrected for measurement error. The proportion of the variance of x which cannot be attributed to measurement error, i.e. its 'reliability' (internal consistency), becomes the square of its loading on F, a^2. In the situation where the theoretical variable F is considered perfectly measured, d is zero and then F and x are identical.

Finally, the model is not restricted to recursive relations; non-recursive relations representing reciprocal dependencies can be encompassed within it. For example, f_2 can be postulated as dependent on f_1 while f_1 is simultaneously dependent on f_2, i.e. $f_1 \rightleftharpoons f_2$. This capability of 'dynamic modelling', which is complicated to achieve with conventional path analysis, is another valuable routine feature of LISREL.

Testing and estimating the model

Once a structural equation model is specified, the next task is to test its
goodness of fit to the observed data, usually comprising correlations or
covariances, and to estimate its structural parameters (factor loadings, path
coefficients, variances and covariances). The distinctive features of LISREL
in achieving these aims are as follows.

First, for the parameters of a model to be capable of estimation, they
must be uniquely determined by the observed data; the set of simultaneous
equations expressing the model must have just one solution. Under this
condition the model is said to be 'identified'. If more than one solution to
the equations is possible and the structural parameters are not uniquely
determined, the model is said to be 'under-identified'. If there are more equations than are needed to find a solution for the unknowns, the model is said
to be 'over-identified'. To achieve identification certain parameters in the
model (e.g. factor loadings) can be constrained to be zero or some other
fixed value, or can be made equal to each other. For example, in principle
in Figure 5.3 all the indicators x and y could have loadings from all the
factors F and f; the constraints imposed on the measurement model force
large numbers of these factor loadings to be zero, as theory dictates. When
a model is not identified, the program points out a particular parameter that
may be causing the problem. But for complex models, to ensure identification, it is also often necessary to work through the algebra (see Duncan,
1975). The aim in LISREL specification and testing is to obtain a model
which is just identified (i.e. not over-identified) and yet fits the observed
data; such a model will produce the most *parsimonious* account of the data.

Second, as the estimation procedure is iterative, all parameters in the
model have to be given initial 'start' values. In the most recent versions of
LISREL these are worked out automatically using the 'instrumental variables' method. The program then goes on to estimate the parameters of the
models by maximum likelihood methods under the conditions of best fit.
In effect, the differences between the correlations (or covariances) implied
by the parameters and the observed correlations (or covariances) will be
minimized.

Third, under the assumption of multivariate normality for the distribution of the observed variables, a statistical (likelihood ratio chi-square) test
is available to test how close the residual correlation matrix is to zero. In a
highly constrained model with many parameters set to zero, the value of chi-
square relative to degrees of freedom is likely to be large. Releasing the
constraints on certain parameters will reduce the value of chi-square; and
as parameters continue to be released, the chi-square drops until one
approaching zero can be achieved.

However, there is a danger in proceeding too far in this direction. Such
'over-fitting' not only capitalizes on chance, but, as with over-identification,
defeats the purpose of scientific theorizing, which has as its aim the most

parsimonious explanation of the observed phenomena in terms of the minimum number of structural relations among explanatory constructs.

Fourth, it is the practice in LISREL work, typically, to decide on a reasonable chi-square value relative to degrees of freedom as an indicator of fit, alongside other indicators of fit such as a goodness-of-fit index (with a range of 0–1) and the observed residual (normalized) correlations, either averaged or used to identify a maximum acceptable value. This rule of thumb approach is adopted in the example presented in this chapter. Ways of introducing a more rigorous 'classical' approach to hypothesis testing in LISREL have been frequently discussed (e.g. Bentler and Bonnett, 1980; Hoelter, 1983). The problem with using them is that only approximations to multivariate normality are likely to be achieved with most observed data which means that the test assumptions will not be met. Goodness-of-fit tests also suffer from the problem that the size of chi-square depends critically on sample size, which means that with large samples it is difficult to construct a parsimonious model. It is virtually impossible to achieve a good fit of a constrained model using strictly statistical criteria (i.e. a small non-significant chi-square). Over-fitting is therefore unavoidable if a non-significant chi-square is adopted rigidly as the criterion for an acceptable model.

Fifth, diagnostic information is obtained from the program whereby 'modification indices' (chi-square values) are given for all the parameters constrained to be zero. These modification indices estimate how much the overall chi-square will be reduced by releasing the constraint on the parameter and allowing it to be estimated. The matrix of residual correlations is also supplied, highlighting those correlations in the original data which the model has been least successful in explaining.

Sixth, as with factor analysis, LISREL assumes that the observed variables are continuous and measured on interval scales. This is the basis on which the product moment correlations or covariances are computed. In practice, many variables of theoretical interest are not measured in this way. Categorical variables are common and, although when converted into 'dummy' (dichotomous) variables they are often treated as if they are continuous, LISREL offers a more rigorous approach to including them in the model. With such data, 'polychoric' and 'polyserial' correlation coefficients can be computed alongside product moment correlation coefficients. These are generalizations of the familiar tetrachoric and biserial correlations. (Tetrachoric correlations occur between dichotomous variables assuming that there is an underlying continuous variable; biserial correlations occur where there is one continuous variable correlated with a dichotomous variable.) Generally if the levels of intercorrelation are in the region of 0.30 or below, product moment correlation coefficients are probably preferred.

Finally, other estimation methods, such as generalized least squares and unweighted least squares, are also available in LISREL as alternatives to maximum likelihood estimation. These may be preferred particularly when the data depart radically from multivariate normality.

Youth in Transition Study: delinquency analysis

To illustrate the use of LISREL in the analysis of longitudinal data, we take an example from the Youth in Transition Study (Bachman et al., 1978). Data were collected in six waves by postal questionnaire for a sample of 1471 American boys starting when they were in the 10th grade of high school (age 16) with follow-ups initially at annual intervals. For the purpose of this analysis we use the data collected for 1400 members of the sample (white males) at two time points, T_1 when they were in 10th grade and T_2 a year later when they were in 11th grade.

Six variables are used, each of which was constructed from a number of questionnaire items: three delinquency variables measured at the two time points, namely delinquency in school (y_2, y_6), aggressive behaviour (y_3, y_7) and theft and vandalism (y_4, y_8); a social life participation variable (y_1, y_5), also measured at the two time points; and two measures of parental influence measured at T_1, namely parental control (x_1) and parental punitiveness (x_2). The correlations among these variables are shown in Table 5.2.

The theoretical variables employed in the analysis are delinquency (f_2, f_4), measured by three indicators, 'delinquency in school', 'aggressiveness' and 'theft and vandalism' (y_2, y_3, y_4 at T_1, and y_6, y_7, y_8 at T_2); social life (f_1, f_3), measured by a single indicator (y_1 and y_5) at each time point; and parental control (F_1) and parental punitiveness (F_2), each of which are also measured by single indicators at T_1 (x_1, x_2).

The theory under test follows Emler (1984) in postulating that delinquency is a form of masculine status seeking that typically takes place in groups. An essential prerequisite therefore is participation in teenage social life; social life exercises a stronger influence on delinquency than delinquency exercises on social life (hypothesis H_1). The alternative hypothesis, following e.g. Eysenck (1964), is that delinquents are pathological individuals who seek out like-minded characters with whom they commit delinquent acts. On these grounds delinquency is likely to precede active participation in teenage social life rather than the other way round; delinquency exercises a stronger influence on social life than social life exercises on delinquency (hypothesis H_2).

Table 5.2 *Correlations between the ten variables (N = 1,400)*

1	Social life (T_1)	y_1	1.00								
2	Delinquency in school (T_1)	y_2	0.36	1.00							
3	Aggressiveness (T_1)	y_3	0.39	0.78	1.00						
4	Theft and vandalism (T_1)	y_4	0.22	0.63	0.61	1.00					
5	Social life (T_2)	y_5	0.51	0.24	0.29	0.16	1.00				
6	Delinquency in school (T_2)	y_6	0.33	0.57	0.49	0.39	0.33	1.00			
7	Aggressiveness (T_2)	y_7	0.24	0.36	0.40	0.26	0.23	0.68	1.00		
8	Theft and vandalism (T_2)	y_8	0.18	0.36	0.38	0.47	0.17	0.61	0.61	1.00	
9	Parental control	x_1	−0.15	−0.07	−0.08	−0.09	−0.12	−0.05	−0.03	−0.07	1.00
10	Parental punitiveness	x_2	0.01	0.25	0.28	0.23	−0.04	0.20	0.20	0.13	0.27	1.00

A final alternative hypothesis is that no sensible causal ordering can be attached to these two variables: they influence each other equally (hypothesis H_3). Underlying the relations between social life and delinquency are the further set of relationships between the boy and his parents. To evaluate the hypotheses adequately, therefore, parental control and parental punitiveness need to be controlled in the analysis.

To evaluate the three competing hypotheses, a cross-lagged regression model (Pelz and Andrews, 1964; Kenny and Harackiewitz, 1979; Plewis, 1985) is implied as in Figure 5.4. Under the assumptions that the cross-lagged variables are 'synchronous' (i.e. f_1, f_2 are measured at the same time point and f_3, f_4 are measured at the same time point) and display 'stationarity' (i.e. equal dispersions at both time points):

For H_1 to be supported, $h_{41} > h_{32}$
For H_2 to be supported, $h_{32} > h_{41}$
For H_3 to be supported, $h_{32} = h_{41}$.

At the most basic level of first-order correlations for the single indicators, H_1 is supported strongly over H_2 and H_3 for the delinquency in school indicator ($h_{41} = 0.33$; $h_{32} = 0.24$) but not for aggressiveness ($h_{41} = 0.24$; $h_{32} = 0.29$) and theft and vandalism ($h_{41} = 0.18$; $h_{32} = 0.16$), where the relationship is more ambiguous (Table 5.2). We need the cross-lagged regression model cast as a structural equation model to see which hypothesis is sustained (a) when delinquency is specified as a single theoretical variable with three indicators and (b) when T_1 measures of social life and delinquency and the parental influence variables are controlled.

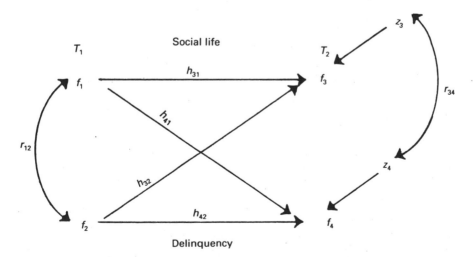

Figure 5.4   *Cross-lagged regression model: r_{12} is the correlation between f_1 and f_2 at T_1, and r_{34} is the correlation between the residuals z_3 and z_4 of f_3 and f_4 at T_2*

To represent the possible effects of the parental influence variables in the model, we make the plausible assumption that although they were both measured at T_1, they precede the T_1 measures of social life and delinquency causally. In other words, parental control and parental punitiveness influence teenage behaviour rather than the other way round. We would assume that the correlation at T_1 between the social life and delinquency variables cannot be fully accounted for by the parental variables, which means that a residual correlation has to be specified for them ($z_1\ z_2$). Although we may expect more of the T_2 correlation between social life and delinquency to be accounted for because of the T_1 measures of these variables, we similarly specify a residual correlation ($z_3\ z_4$).

The model with these assumptions incorporated is shown in Figure 5.5. Note that paths are included from the parental influence variables to the measures of the social life and delinquency variables at both time points, referred to as lag 1 and lag 2 paths respectively. Note also that, as previously stated, correlations are specified for the residual z of f_1, f_2 and f_3, f_4 but not initially for the residual measurement errors in the delinquency

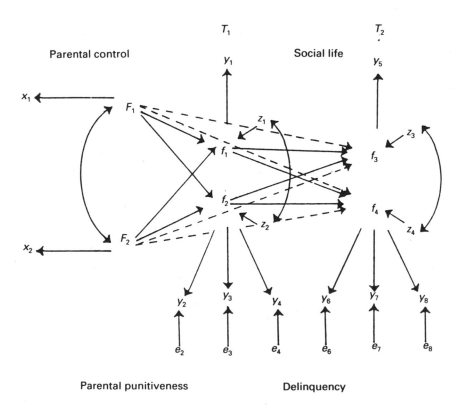

Figure 5.5 *Delinquency, social life and parental influence model*

indicators *e*. We now proceed to test various versions of this model with two aims: (a) to achieve an optimum fit of the model to the data, while at the same time minimizing, in accordance with the principles of scientific parsimony, the number of parameters to be estimated; (b) under the conditions of optimum fit, to compare the estimates of the cross-lagged path coefficients h_{41} and h_{32} to see which of the hypotheses H_1, H_2, H_3 can be sustained.

In evaluating the fit of the models, we observe the effect on indices of fit of removing or imposing certain constraints on the model. As we have seen, there are a number of indices of fit provided by the LISREL program which can be used additionally to assess fit but, as they would not substantially affect the conclusions here, for simplicity they are not all presented. For our purpose only two indices of fit are used; chi-square divided by degrees of freedom (DF) (as recommended by Wheaton et al., 1977); and the maximum residual correlation left after fitting the model to the data (max *r*). With improved fit, the value of chi-square reduces relative to degrees of freedom. Consequently the chi-square ratio declines and the maximum residual correlation also gets smaller. In large-sample work of this kind, a simple statistical test of chi-square assessed against the criterion probability value ($p > 0.10$, $p > 0.01$) is not appropriate, because, as noted earlier, use of such a criterion inevitably leads to over-fitting, i.e. capitalizing on random sampling error in the data and ending up with a model that is theoretically unsatisfying because it has too many parameters. In model evaluation using LISREL the approach is to observe the effect of changes in a model on its fit and take as the optimal model one where only marginal further improvements in fit can be achieved through releasing the constraints on single parameters. In some ways the maximum residual correlation value is the most intuitively satisfying for doing this because the aim of LISREL can be seen most simply as reducing all the original observed correlations among the measured variables to zero.

The results of testing different models are shown in Table 5.3. Model 1 is the model represented in Figure 5.5, and model 2 is a simple variation on it in which the lag 2 paths from the parental influence variables (F_1 and F_2) to the T_2 measures of social life and delinquency (f_3 and f_4) (represented by the dashed lines on Figure 5.5) are removed. Although the maximum residual correlation is the same for both models, 0.15, the chi-square ratio is marginally improved for model 2, reducing from 18.8 to 16.8. Accordingly, model 2 is preferred and in all subsequent models the paths from the parental influence variables to the T_2 measures (lag 2 paths) are constrained to be zero.

The difficulty with model 2 is the high residual correlation, 0.15. LISREL's modification indices point to the places in the model where the fit is weakest. These turn out to be the zero correlations between the measurement errors in the delinquency indicators across time. There are two ways of modelling these residual correlations: one is to specify a method/memory factor underlying all the indicators, *e* (model 3); the other is simply to remove

Table 5.3 *Statistics for models (N = 1,400)*

Model	χ^2	DF	$\dfrac{\chi^2}{DF}$	Max r
1	452	24	18.8	0.15
2	469	28	16.8	0.15
3	465	27	17.2	0.14
4	163	25	6.5	0.08
5	166.9	26	6.4	0.08
6	765	28	27.3	0.37
7	166.9	26	6.4	0.08

Models
1 All possible causal paths included but no correlated residuals: as in Figure 5.5.
2 Model 1 with lag 2 paths $F_1 f_3$, $F_1 f_4$, $F_2 f_3$, $F_2 f_4$ removed.
3 Model 2 with a single method factor specified to underlie all the delinquency indicators at both time points, $Y_1, Y_2, Y_3, Y_4, Y_5, Y_6$.
4 Model 2 with residual correlations specified between the residuals for two measures of *each* indicator across the two time points, $e_2 e_4$, $e_3 e_5$, $e_4 e_6$.
5 Model 4 with causal path $F_2 f_1$ removed, as in Figure 5.6.
6 Model 5 with stabilities $f_1 f_3$ and $f_2 f_4$ removed and reciprocal causal paths $f_1 f_2$, $f_3 f_4$ replacing the correlations $f_1 f_2$ and $f_3 f_4$.
7 Model 6 with stabilities $f_1 f_3$ and $f_2 f_4$ included.

the constraint that the correlations between the measurement errors for each indicator between the two time points (e_2 and e_6, e_3 and e_7, e_4 and e_8) should be zero (model 4). This latter approach restricts the issue to one of a possible measurement bias in each indicator brought about by a carry-over memory effect.

The result for model 3 shows no improvement in fit by the inclusion of the method/memory factor: the chi-square ratio actually goes up marginally. For model 4, however, a marked improvement in fit is achieved. Chi-square drops to a third of its size for model 2, the chi-square ratio drops from 16.8 to 6.5, and, perhaps most significant of all, the maximum residual correlation falls to 0.08, almost half the previous level. This model is clearly now close to the optimum fit for these data. But a further improvement can be made. Inspection of the paths between the parents' influence variables and the T_1 social life and delinquency variables (F_2 to f_1 and F_1 to f_2) identifies a path of only 0.01 between parental punitiveness (F_2) and social life (f_1). Constraining this path to be zero (model 5) produces a further small improvement in fit with the chi-square ratio dropping to 6.4: the maximum residual correlation remains unchanged at 0.08. This is the preferred model for the data.

We are now in a position to make substantive interpretations of the cross-lagged path coefficients in the model to evaluate the original hypotheses. These are shown in Figure 5.6. It is clear that imposing all the controls in the model reduces the cross-lagged regression coefficients to near zero. There is no evidence to support either H_1 or H_2, which means that H_3 (equal and reciprocal effects between the two critical variables) cannot be rejected:

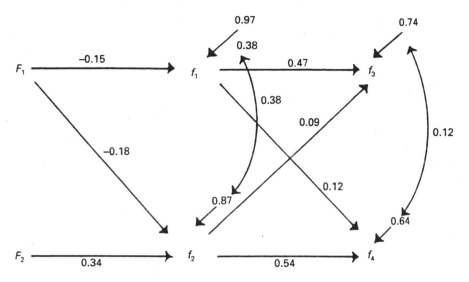

Figure 5.6 *Path coefficients for model 5*

$$H_1: \quad h_{41} > h_{32}$$
$$H_2: \quad h_{32} > h_{41}$$
$$H_3: \quad h_{32} = h_{41}.$$

The loss of evidence for any substantial cross-lagged effects in longitudinal regression models of this kind is not uncommon (Mark, 1979) and occurs primarily because of the substantial regression effect of each variable on itself across the two time points; this defines its 'stability' (Wheaton et al., 1977). This raises the more speculative possibility, which can be tested by LISREL, that suppression of these effects, the stabilities, might draw out in stronger relief the cross-lagged effects. Moreover, the correlations between the residuals for social life and delinquency (f_1, f_3 and f_2, f_4) at each time point can be replaced by reciprocal paths expressing the mutual dependence between these two variables at each time point ($f_1 = f_2$ and $f_3 = f_4$) (model 6).

As Table 5.3 shows, such a model cannot be sustained by the data. The chi-square is massively increased. The chi-square ratio quadruples and the maximum residual correlation rises to 0.37. Clearly LISREL is saying that a model without stability is difficult to justify, but, most important from the methodological point of view, the program demonstrates this unequivocally. In the final model the stabilities are restored (model 7), but the reciprocal paths are retained (model 7). Figure 5.7 shows the model with the parameter estimates. As Table 5.3 shows, the fit of the model returns to its previous level and we now have the additional estimates of the reciprocal paths in place of the correlations between residuals. Once more the cross-lagged regression effects are both about equal and now even closer to zero than they were in model 5. On the other hand, the reciprocal paths do

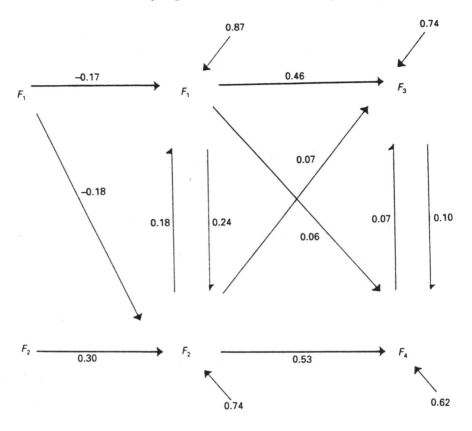

Figure 5.7 *Path coefficients for model 7*

show differential effects. The path from social life to delinquency is stronger than the path from delinquency to social life at both time points, providing some limited evidence that, at least within a given time point, H_1 is sustained. It seems that over the particular period covered by the study, changes in the values of the variables are too small to produce significant cross-over effects, as the majority of the sample are not changing their reported behaviour between the two time points. This result makes the case for taking measurements over much longer periods to test theories of this kind.

Conclusion

The Youth in Transition example demonstrates the value of the LISREL structural equation modelling approach in the analysis of longitudinal data. In LISREL we have the opportunity to formulate a cross-lagged (longitudinal) regression model precisely, estimate its parameters corrected for attenuation under a range of theoretical constraints, and test the goodness of fit of the model to the data.

Some of the LISREL features could have been exploited more fully in the present example. Most obviously, we could have replaced the variance of 1 of the indicators for social life and parents' influence by the square roots of their reliabilities (available for all the Youth in Transition variables), to correct them for attenuation. We could also have included a much wider range of exogenous variables as controls in the model. Goodness of fit could also have been assessed in other ways. It seems unlikely though that any of these enhancements would fundamentally affect our conclusion. Cross-lagged regression effects are difficult to establish with these data. All we can say is that weak mutually reinforcing synchronous effects exist between the two central variables, delinquency and social life, with the latter being the more dominant. Within its limits the LISREL methodology employed here has enabled us to subject the original hypotheses to a much more rigorous test than would usually be the case.

A more difficult problem is inherent in the linear model methodology, whether applied as in LISREL or through any of the multivariate analysis techniques. It has been argued that regression methods are inappropriate to assess change across time and that the causal interpretations placed on them are not justified, e.g. Rogosa and Willett (1985) (also see alternatives such as Collins et al., 1988). This issue is beyond the scope of this chapter (see Plewis, 1985 for an earlier justification of the regression approaches). What we are entitled to conclude is that if the researcher is convinced of the legitimacy of applying regression methods in the analysis of longitudinal data, then structural equation modelling can be a most effective way of doing it. In other words, if regression coefficients are to be used as the indicators of structural relations across time, then a program like LISREL is the best way to estimate them.

But in using LISREL we need to be aware of some of the problems that have to be confronted. To use the method effectively, the researcher needs a good theory which not only is plausible, but can be represented by an identified model (Duncan, 1975).

Use of chi-square as a goodness-of-fit measure or index rather than as the basis for a statistical decision leaves many researchers uncomfortable. Numerous attempts have been made to solve this problem, such as Bentler and Bonnett's (1980) use of a highly constrained 'null model' against which to compare different models, but none of them fully solve the problem. In large-scale survey analysis, any conventional criterion for testing fit will produce an over-fitted model. Consequently, for progress to be made it is essential to use scientific judgement as to when the specification of an optimum model has been achieved. Judgement is typically guided by the data as expressed in the LISREL output, but also in terms of previous research and consequently the plausibility of the theory that the model represents. There is a great danger in LISREL in working blindly towards a well-fitting model which is then justified *ex post facto* in causal terms. As Cliff (1983) points out, the language of causal modelling may trap the naïve researcher into thinking that causes have been established when a LISREL model fits the data, rather than certain possible causal explanations ruled out. Causal inference, of course, depends ultimately on the internal validity of the research design, not the particular analysis method employed.

The experienced user of LISREL realizes that the program is an invaluable tool for refining theoretical concepts, the methods of measuring them and the estimation of the structural relations between them. Used heuristically in this way, missing variables in a model and the need for new data may be identified. Frequently, rethinking of theoretical positions is indicated. None of these steps in the development of a theory fit precisely into the classical approach to statistical method but they are nevertheless an important aid to scientific progress.

References

Bachman, J.G., O'Malley, P.M. and Johnston, J. (1978) *Youth in Transition*, vol. 6, *Adolescence to Adulthood*. Ann Arbor: Institute for Social Research.

Bentler, P.M. (1980) 'Multivariate analysis with latent variables: causal modelling', *Annual Review of Psychology*, 31: 419–56.

Bentler, P.M. and Bonnett, D.G. (1980) 'Significance tests and goodness of fit in the analysis of covariance structures', *Psychological Bulletin*, 88: 588–606.

Bynner, J.M. and Romney, D. (1985) 'LISREL for beginners', *Canadian Psychology*, 26: 43–9.

Cliff, N. (1983) 'Some cautions concerning the applications of causal modelling methods', *Multivariate Behavioural Research*, 18: 115–26.

Collins, L.M., Cliff, N. and Dent, C.W. (1988) 'Methodology for measurement of dynamic constructs in longitudinal panel studies', *Applied Psychological Measurement*, 12: 217–30.

Duncan, O.D. (1975) *Introduction to Structural Equation Models*. New York: Academic Press.

Emler, N. (1984) 'Differential involvement in delinquency: towards an interpretation in terms of reputation management', *Progress in Experimental Personality Research*, 13: 173–239.

Eysenck, H.J. (1964) *Crime and Personality*. London: Routledge and Kegan Paul.

Hoelter, J.W. (1983) 'The analysis of covariance structures: goodness of fit indices', *Sociological Methods and Research*, 11: 325–44.

Joreskog, K.G. and Sorbom, D. (1979) *Advances in Factor Analysis and Structural Equation Models*. Cambridge, MA: Abt Books.

Joreskog, K.G. and Sorbom, D. (1981) *LISREL V Users Guide*. Chicago: International Methods and Research.

Kenny, D.A. and Harackiewicz, J.M. (1979) 'Cross lagged panel correlation: practice and promise', *Journal of Applied Psychology*, 64: 372–9.

McDonald, R.P. (1978) 'A simple comprehensive model for the analysis of covariate structures', *British Journal of Mathematical and Statistical Psychology*, 31: 59–72.

Mark, M.M. (1979) 'Inferring cause from passive observation', in T.K. Cook and D.J. Campbell (eds), *Quasi-Experimentation: design and Analysis Issues in Field Settings*. Chicago: Rand McNally.

Pelz, D.C. and Andrews, F.M. (1964) 'Detecting causal priorities in panel data', *American Sociological Review*, 29: 836–48.

Plewis, I. (1985) *Analysing Change: using Longitudinal Data for the Measurement and Explanation of Change*. London: Wiley.

Rogosa, D. and Willett, J.B. (1985) 'Understanding correlates of change by modelling individual differences in growth', *Psychometrika*, 50: 203–28.

Saris, W.E. and Stronkhorst, L.H. (1984) *Causal Modelling in Non-Experimental Research: an Introduction to the LISREL Approach*. Amsterdam: Sociometric Research Foundation.

Spearman, C.E. (1904) 'General intelligence objectively determined and measured', *American Journal of Psychology*, 15: 206–21.

Wheaton, B. , Muthen, B., Alwin, D.E. and Summers, G.F. (1977) 'Assessing reliability and stability in panel models', in D. Heise (ed.), *Sociological Methodology 1977*. San Francisco: Jossey-Bass.

Wright, S. (1921) 'Correlations and causation', *Journal of Agricultural Research*, 20: 557–85.

6
Longitudinal Multilevel Models

Editors' introduction

Multilevel modelling may be seen as an extension of conventional regression analysis for data which have a hierarchical or clustered structure. The major impetus for the development of multilevel modelling methods has come from educational research where education authorities, schools, classes and pupils constitute a natural hierarchy and conventional regression analysis has been demonstrably misleading. However, the methods are diffusing rapidly through other areas of social science research in which data have a natural or artificial hierarchical structure.

One feature of clustered data is that individuals in a cluster tend to be more similar on unobservable characteristics than individuals in different clusters, and if this is ignored, as in conventional regression analysis, the standard errors of parameter estimates will be underestimated. Multilevel methods address this problem within a much more general modelling framework which also allows the slopes of regression lines to vary between clusters. Thus, for example, not only may schools, geographical areas, or industrial sectors have different levels of outcome over and above those attributable to explanatory variables, but the outcomes may vary in their responsiveness to different explanatory variables.

Multilevel modelling methods are usually associated with cross-sectional analysis, but they are also relevant to longitudinal data because repeated measures over time on an individual constitute a natural data cluster. In this context, multilevel methods have close similarities to the longitudinal data analysis methods discussed in Chapter 2 and both approaches use individual specific error terms to represent the effects of omitted explanatory variables.

The first section of this chapter explains the rationale for using multilevel modelling and includes some examples of the kinds of questions that can be addressed. The next section demonstrates how the approach relates to conventional regression and introduces an appropriate notation. The substantive example guides the reader through an important educational research application of multilevel modelling, and the final section includes some advice on software.

Longitudinal Multilevel Models: Understanding Educational Progress in Relation to Changes in Curriculum Coverage

Ian Plewis

Quantitative researchers in the social sciences who ignore the structure of their data do so at their peril. Not only might they be led into false inferences about relations between variables; they might also deprive themselves of insights about the social processes they are studying. However, in at least one field of social science, educational research, the recognition is spreading that most data are located within a structure which is hierarchical, or nested. Consider the organization of state education in England. Local education authorities (LEAs) are usually placed at the top of the hierarchy, followed by schools within LEAs, then teachers or classes within schools, sometimes then groups within classes, with individual pupils at the bottom of the hierarchy. Moreover, it is also acknowledged that this structure, which is a property of the population and is not induced by sampling, should be exploited in any statistical analysis through the use of multilevel models as developed by Aitkin and Longford (1986), Goldstein (1987), Raudenbush (1988) and others.

Although most applications of multilevel models to date are to be found in educational research (Bock, 1989; Raudenbush and Willms, 1991), it is not only educational data for which these methods can be used. A good deal of social science data are structured hierarchically. For example, local authorities contain neighbourhoods which in turn contain households in which individuals live. We might then want to ask whether morbidity varies more between individuals in a household than it does between neighbourhoods in a local authority. Mason et al. (1983) apply multilevel models to an analysis of fertility data. The lower-level units are married women aged 40–44, the upper-level units are 15 developing countries. At the lower level, the response variable 'children ever born' is related to explanatory variables such as years of education; at the upper level, differences between countries in mean fertility levels are related to GNP and a family planning variable.

Sometimes the data are structured within an individual. Thus, in the systematic observation methods used by psychologists and others, individuals' time in an activity varies, for example, between days within a week and between weeks. Individuals are then at the top of the hierarchy, days at the bottom. Plewis (1988) and Plewis et al. (1990) describe how estimates of stability over time in such studies can be obtained using multilevel models, and how these ideas can be applied to time budget studies. Goldstein (1987: Chapter 4) shows that the same ideas can be applied to particular kinds of longitudinal data; an application to earnings in engineering firms over a six-year period is discussed by Davies et al. (1988).

Multilevel models (sometimes called variance component models and hierarchical linear models, or HLMs) can be used in a number of ways. One, not especially informative, way is to ensure that the standard errors (i.e. the precision) of estimates in statistical models specified at the individual level are calculated properly, by taking account of the clustering created by the hierarchical structure of the data. Often (see, for example, Aitkin et al., 1981), estimates which appear to be statistically significant when clustering is ignored turn out to be much less precise in a properly specified multilevel model. More valuably, multilevel models can provide answers to interesting questions such as: are there any substantively important differences in examination results between schools within LEAs, and are these differences greater than the differences between LEAs? And they allow us to focus much more explicitly than in the past on whether, how, and why within-group relations between variables differ across groups, and how within-group and between-group associations differ. This is an issue which goes back at least to Robinson's (1950) paper on the 'ecological fallacy', which showed that the correlation between 'illiteracy' and 'nativity' (born or not born in US) in 1930 was small and positive for individual-level data, but large and negative for state-level and region-level data. Multilevel modelling shows how conclusions drawn from data collected (or analysed) only at the group level can be misleading. Although the techniques often use group-level variables, the multilevel approach stresses the importance of collecting data at the individual level (or, more generally, at the lowest level of the hierarchy).

In principle there is no restriction to the number of levels in a multilevel model, although in practice examples using more than three levels are rare, and in this chapter the exposition is restricted to just two levels in an educational context. Pupil variables are called level 1 variables and school (or teacher) variables are called level 2 variables. In other words, the ordering of the levels is from the bottom to the top of the hierarchy. In general, variables at levels above level 1 can be obtained by aggregating level 1 variables (the mean mathematics attainment in a class is one example, the mean income in a neighbourhood is another) or they can be defined at the higher level such as class size or an index of pollution for a neighbourhood.

It may be helpful at this stage to consider the motivation for using multilevel models in the research context which provides the detailed example discussed in a later section. One of the major findings from the longitudinal research reported in Tizard et al. (1988) was the substantial association between pupils' progress in the three Rs in infant school and their coverage of the curriculum; for a particular test score at the beginning of the school year, those pupils covering more of the curriculum had higher attainments at the end of the year. This finding, which held for all three infant years for both the written language and mathematics curricula, was provocative, but the data were not sufficiently extensive to establish what the processes underlying this association might be. In particular, it was not possible to distinguish processes operating at level 1 (i.e. pupils) from those operating either just at level 2 or at both levels. Did the association arise from the substantial *between-school* differences in curriculum coverage that were found? In other words, was more progress made in those classes and schools where more of the curriculum was covered? Or did it hold only *within classrooms* because those pupils given more of the curriculum, perhaps because their teachers had higher expectations of them, get on faster? Or did the association merely reflect the fact that teachers are experts at picking out pupils likely in any case to do well during the year, thus exposing them to appropriate amounts of the curriculum? Tackling this set of questions with a multilevel approach offered the prospect of understanding these educational processes better.

We now outline the theory of multilevel modelling before proceeding to describe the results on curriculum coverage given in Tizard et al. (1988), to present some more analyses of those data, and to consider the limitations of the results. We then describe the study which followed on from Tizard et al., the statistical models used, and some of the results obtained. Methodological implications of the work are raised in the concluding section, along with a discussion of the available software.

Basic theory of multilevel modelling

This section consists of a short discussion of how multilevel models are specified and estimated, dealing only with relatively simple models. A more leisurely introduction to these topics is given by Paterson (1991), a more rigorous and extensive one by Goldstein (1987: Chapter 2).

Consider first a conventional multiple regression model with a response variable **y** and two explanatory variables, x_1 and x_2:

$$y_i = \beta_0 + \beta_1 x_{1i} + \beta_2 x_{2i} + e_i \tag{6.1}$$

where $i = 1, 2, \ldots, n$ and n is the sample size. In this equation, **y** might be a measure of pupils' educational attainment, x_1 a measure of parental education, and x_2 a measure of family income, with **e**, the error term, representing all the unexplained variation in **y**. The coefficient β_1 shows how attainment varies as parental education varies for fixed values of family income; β_2 shows how attainment varies as family income varies for fixed values of parental education. Estimates of β_0, β_1 and β_2 can be obtained by using ordinary least squares (OLS) as incorporated into all the well-known statistical packages.

Suppose, however, that the sample of n pupils is, like the population from which it was selected, structured by school. Let us now use the label y_{ij} for the attainment of an individual pupil; j ($j = 1,2,...,S'$) represents the pupils' school (and so j is the level 2 subscript) and i ($i =1,2,...,n_j$) represents the pupil within the school (and so i is the level 1 subscript), and $\Sigma_j n_j = n$. Note that the number of pupils per school can vary across schools. We now change equation (6.1) to

$$y_{ij} = \beta_{0j} + \beta_1 x_{1ij} + \beta_2 x_{2ij} + e_{ij} \qquad (6.2)$$

The addition of subscript j to β_0 means that the intercept is allowed to vary from school to school, which in turn means that the mean attainment level, adjusted for parental education and family income, varies from school to school (perhaps, although not necessarily, because some schools are more effective than others). However, the slope coefficients, β_1 and β_2 in (6.2), are assumed not to vary across schools in this model; they represent the pooled (or averaged) within-school slopes and will not in general be the same as β_1 and β_2 in equation (6.1) (see Aitkin and Longford, 1986: 11).

Equation (6.2) is the simplest of the set of two-level models which follow from (6.1), and is often referred to as a variance components model. In order for OLS to be appropriate for equation (6.1), the error terms e_i must be uncorrelated across pupils. This cannot be true in general if equation (6.2) is true because β_{0j} introduces a correlation between pupils within schools, often known as the intra-unit or intra-class correlation. In other words, since school means differ, pupils within a school tend to be more alike than those in different schools. The intra-unit correlation is defined as the ratio of between-school variance to total variance (or level 2 variance divided by the sum of level 1 and level 2 variances), and will be familiar to survey researchers for its role in the calculation of design effects for clustered samples (Kish, 1965: 170). Hence, OLS cannot, or rather should not, be used and alternative methods for estimating the coefficients, and the variance components, are needed. A number of iterative algorithms have been proposed and incorporated into statistical packages for multilevel models, and these are discussed in more detail in the final section.

Estimating model (6.2) using one of these packages will produce the correct standard errors for the coefficients β_1 and β_2 and would enable us to decide whether there was significant variation between schools. However, we can extend (6.2) by trying to account for variation between schools in (adjusted) attainment by explanatory variables defined at the school level, such as mean expenditure per pupil or mean family income:

$$\beta_{0j} = \gamma_{00} + \gamma_{01} z_{1j} + u_{0j} \qquad (6.3)$$

The error term u_{0j} represents whatever variation between schools is unaccounted for by the school-level variable, z_1.

A further extension of model (6.2) occurs if we now allow one or both of the slope coefficients, β_1 and β_2, to vary across schools. In other words, we allow for the possibility that the associations between attainment and the level 1 variables of parental education and family income are stronger in some schools than in others. Thus,

$$y_{ij} = \beta_{0j} + \beta_{1j}x_{1ij} + \beta_{2j}x_{2ij} + e_{ij} \tag{6.4}$$

Now each school has its own siope coefficients as well as its own intercept and we can try to account for any variation in β_{1j} and β_{2j} due to further, but not necessarily different, school-level variables z_2 and z_3:

$$\beta_{1j} = \gamma_{10} + \gamma_{11}z_{2j} + u_{1j} \tag{6.5}$$

$$\beta_{2j} = \gamma_{20} + \gamma_{21}z_{3j} + u_{2j} \tag{6.6}$$

Note that we can substitute equations (6.3), (6.5) and (6.6) into (6.4); the resulting rather complicated equation is not reproduced here, but would show that attempting to account for variation in β_{1j} by z_{2j}, for example, is equivalent to estimating the coefficient of a between-level interaction $x_{1ij} z_{2j}$ between the pupil (or level 1) variable x_1 and the school (or level 2) variable z_2.

A graphical illustration of the increasing complexity of the models as we move from equations (6.1) to (6.2) to (6.4) is given, for just one explanatory variable, in Figures 6.1, 6.2 and 6.3. The data are the same in each figure: 20 data points from three groups ($n_1=4$, $n_2=6$, $n_3=10$). Figure 6.1 shows the

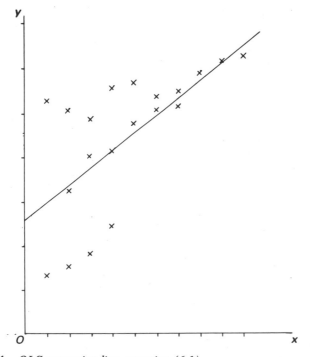

Figure 6.1   *OLS regression line, equation (6.1)*

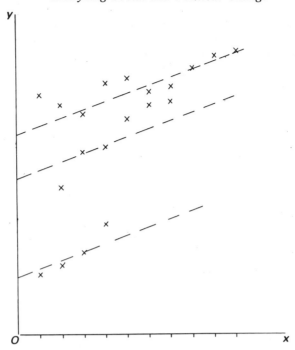

Figure 6.2   *Variance component model, equation (6.2): random intercept, constant slope*

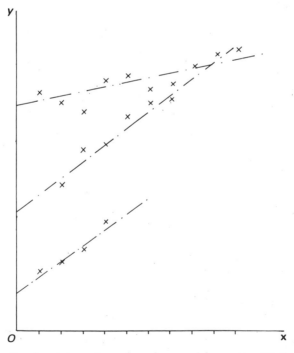

Figure 6.3   *Random intercept, random slope model, equation (6.4)*

overall regression line corresponding to equation (6.1) and thus not taking into account the grouping. This line is considerably steeper than the average within-group regression shown in Figure 6.2, i.e. equation (6.2). However, the slopes vary as shown in Figure 6.3; two of the groups essentially have the same slope, but the third has a flatter one. Figure 6.3 also shows that the differences between groups in *y* for particular values of *x* are no longer constant, as they were in Figure 6.2, but vary with *x*. When slopes vary from group to group in this way, the between-group variation for the intercept is often not easy to interpret; there is a different between-group variation for each value of *x*.

It is also possible to estimate the residuals $\hat{u}_{0j}$, $\hat{u}_{1j}$ and $\hat{u}_{2j}$ for each school from equations (6.3), (6.5) and (6.6) and they can be used in various ways. Aitkin and Longford (1986) used the estimated residuals for the intercept (i.e. $\hat{u}_{0j}$) to rank schools on their exam results adjusted for intake, and the example used in this chapter shows how both $\hat{u}_{0j}$ and $\hat{u}_{1j}$ can be used. It could be argued that rather than estimating these apparently complicated multi-level models, it would be possible to estimate a separate regression for each school and hence get separate estimates of β_{0j}, β_{1j} and β_{2j}. Although more satisfactory than ignoring the structure of the data altogether, this approach is nevertheless both less informative and less efficient than multilevel modelling. The great advantages of the multilevel approach described here are, first, that we get estimates of the variances of β_{0j}, β_{1j} and β_{2j} and the standard errors of these variances and can thus decide whether the observed variation is greater than would be expected by chance; and, second, that the estimated residuals depend not only on the data for that school, but also on data from other schools. Thus, for example, a particularly discrepant estimate of β_{1j}, especially one based on few data points, will be 'shrunk' towards the overall mean of β_1 and, consequently, the variation between the slope coefficients will have taken account of the sampling error for each separate within-school estimate. For further discussion of 'shrinkage', see Aitkin and Longford (1986: 16) and Goldstein (1987: 21).

An example

Curriculum coverage and progress: initial findings

The sample for the Tizard et al. (1988) study consisted of all pupils entering, in September 1982, the reception classes of a sample of 33 multi-ethnic inner London infant schools. These pupils were tested at the end of each year, and curriculum coverage data were obtained for each pupil for each of their three years in infant school. The sample size was about 400 pupils and 50 teachers. Because entry to inner London infant schools is termly, and because the sample was restricted to September entrants, it was not possible to obtain reliable school-level and class-level data by aggregating pupil-level variables.

The construction of the measure of curriculum coverage used throughout this chapter is described in detail in Farquhar et al. (1987). Briefly, all teachers in the sample completed checklists for each sample pupil separately for written language and mathematics. A score was derived for each pupil, which was a weighted sum of those items on the checklist said by the teacher to have been experienced by the pupil, the weights determined by the proportion of pupils in the sample experiencing an item. An item experienced by only a small proportion of pupils was weighted higher than one experienced by the majority of pupils. Weights varied between zero and five and to this extent the score reflected both the relative range and relative difficulty of the curriculum reported to have been experienced by each pupil. For mathematics in year 1 (i.e. middle infants), the curriculum coverage variable had a range of 0–116 and a mean of 43. There were considerable differences both within and between schools: variation between children within schools was 240 and variation between schools was 289, giving an intra-unit correlation of 0.55.

The model used in this study to examine the link between curriculum coverage and progress was essentially equation (6.2), with $\mathbf{y}$ as the appropriate attainment test score at the end of the year, $\mathbf{x}_1$ as the attainment test score at the end of the previous year (i.e. the 'intake' measure) and $\mathbf{x}_2$ as the curriculum coverage score for the year. This is a simple two-level version of the conditional model for change given in Plewis (1985: Chapter 3). No attempt is made here to explain the variation in β_{0j}. The estimate of β_2, the pooled within-school coefficient for curriculum coverage, was consistently greater than zero and statistically significant for each year and for the two areas of the curriculum.

This model is not however a complete model for change in that, although it includes measures of attainment at two occasions, there is only one measure of curriculum coverage. Assuming that the causal link runs from curriculum coverage to progress (i.e. assuming a recursive model), then two other models can be considered. The first is a simple extension of equation (6.1), ignoring, for simplicity, variation between schools:

$$y_i = \alpha_0 + \alpha_1 x_{1i} + \alpha_2 x_{2i} + \alpha_3 x_{3i} + e_i \tag{6.7}$$

where $\mathbf{x}_2$ and $\mathbf{x}_3$ are curriculum coverage scores for two successive years and interest focuses on α_3, the effect of a change in curriculum coverage on progress.

The second is a simple difference model:

$$y_i - x_{1i} = \gamma_0 + \gamma_1(x_{3i} - x_{2i}) + e_i \tag{6.8}$$

with each of the variables standardized to have a mean of zero and a standard deviation of one. The advantages and disadvantages of these two models for change are discussed in Plewis (1985: Chapter 4). An additional possible advantage of (6.8) is that, if differences between schools are constant over time, then differencing eliminates them and hence, providing the slopes do not vary, there is then no need for a two-level model.

The results from models (6.7) and (6.8) are given in Table 6.1. The estimates of α_3 and γ_1 are consistently positive, with $\hat{\alpha}_3$ always larger than $\hat{\gamma}_1$. They suggest that a one standard deviation unit change in curriculum coverage leads to between 0.1 and 0.2 standard deviation units change in progress, values which are somewhat smaller than those obtained from the model with just one measure of curriculum coverage.

It is also possible with these data, at least in principle, to test the assumption about causal direction by fitting non-recursive models (see Plewis, 1985: Section 4.6). In other words, both causal directions, from curriculum coverage to progress and from progress to curriculum coverage, are specified in the model. However, no consistent results were obtained from this approach, either from year to year or across the two areas of the curriculum, and so this analysis was inconclusive.

The evidence presented in this section is consistent with the hypothesis that curriculum coverage is, in some way, causally related to progress in written language and mathematics. But, if there is indeed a causal link, we have not learned a lot about how it operates. The analyses have focused on pupils' scores on curriculum coverage, and on within-school relationships with progress as given by, for example, β_2 in equation (6.2). They have not, however, explored all the potential of multilevel modelling. A more complete understanding of the underlying process would not come only from pupil-level models. It would also come from testing whether any of the variation between schools in, say, mathematics progress (assuming there is some) could be accounted for by curriculum coverage variables defined at the school level such as the school mean and standard deviation. Also the models might be improved by including teachers (or classes) as a third level between schools and pupils; it could be variation between teachers in curriculum coverage (which masquerades as variation between pupils in a two-level model), rather than variation between schools, which is important for understanding progress. Another limitation of models such as equation (6.2) is that the association between curriculum coverage and progress is assumed to be the same for all schools, which is an assumption which ought, if possible, to be tested. Finally, attempts to test the direction of the causal link were not successful and ideally one would like to do this within the framework of a multilevel model. It was to try to overcome at least some of these limitations that the study described in the next section was undertaken.

Table 6.1 *Parameter estimates for models (6.7) and (6.8) using data from the original study*[1]

Years	Written language		Mathematics	
	$\hat{\alpha}_3$	$\hat{\gamma}_1$	$\hat{\alpha}_3$	$\hat{\gamma}_1$
Middle–reception	0.18	0.11	0.34	0.15
Top–middle	0.19	0.08	0.15	0.07

[1] Regression coefficients have been standardized.

Design of second study

As we have seen, the design of the first study was not ideal for trying to understand the link between curriculum coverage and progress. This was partly because variables defined as aggregates of level 1 variables were not available, and partly because a three-level approach was deemed preferable with pupils as level 1 as before, but with teachers as level 2 and schools as level 3. Thus, for the second study, 20 schools were selected with each school having at least two year 1 classes at the time of selection. Two classes were randomly chosen in those schools with more than two year 1 classes. Of the 20 schools, 18 had been in the first study; the other two served similarly multi-ethnic areas.

All pupils in the selected classes were tested in reading and maths during the summer term in 1987 and again a year later. The tests were the same as those used in the first study. Curriculum coverage data, for mathematics only, were obtained during the second half of the summer term in 1988. Other contextual information, such as class size and the proportion of children having English as a second language, was also collected. The number of schools in the second study was smaller than in the first but the number of pupils was considerably greater, 1067 pupils being tested at least once and 776 on both occasions. This strategy enabled us to obtain good estimates of class-level and school-level variables, defined as aggregates over pupils, which had not been possible in the first study.

Stages of analysis

The second study was designed with three levels. However, it soon became clear from preliminary analyses that there was little need to include both teachers within schools, and schools themselves, in the models. For a number of mainly substantive reasons given in Plewis (1991) it was decided to use teachers rather than schools to define level 2. Hence the analysis proceeded along the general lines already described, with level 2 variation being all the variation between teachers, both teachers in the same school *and* teachers in different schools. Between-teacher within-school and between-school variations were thus amalgamated.

The logic driving the data analysis is shown in Figure 6.4; the statistical models underpinning Figure 6.4, and the estimates from these models, are given in the next section. The main aims of the analysis were to establish, first, if there were between-teacher differences in mathematics progress over year 1; and second, if there were, whether any of these differences could be accounted for by the curriculum coverage measure.

From now on, the response variable **y** is either MATH6 (mathematics attainment at the end of year 1, when the pupils were six years old) or CURRIC COVERAGE, and the explanatory variables are MATH5 (mathematics attainment one year earlier) and READ5 (reading attainment then). READ5 (the class mean reading attainment) is also used. Basic descriptive data for these variables are given in Table 6.2. When we talk about mathe-

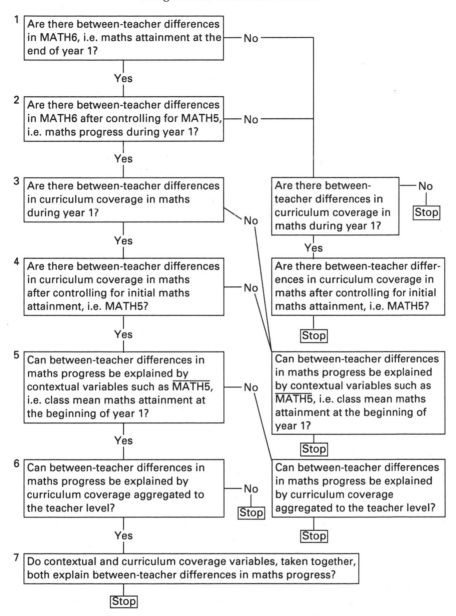

Figure 6.4 *Stages of analysis*

matics progress, we mean that MATH6 is the response variable and one of the explanatory variables is MATH5; this is the most usual way of defining progress for educational data (see Tizard et al., 1988: 29).

Stage 1 (Figure 6.4) is concerned merely with differences in attainment, which means a model with no explanatory variables and just two variance components. If there were no between-teacher variation in mathematics attainment at the end of the year, then it was most unlikely that there would

Table 6.2   *Descriptive statistics for the main data set used in this chapter*

		Raw scores	
	n	Mean	Standard deviation
Maths attainment at the beginning of year 1 (MATH5)[1]	897	17.1	6.6
Class mean maths attainment at the beginning of year 1 (MATH5)	43	16.6	3.1
Reading attainment at the beginning of year 1 (READ5)	897	23.7	18.7
Class mean reading attainment at the beginning of year 1 (READ5)	43	22.2	9.1
Maths attainment at the end of year 1 (MATH6)	882	13.1	9.2
Curriculum coverage year 1	867	51.7	26.3

[1] MATH5 and MATH6 are different maths tests.

have been anything interesting to model. Stage 2 is concerned with progress (MATH6 for fixed values of MATH5); it is possible that any differences between teachers found at stage 1 could have been accounted for by intake differences in the classes so that pupils made the same amount of progress, regardless of the class (and school) they were in. If so, then again the main analysis ends at this point. Stages 3 and 4 are similar to stages 1 and 2 but they focus on curriculum coverage as the response variable. Clearly, curriculum coverage would not have featured in the analysis if it varied only between pupils within a class and not between teachers. Also, if all the variation between classes were accounted for by intake differences in mathematics attainment then curriculum coverage has little to offer in the way of explanation.[1]

At stage 5, so-called contextual variables (such as class or school mean attainment at the beginning of the year and the spread of attainment then) are considered as potential explanatory variables for mathematics progress along with 'fixed' characteristics of the class or teacher such as class size and teacher experience. Stage 6 is the crucial stage for this analysis: did aggregate versions of curriculum coverage (specified in more detail below) account for any of the between-teacher variance in progress? Stage 7 is an amalgamation of stages 5 and 6 to give a clearer picture of the most powerful influences on teacher differences.

Note that the focus in Figure 6.4 is on between-teacher differences in means, either test scores or curriculum coverage. However, more sophisticated models are also considered below including models in which, for example, the relation between curriculum coverage and initial attainment is allowed to vary between classes as in equation (6.4).

Results from second study

Estimating the model at stage 1 of Figure 6.4, which is just a simple two-level variance components model, gave a between-teacher variance of 10.8, about 13 per cent of the total variation in MATH6. The estimate of the between-teacher variance component was about three times its standard error, suggesting strongly that there are systematic differences.

The model at stage 2 is:

$$(MATH6)_{ij} = \beta_{0j} + \beta_1 (MATH5)_{ij}^2 + \beta_2 (READ5)_{ij} + e_{ij} \qquad (6.9)$$

Note that a quadratic term in MATH5 gives a better fit to the data than the linear term. Also, initial reading attainment is associated with mathematics progress and should therefore be included in the model in order to control adequately for initial attainment. The variation between teachers for β_1 and β_2 was small compared with their standard errors and could be ignored. The estimates for equation (6.9) are given in Table 6.3. The variation between teachers s_t^2 is statistically significant and is clearly sufficiently large to be explained potentially by other variables defined at level 2.

The variance components model at stage 3 produced an estimate of 0.49 for the intra-unit correlation for curriculum coverage, a value close to that obtained in the first study. It was found that READ5 was related to mathematics curriculum coverage, as well as MATH5 at level 1, and that READ5 (the class mean reading attainment at intake) accounted for some of the between-teacher (i.e. level 2) differences in curriculum coverage. This resulted in the following model for curriculum coverage at stage 4:

$$(CURRIC\ COVERAGE)_{ij} = \beta_{0j} + \beta_{1j} (MATH5)_{ij} + \beta_2 (READ5)_{ij} + e_{ij} \qquad (6.10)$$
$$\beta_{0j} = \gamma_{00} + \gamma_{01} (READ5)_j + u_{0j} \qquad (6.11)$$
$$\beta_{1j} = \gamma_{10} + u_{1j} \qquad (6.12)$$

The estimates are given in Table 6.4. The coefficients for MATH5 and READ5 (γ_{10}, the mean of β_{1j}, and β_2, respectively) show that individual pupils have higher curriculum coverage scores the higher their initial attain-

Table 6.3   *Parameter estimates for model (6.9) (mathematics progress)*

	β_1	β_2	s_t^2	s_e^2
Estimate	0.022	0.15	4.0	26
Standard error	0.001	0.014	1.2	1.4

Table 6.4   *Parameter estimates for models (6.10) to (6.12) (curriculum coverage)*[1,2]

	γ_{10}	β_2	γ_{01}	$s_{\beta_1}^2$	s_t^2	s_e^2
Estimate	1.0	0.51	0.79	0.54	200	146
Standard error	0.15	0.04	0.21	0.18	47	8.0

[1] The covariance between the two variance components is omitted from the table.
[2] MATH5 was centred around the sample mean, so s_t^2 gives the intercept variance at the sample mean.

ments, but also, regardless of their initial attainments, if they are in initially higher attaining classes ($\hat{\gamma}_{01} = 0.79$). READ5 accounts for 19 per cent of between-teacher variation in curriculum coverage after allowing for the influences of MATH5 and READ5. The association between curriculum coverage and MATH5 does vary across teachers as shown by the value of $s_{\beta_1}^2$ in Table 6.4; indeed, taking plus and minus two standard errors shows that β_{1j} ranges from about -0.5 to 2.5.

The analysis up to this point established that there was between-teacher variation in mathematics progress to be explained, and there was variation in curriculum coverage which might explain it. Two sets of residuals may be estimated from equations (6.11) and (6.12): $\hat{u}_{0j}$, reflecting differences between teachers in the amount of curriculum coverage (adjusted for intake); and $\hat{u}_{1j}$, reflecting differences *between* teachers in the *within-teacher* association between initial attainment and curriculum coverage. These are potentially important explanatory variables for understanding variation between teachers in mathematics progress. They represent differences in the way teachers deliver the maths curriculum to their pupils after allowing for the different attainments of these pupils. One might expect pupils to make more progress if they are in classes with higher values of $\hat{u}_0$ and $\hat{u}_1$ because they will cover more of the curriculum or because the curriculum they are exposed to will be more closely matched to their ability than for pupils in other classes.

We found no evidence that the contextual effect represented by initial class mean attainment was related to mathematics progress (stage 5), although, as we have seen in equation (6.11) and Table 6.4, there was a contextual effect represented by READ5 and associated with curriculum coverage. The model at stage 6 was:

$$(\text{MATH6})_{ij} = \beta_{0j} + \beta_1 (\text{MATH5}^2)_{ij} + \beta_2 (\text{READ5})_{ij} + e_{ij} \tag{6.13}$$
$$\beta_{0j} = \gamma_{00} + \gamma_{01} \hat{u}_{0j} + v_{0j} \tag{6.14}$$
or
$$\beta_{0j} = \gamma_{00} + \gamma_{01} \hat{u}_{1j} + v_{0j} \tag{6.15}$$

Because $\hat{u}_{0j}$ and $\hat{u}_{1j}$ are highly correlated ($r = 0.8$), entering them jointly into an equation produced unstable estimates. Entering them separately into equations (6.14) and (6.15) produced estimates of 0.025 (SE = 0.027) for γ_{01} in (6.14) and 0.55 (SE = 0.58) for γ_{01} in (6.15). Although in the expected direction, these estimates are small compared with their standard errors, and so there is little support from these results for the belief that between-teacher differences in curriculum coverage are related to pupils' progress.[2]

Discussion

If we refer to the competing explanations given earlier for the association between curriculum coverage and progress, these results tend to support the idea that it is the processes within classes which are important, rather than those between classes. On the other hand, the sizes of the effects given by γ_{01} in equations (6.14) and (6.15) are not substantively unimportant, even though they are not statistically significant. The ranges of effect (the differences in progress between pupils in classes with the highest and lowest values of $\hat{u}_{0j}$ and $\hat{u}_{1j}$) are around 20 per cent of the standard deviation of MATH6. The estimates are imprecise because the sample of *teachers* is small (only 40) even though the sample of pupils is relatively large. Standard errors for variables defined at level 2 will be determined by the size of the sample of level 2 units and not that of level 1 units. This raises questions about the design of studies which intend to use multilevel techniques in their analysis, which have yet to be addressed in the literature.

Model specification is always important and nearly always controversial in quantitative social science. For multilevel models, a crucial issue is the specification of the model at level 1. Inadequate specification at level 1 can lead to false inferences about the effects of level 2 variables. We found in the above example that the variation between teachers for mathematics attainment (i.e. 10.8) was considerably greater than it was for progress (i.e. 4.0); it is always important to take account of so-called intake differences in this kind of research. Here, the variation between teachers in MATH6 after controlling for MATH5[2] but before controlling for READ5 was 5.2, and so it would not have been adequate to have controlled solely for initial mathematics attainment when looking for explanations of differences between teachers in pupils' mathematics progress. There may still not be sufficient control for intake in equation (6.9); for example, socio-economic status is often found to be related to progress. Such information was not available for individual pupils in this study although, as the sample was a mainly working-class inner-city one, the omission of socio-economic status is unlikely to have been important. Such questions about the processes governing the selection of individuals into different groups and about statistical control will always be raised when analyses of data are reported from observational studies.

There is another way in which the models in this chapter are misspecified: no account has been taken of measurement error in the analysis. In fact, the reliabilities of each of the variables are high.[3] Nevertheless, the between-teacher variation in curriculum coverage and in mathematics progress may be overestimated given that $\hat{\gamma}_{10}$ in equation (6.12) and $\hat{\beta}_1$ and $\hat{\beta}_2$ in equation (6.13) are likely to be biased downwards, if only slightly, by the failure to account for measurement error. Goldstein (1987) shows how corrections for measurement error can be built into multilevel models but at present we have little experience of these techniques.

The model at stage 6, like the initial model estimated for the first study, is based on just one measure of curriculum coverage and so is not truly longitudinal. It would be useful to consider how inferences about change could be strengthened if extra measures were available by specifying multilevel versions of equations (6.7) and (6.8). However, this would take us into the territory of multilevel causal modelling or multilevel path analysis.

Software

Multilevel modelling is a rapidly developing area of research with attention now being directed to, for example, models for categorical data and to multivariate data (i.e. more than one response variable). Introductions to these topics can be found in Goldstein (1987). Advances in available computer software are closely following these theoretical developments. Indeed, multilevel modelling would still only be of theoretical interest were it not for the marketing in the past few years of a number of specialized packages. There were, in 1991, four stand-alone packages for multilevel modelling. All the results in this chapter were obtained using ML3 (Rasbash et al., 1989) and VARCL (Longford, 1988). The other two major packages are HLM (Bryk et al., 1988) and GENMOD (Mason et al., 1988). Kreft et al. (1990) give a review of the four packages, although it should be stressed that they are continually being revised and expanded.[4]

A limited amount of analysis in this area is possible using some of the well-known statistical packages. The VARCOMP procedure in SAS (1985) can provide estimates of variance components for nested designs using different methods of estimation, but cannot deal with explanatory variables or random slopes. The BMD suite has P5V;[5] this does allow explanatory variables and random slopes but only two levels, and is really designed for small data sets (Schluchter, 1988).

Conclusion

This chapter has shown how hierarchically structured longitudinal data can be used to investigate links between variables. Methods for analyzing such data are particularly suitable for, but are not restricted to, questions in educational research. A good deal of social science data, both longitudinal and cross-sectional, can be looked at from a hierarchical perspective. Doing so offers the prospect of greater insights about social processes than can be obtained from the more traditional single-level models.

Notes

This research was funded by the ESRC as part of an extension of its grant to the Thomas Coram Research Unit as a Designated Research Centre. The studies were carried out in Inner London Education Authority schools and the author would like to thank the staff for their cooperation, and to acknowledge the contributions to the research of Rosemary Creeser and Ann Mooney. The author would also like to thank Harvey Goldstein and Barbara Tizard for comments on earlier drafts of this paper.

1 Although the main analysis ends if there is a negative answer at stages 1 or 2, one might nevertheless wish to estimate the teacher variance component for curriculum coverage. Not in Figure 6.4, but also of some interest, is whether the result from the earlier study on the within-class association between progress and curriculum coverage is replicated.

2 Further analysis of these data, reported in Plewis (1991), suggests that there are other, more fruitful, ways of using the curriculum coverage data at the teacher level.

3 For example, the test-retest reliabilities of MATH5 and MATH6 are 0.92 and 0.91 respectively; the split-half reliability of curriculum coverage is 0.93.

4 One way of keeping up with the developments is to subscribe to the newsletter produced by the Multilevel Models Project at the Institute of Education, University of London, WC1H 0AL, UK.

5 Formerly P3V, which was used for some of the analysis in Tizard et al. (1988).

References

Aitkin, M., Anderson, D. and Hinde, J. (1981) 'Statistical modelling of data on teaching styles (with discussion)', *Journal of the Royal Statistical Society, Series A*, 144: 419–461.

Aitkin, M. and Longford, N. (1986) 'Statistical modelling in school effectiveness studies (with discussion)', *Journal of the Royal Statistical Society, Series A*, 149: 1–43.

Bock, R.D. (ed.) (1989) *Multilevel Analysis of Educational Data*. San Diego: Academic Press.

Bryk, A.S., Raudenbush, S.W., Seltzer, M. and Congdon, R.T. (1988) *An Introduction to HLM: Computer Program and Users' Guide*. Chicago: University of Chicago Press.

Davies, R.B., Martin, A.M. and Penn, R. (1988) 'Linear modelling with clustered observations: an illustrative example of earnings in the engineering industry', *Environment and Planning A*, 20: 1069–84.

Farquhar, C., Blatchford, P., Burke, J., Plewis, I. and Tizard, B. (1987) 'Curriculum diversity in London infant schools', *British Journal of Educational Psychology*, 57: 151–165.

Goldstein, H. (1987) *Multilevel Models in Educational and Social Research*. London: Griffin.

Kish, L. (1965) *Survey Sampling*. New York: Wiley.

Kreft, I.G.G., de Leeuw, J. and Kim, K.S. (1990) *Comparing Four Different Packages for Hierarchical Linear Regression: GENMOD, HLM, ML2 and VARCL*. Centre for the Study of Evaluation, University of California, Los Angeles, CSE Report 311.

Longford, N. (1988) *VARCL Manual*. Princeton, NJ: ETS.

Mason, W.M., Anderson, A.F. and Hayat, N. (1988) *Manual for GENMOD*. Population Studies Center, University of Michigan.

Mason, W.M., Wong, G.Y. and Entwisle, B. (1983) 'Contextual analysis through the multi-level linear model', in S. Leinhart (ed.), *Sociological Methodology 1983–84*. San Francisco: Jossey-Bass.

Paterson, L. (1991) 'An introduction to multilevel modelling', in S.W. Raudenbush and J.D. Willms (eds), *Schools, Classrooms and Pupils: International Studies of Schooling from a Multilevel Perspective*. San Diego: Academic Press.

Plewis, I. (1985) *Analysing Change*. Chichester: Wiley.

Plewis, I (1988) 'Estimating generalisability in systematic observation studies', *British Journal of Mathematical and Statistical Psychology*, 41: 53–62.

Plewis, I. (1991) 'Using multilevel models to link educational progress with curriculum coverage', in S.W. Raudenbush and J.D. Willms (eds), *Schools, Classrooms and Pupils: International Studies of Schooling from a Multilevel Perspective*. San Diego: Academic Press.

Plewis, I., Creeser, R. and Mooney, A. (1990) 'Reliability and validity of time budget data: children's activities outside school', *Journal of Official Statistics*, 6: 411–19.

Rasbash, J., Prosser, R. and Goldstein, H. (1989) *ML3 Manual*. London: Institute of Education.

Raudenbush, S.W. (1988) 'Educational applications of hierarchical linear models: a review', *Journal of Educational Statistics*, 13: 85–116.

Raudenbush, S.W. and Willms, J.D. (1991) (eds) *Schools, Classrooms and Pupils: International Studies of Schooling from a Multilevel Perspective*. San Diego: Academic Press.

Robinson, W.S. (1950) 'Ecological correlations and the behaviour of individuals', *American Sociological Review*, 15: 351–7.

SAS (1985) *SAS Users' Guide*. Cary, NC: SAS Institute.

Schluchter, M.D. (1988) *BMDP5V: Unbalanced Repeated Measures Models with Structured Covariance Matrices*. BMDP Statistical Software, Los Angeles, Technical Report 86.

Tizard, B., Blatchford, P., Burke, J., Farquhar, C. and Plewis, I. (1988) *Young Children at School in the Inner City*. Hove: Lawrence Erlbaum.

7

Event History Analysis

Editors' introduction

This chapter explains the basic methods that may be used to investigate and model the timing of events. It also reviews the main problems that have been encountered in applying such methods to social science event history data, and Tuma is quite candid about the fact that some of the problems have yet to be resolved adequately. Illustrative analyses of the timing of births provide the empirical focus.

In contrast to the earlier chapters in this volume, which show how methods more usually associated with cross-sectional analysis may be extended to include a temporal dimension, this chapter is concerned with a methodology which has an explicit longitudinal perspective. Indeed, the response variable is the time between events. This is a continuous response variable and, as Tuma emphasizes, conventional regression methods could be used to model the relationship between explanatory variables and duration. This approach is sometimes advocated; see, for example, Aitkin et al. (1989: Chapter 6). However, for a variety of technical and substantive reasons, it has proved convenient in most circumstances to adopt a rather different approach to formulating models for duration data and for interpreting the results. It is for this reason that the chapter has so much notation and terminology which will be unfamiliar to those new to longitudinal data analysis. However, the chapter is written in a style which enables the reader to skip over the more technical material while still obtaining a good grasp of the main concepts.

One reason why conventional regression methods are rarely used with duration as a response variable will become apparent on reading Tuma's introduction to exploratory methods in the first section of the chapter: researchers often have a substantive interest in the distributional characteristics of duration. This is quite different from the typical situation in regression analysis where the distribution of the error term (and hence the distribution of the response variable for given values of the explanatory variables) is only of concern in so far as it might infringe the normality assumption and thereby prejudice inference on the explanatory variables. One consequence is that, whereas conventional regression analysis is dominated by a single probability distribution (the normal or Gaussian), a large variety of probability distributions are used in duration analyses to represent the different duration characteristics which occur in practice. Tuma provides details of the main distributions which have found favour in social science work, including the Weibull, gamma, and log-Gaussian (often called the log-normal).

In the editors' introduction to Chapter 4, we explained that there are several entirely equivalent ways of representing a probability distribution, and the representations used in that chapter included the probability density function and the distribution function. Tuma adopts standard notation $f(t)$ and $F(t)$ for these two functions, with the alternative terminology 'cumulative distribution function' for the latter. She also explains that other representations of probability distributions are important in analyzing event history data. These include the survival function $S(t)$, which is just the probability of the duration exceeding t, and the hazard function $h(t)$. The hazard function is particularly important because it makes explicit the relationship between the probability distribution of duration, a concept somewhat abstract and difficult to interpret, and the rate at which events occur. The hazard function therefore tends to provide the link between substantive considerations and the technical details of the model; it plays a central role in model formulation and model interpretation. Moreover, for similar reasons, it is usual to assume that explanatory variables affect duration by having a scaling effect on the hazard function. This is the widely used *proportional hazard* formulation which is quite different from the conventional regression assumption that the effect of the explanatory variables is confined to the mean of the response.

The proportional hazard formulation has an additional advantage when interest focuses solely upon the effects of explanatory variables: the Cox partial likelihood approach enables the scaling effects of explanatory variables to be estimated without making any assumptions about the 'baseline' probability distribution of the durations.

An important characteristic of duration data is that, by the end of the study, the outcome of interest has often not yet occurred for some respondents. This means that a proportion of the durations are 'right-censored'; we know that they exceed the recorded time but do not know by how much. Allowing for right-censored observations introduces a further level of complication into methods for analyzing duration data and is one of the reasons why even exploratory data analysis methods can involve comparatively complex formulae. Again, we would emphasize that the non-statistician need not linger over formulae but may rely on the text and figures. For example, it is not necessary to follow the algebra of the Kaplan-Meier estimates to understand from Figure 7.2 that the relationship between the probability of remaining childless and age, complete with confidence intervals, may be estimated directly from the data.

Finally, we would note a potentially confusing feature of event history analysis: although the statistical methods used have been developed to model *durations*, the main research focus in event history analysis is upon the *timing* of events.

Event History Analysis: An Introduction

Nancy Tuma

My goal in this chapter is to provide a general introduction to the set of statistical tools called event history analysis, giving primary emphasis to the aspects of most interest to social scientists: when one should apply various techniques, and what one can learn from them. My first sections concentrate on statistical methods for analyzing event history data that assume minimal difficulties in the data collection phase. To date most statistical work on event history analysis falls into this category. Thus, this part of my discussion provides an overview of what is currently known about event history analysis. My final section identifies some of the common ways that event history data do not meet the usual assumptions of statisticians. It has several objectives. First, I hope that it will help those who collect event history data to become more aware of the consequences of certain aspects of their observation schemes that cause data analysts grief and perhaps to avoid some of these unfortunate features in the future. Second, I hope that it may generate interest in developing statistical methods for dealing with some of the common deficiencies in event history data collected by social scientists. Finally, I hope that it will lead analysts of event histories to interpret results based on methods that ignore these problems with suitable caution until data collectors or statisticians have overcome them.

Fundamentals of event history analysis

What is event history analysis? By definition it refers to the analysis of event history data – data on the timing of 'events' for some sample within a given observational period, which may vary across members of the sample. An 'event' is a change in the value of some discrete random variable $Y(t)$ that is defined over some time interval and that has a countable number of exhaustive and mutually exclusive values. To give a few examples, the discrete variable may be a person's marital status, number of children, employment status, place of residence, religious affiliation, or political party. Indeed, even history analysis has been frequently and fruitfully applied in demography (for a review, see Hobcraft and Murphy, 1986) and in studies of the life course (for many applications and an extensive bibliography, see Mayer and Tuma, 1990).

It is important to stress that the units in a sample need not be people. They may be territories, political entities, firms, clubs, relationships between social entities, documents, cultural artifacts, and so forth. Thus, event history analysis has been used to study changes in the political structure of nations and other territorial units (for example, Bienen and Van de Walle, 1989; Carroll and Hannan, 1981; Knoke, 1982; Strang, 1990), occurrence of collective events (for example, Olzak, 1987; 1989a; 1989b), changes in organizational forms (for example, Barnett, 1990; Carroll and Hannan, 1989; Halliday et al., 1987), occurrence of various types of interpersonal behaviours (for example, Drass, 1986; Felmlee et al., 1990; Griffin and Gardner, 1989; Robinson and Smith-Lovin, 1990), and adoption of laws, policies, and various social innovations (for example, Edelman, 1990; Marsden and Podolny, 1990; Strang and Tuma, 1993; Sutton, 1988).

Figure 7.1 gives a pictorial illustration of an event history for a hypothetical member of some sample. In this illustration, $Y(t)$, the discrete variable being studied, is a person's marital status, where 'death' is included as a possible value of $Y(t)$ for completeness. The hypothetical person is born at t_0 and is initially unmarried. At t_1, he marries. Later, at t_2, he divorces his spouse and enters the status of divorcee. Then he remarries at t_3. At time t_4 his spouse dies: he becomes a widower. Still later, at t_2, he himself dies. Over the time span for which this process is defined, this individual occupies five distinct statuses (one of which, 'married', is occupied twice), and he has five events, not counting his birth. Other individuals may experience more or fewer events and different combinations of events in different orders, as well as at different times.

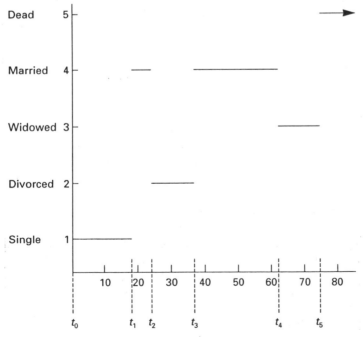

Figure 7.1 *A hypothetical event history of an individual's changes in marital status*

Event history data contain information on all events and times in some observational period τ_1 to τ_2, for example birth to death. It is worthwhile contrasting them with a few other common types of data. Cross-sectional data record the status of sample members at a particular point in time. Panel data, sometimes called state histories, record the status of sample members at a series of discrete points in time, for example, marital status at ages 20, 30, and 40, but not at points between these ages. Event count data tell how many events have occurred in some interval τ_1 to τ_2, but do not tell when events occurred or in what order. Current status data indicate whether or not some event has occurred by a given time, for example if the person has married by age 25. Finally, backward recurrence time data give the length of time since entering the most recent state – for example the person's current marital status at the time of an interview and how long he or she has been in this status – but nothing about previous marital events.

It may seem tempting to formulate separate models for each type of data, using whatever statistical model is most convenient. This common approach ignores the fact that a single reality is being studied, and that apparent differences arise only because of the use of different observation schemes. In my view a better approach is to develop methods that recognize that we are all studying the same reality. Too often we act like the famous group of blind men who felt different parts of an elephant and thought that they had experienced different objects, leading them into unproductive arguments about the nature of reality. Developing such methods is admittedly easiest when event history data are available because one then has complete information in some period; all of the other types of data I mentioned lack some information. The completeness of information in event history data can be of great value in discriminating among alternative hypotheses.

For purposes of analyzing data based on Figure 7.1, it is customary to imagine that Figure 7.1 depicts 'reality' for this hypothetical person. Nevertheless, it is important to stress that my conceptualization of the process of marital formation and dissolution has greatly influenced this picture. Some would argue that we should distinguish additional statuses, for example cohabitation and separation. Others might wish to combine 'divorced' and 'widowed' into one status called 'formerly married'. This picture also assumes that the transition from one status to another occurs at a given moment. This may be fairly reasonable for changes in marital status if one ignores cohabitation and separation. But, addition of these two statuses might make it hard to claim that transitions from one status to another are instantaneous. All of these potential difficulties with Figure 7.1 as a picture of reality stem from this particular conceptualization of this phenomenon. They are issues about which social scientists tend to worry, but to which statisticians are usually indifferent.

Ignoring these caveats for the moment (though in my view they are not trivial), the data analyst has the problem of converting information like that in Figure 7.1 for some number of cases into a form suitable for statistical analysis. Note that all of the information in Figure 7.1 can be summarized by

N pairs of variables, the time of an event and its outcome, where N is the total number of events that occurs for a given case. One also needs information on the starting time and state, and on the start and end of the observation period. Just how all of this information is coded depends on the requirements of the particular computer software being used. From a statistical viewpoint, one is no better or worse than another. From a computational viewpoint, some require more storage space or are easier to manipulate than others.

From the perspective of data analysts, it is useful to divide methods of analyzing such data into two broad categories related to the purpose of the analysis. One is to describe or summarize basic patterns in the data. This may be the ultimate purpose or the prelude to a second, which is to investigate the effects on the outcome being studied of certain explanatory variables.

Before reviewing techniques used for each purpose, I will digress briefly to describe the relationship of event history analysis to some similar methods of analysis. *Failure-time analysis* refers to a set of techniques for analyzing data on the time of a single event or 'failure'. The name arose because the techniques were developed mainly for engineers, who were often interested in the effect of some factor on the likelihood of failure of certain equipment (for example, light bulbs, engines, and so forth) over time. *Survival analysis* refers to essentially the same techniques, which are often used by biostatisticians and medical researchers to examine the effect of some treatment (for example, a new drug) on survival or its opposite, mortality. Event history analysis subsumes survival (failure-time) analysis because it studies the process leading not only to a single event but also to multiple events, some of which may be repeated over time. Nevertheless, survival (failure-time) analysis provides a good introduction to event history analysis. Concepts and methods are very similar but often simpler because they refer only to a single, non-recurring event. Consequently, I introduce various ideas in terms of analysis of the occurrence of a single event and only suggest how they are extended in event history analysis.

Consider the first event in an individual's lifetime, assumed to begin at t_0. The time of this event is a random variable T_1, or simply T when we consider a single non-repeatable event, such as death. One fundamental concept that describes the timing of this event is the *cumulative distribution function* (CDF),

$$F(t) \equiv \Pr(T \leq t)$$

In words, $F(t)$ is the probability that the event occurs *before* time t.

The complement of $F(t)$ is called the survivor function,

$$S(t) \equiv 1 - F(t) \equiv \Pr(T > t)$$

In words, $S(t)$ is the probability of survival until time t. The survivor function turns out to be used more than the CDF in empirical analyses.

At the starting time t_0, the probability of survival is one: $S(t_0) = 1$. Ordinarily, $S(\infty) = 0$. But sometimes $S(\infty) > 0$, which means that there is a non-zero probability that the event does not occur, even if an infinite amount of time passes. In this situation, the distribution of T is said to be *defective*. Defective distributions are fairly common in empirical applications; an example is given below.

Associated with $F(t)$ is a *probability density function* (PDF),

$$f(t) \equiv dF(t)/dt \equiv -d\ S(t)/dt$$

The probability density function is a measure of the unconditional probability that the event happens at time t. The relative frequency distribution (histogram) of t gives an empirical approximation to the PDF.

Another extremely important concept is the *hazard rate* or *failure rate*,

$$h(t) \equiv f(t)/S(t) = -d\ \log S(t)/dt$$

The hazard rate is a measure of the probability that an event occurs at time t, *conditional* on it not having occurred before t. (It is this 'conditioning' that distinguishes the hazard rate from the PDF.) When social scientists seek to explain change over time in the occurrence of some event, they usually express their ideas in terms of factors that raise or lower the hazard rate.

When there is more than one possible outcome – competing risks, as they are usually called – then additional quantities are introduced. One is $m_k(t)$, the probability of outcome k conditional on the occurrence of some event at time t. Another important concept is the transition intensity or instantaneous rate of transition to k,

$$r_k(t) \equiv h(t)\ m_k(t)$$

Explanations often focus on the transition rate rather than the hazard rate when there are competing risks.

One other quantity is mentioned fairly frequently in this literature, namely the integral of the hazard rate (or integrated hazard rate) $H(t)$; it can be shown to equal minus the natural logarithm of $S(t)$,

$$H(t) \equiv \int_{t_0}^{t} h(u)du = -\log S(t)$$

At this point it may seem that there is nothing special about the random variable T. After all, we could compute its mean and its standard deviation, and perform various multivariate analyses of data on it based on the well-developed theory of linear models. Why have a special set of techniques arisen to analyze samples of data on T?

One reason is that T is often defined on only a portion of the real line – often on non-negative numbers. For example if T refers to the age at death, it can never be less than zero. A second reason is that the probability density function associated with T is usually highly skewed. But neither reason is sufficient to justify a distinctive name like 'survival analysis' since many real random variables take only non-negative values and are skewed. Usually one just transforms the original variable in some way (for example, by taking its logarithm) to alter both its range and shape in a way that makes it easy to analyze.

One distinctive (though not unique) feature of data on the time to an event, perhaps accounting for the distinctive literature on this topic, is that information on the sample is often incomplete in a well-defined way that can be subjected to statistical treatment. In particular, we often observe the time of an event only if it occurs within a given observational period that ranges from some time τ_1 to a later time τ_2. The observational period may end without the event occurring. This may be either because the event will never occur, or because the event will occur but at some unknown future date. When the value of T is unknown after some τ_2, the data are said to be censored on the right. When data on the times of events or outcomes are incomplete before τ_1, the data are said to be censored on the left. Left censoring is a more serious problem than right censoring and involves more complex statistical issues, so I will not say much about it.

Statisticians distinguish among different types of censoring patterns or rules (for a discussion, see Miller, 1981). I do not review these because social scientists do not encounter most of them very often. In social research, the most common type is censoring based on the times (or length) of the observation period, which is assumed to be independent of the phenomenon studied. Unfortunately, this assumption is often not valid in social research, as I discuss further in the final section.

Exploratory methods

The concepts of survivor function, integrated hazard rate, and hazard rate are of value not only in the statistical theory behind event history analysis, but also in exploratory analyses of event history data.[1]

When right censoring *is* independent of the occurrence of the event being studied, Kaplan and Meier's (1958) product-limit estimator of $S(t)$ is unbiased and asymptotically consistent:

$$\hat{S}_{KM}(t) = \prod_{t_{(i)} < t} \left[1 - \frac{d_{(i)}}{n_{(i)}} \right], \quad t_{(i-1)} < t < t_{(i)}$$

where (i) denotes the ith event when events are arranged in non-descending temporal order; $t_{(i)}$ refers to the time of the (i)th event; $d_{(i)}$ is the number of events occurring at $t_{(i)}$; and $n_{(i)}$ is the number at risk just before $t_{(i)}$, which by convention includes those censored at $t_{(i)}$. $\hat{S}_{KM}(t)$ is a step function, but people often connect the empirical point estimates to obtain a picture that better reflects the (presumed) underlying smooth survivor function.

Greenwood's formula is the most common estimator of the asymptotic variance of $S(t)$:

$$\text{var}[\widehat{S_{KM}}(t)] = [\hat{S}_{KM}(t)]^2 \sum_{t_{(i)} < t} \frac{d_{(i)}}{n_{(i)} [n_{(i)} - d_{(i)}]}, \quad t_{(i-1)} < t < t_{(i)}$$

Thus, the Kaplan-Meier estimator of the two-sided 95 per cent pointwise confidence interval of the survivor function at time t is

$$\hat{S}_{KM}(t) \pm 1.96 \sqrt{[\text{var}(\widehat{S_{KM}}(t))]}$$

A pointwise confidence interval gives the confidence interval at only a single point or time t, but usually one wants to estimate a *simultaneous* confidence band around $\hat{S}(t)$, that is, confidence intervals for some set of time points. Since the pointwise confidence interval at one time is not statistically independent of that at another time, repeated application of Greenwood's formula to a set of time points overstates the true confidence level: the true simultaneous confidence band is wider. Hall and Wellner (1980) and Nair (1984) have developed different ways of estimating a simultaneous confidence band around $\hat{S}(t)$.

Figure 7.2 illustrates the application of this estimation procedure to data on the birth of the first child of German men and women born in 1949–51 who were interviewed in 1981–3. In this example, the 95 per cent pointwise confidence intervals do not overlap except at very young ages (for example, under age 16); one may be confident that the distribution of T differs for German men and women. This finding is not surprising, of course.

In this case, the curves for men and women are fairly similar in shape, with the curve for men clearly further to the right than the one for women. In other applications, two such curves may cross. But, the differences between survivor curves for two groups are not always as clear-cut as in this figure. It is then useful to be able to test whether the survivor curves of g groups differ significantly. Most such tests are generalizations of familiar rank tests. Such tests are often important tools for medical researchers and engineers, who tend to have small samples and few explanatory variables (some of which may represent experimental treatments). They are usually less useful to social scientists, who are more likely to have large samples, many explanatory variables, and no experimental controls. Consequently, I simply refer those interested in such tests to one of the texts covering this topic (for example, Kalbfleisch and Prentice, 1980; Miller, 1981).

Several comments about Figure 7.2 are in order. First, the curve stops abruptly around age 33 because respondents were interviewed when they were in their early thirties. Thus, the data are censored on the right at this age. Second, at this age, nearly a fifth of the women and a third of the men are estimated to be childless. Though it is reasonable to expect the propor-

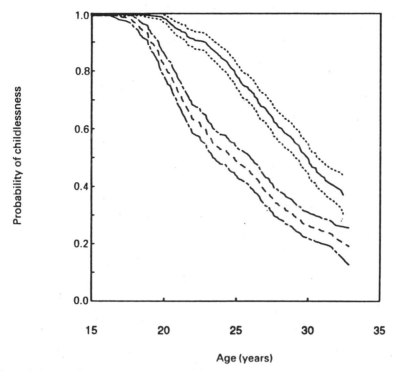

Figure 7.2 *Kaplan-Meier estimates of the survivor function for the first birth of West Germans born in 1949–51 versus age by gender: men (solid), men 95 per cent confidence interval (dot), women (dash), women 95 per cent confidence interval (long dash)*

tion who are childless to fall substantially as age increases, it is unlikely to reach zero, no matter how long the observational period, since some people are biologically incapable of bearing children. Thus, the distribution of age at first birth is defective. An attractive feature of event history analysis is that this does not obviate the scientific value of a curve like that displayed in Figure 7.2. Third, the first birth is not necessarily the first noteworthy event in a person's life. For one thing, he may die first – a type of censoring that is random and probably almost (but not quite) independent of the likelihood of having a child at a given age. Or, he may marry at some time prior to the child's birth, which surely alters the likelihood of a birth. Thus, there may be multiple events (competing risks), and not just a single event. Finally, a first birth holds promise of additional births – births 2, 3, and so forth. So, analysis of the time to the first birth provides a start on the analysis of a person's entire fertility history. More generally, subsequent events can be analyzed as well as the first one.

An examination of a *survivor plot* like that in Figure 7.2 is very useful for telling whether two or more groups differ in the timing of some event, but it is not the most helpful way of telling whether there is time variation in the likelihood of the event occurring, given that it has not yet happened. As the complement of the cumulative distribution function, all survivor curves tend to look fairly similar. In particular, all of them have a backward S shape; they begin at one and tend to decline towards zero over time. Because of the similarity in shape, it is often hard to tell much about the process being studied merely by examining survivor plots.

One way to investigate time variation in the likelihood of an event's occurrence is to examine a plot of the integrated hazard rate $H(t) \equiv -\log S(t)$ versus time t. An estimator of $H(t)$ that has good asymptotic properties was first proposed by Nelson (1972) and later shown to be unbiased by Aalen (1978). This estimator, usually termed the Nelson-Aalen estimator, is

$$\widehat{H}_{NA}(t) = -\log \widehat{S}_{NA}(t) = \sum_{t_{(i)} < t} \frac{d_{(i)}}{n_{(i)}}, \quad t_{(i-1)} < t < t_{(i)}$$

This estimator differs only slightly from minus the logarithm of the Kaplan-Meier estimator of $S(t)$, except when the sample is very small, or in the extreme right tail when the sample is large. Like the Kaplan-Meier estimator of the survivor function, the Nelson-Aalen estimator of the integrated hazard rate is a step function, but again people often connect the points to give a picture that resembles more closely the (presumed) underlying smooth function. One can also compute pointwise confidence intervals of the integrated hazard rate using its estimated variance,

$$\text{var}[\widehat{H}_{NA}(t)] = \sum_{t_{(i)} < t} \left[\frac{d_{(i)}}{n_{(i)}} \right]^2, \quad t_{(i-1)} < t < t_{(i)}$$

Figure 7.3 displays the plot of the Nelson-Aalen estimates of the integrated hazard rate of first birth versus age for the German first-birth data. A constant slope would mean that the hazard rate of first birth does not vary over time. Clearly the slope does vary over time: it is close to zero under age 17 for women and under age 20 for men. Even above this age the slope varies with time, especially for men. In short, the hazard rate of first birth varies with age, as expected. Although this conclusion is not surprising in this application, prior knowledge about time variation in hazard rates is very limited in many other applications.

A plot of the integrated hazard rate does not give a very good picture of the *manner* of variation in the hazard rate over time. It is better to estimate the hazard rate directly. However, it is less clear-cut how to estimate the hazard rate because empirical plots of estimates versus time tend to give a series of spikes, yet we typically believe that the hazard rate is a smooth function of time. Several estimators of the hazard rate are available (see Cox and Oakes, 1984), including one based on the Kaplan-Meier estimator of the survivor function. The illustration in Figure 7.4 is based on the Nelson-Aalen estimator:

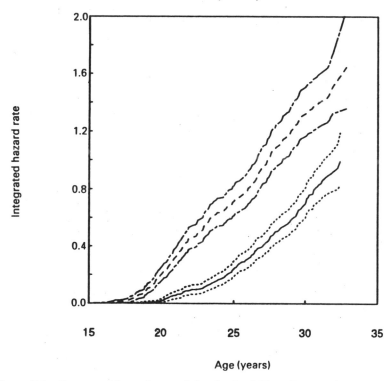

Figure 7.3 *Integrated hazard rate of first birth of West Germans born in 1949–51 versus age in years: men (solid), men 95 per cent confidence interval (dot), women (dash), women 95 per cent confidence interval (long dash)*

$$\widehat{h_{NA}}(t) = \frac{1}{\Delta t_{(i)}} \frac{d_{(i)}}{n_{(i)}}, \quad t_{(i-1)} < t < t_{(i)}$$

Estimation of this quantity from the German data produces a very erratic picture, which is probably a consequence of the relatively small sample size and reporting errors (for example, heaping, rounding, and so forth). To obtain a picture that compensates for this erraticness, it is common to smooth estimated hazard rates in some way. For example, to produce Figure 7.4, I grouped data into one-year age intervals. This yields a step function, but I connected the midpoints of intervals to make the overall pattern easier to decipher. More sophisticated procedures for smoothing hazard rates are also available (for example, see Wu, 1989).

This figure again displays the hazard rate of first birth, but for women born in different years – the birth cohorts of 1929–31, 1939–41, and 1949–51. I have truncated the time scale on the left at age 15 because no woman in this sample had a birth before age 17. Hence, the estimate of $h(t)$ equals zero below age 17. The pattern of variation in the first-birth rate of women for the 1929–31 and 1939–41 cohorts is similar to that found across almost all

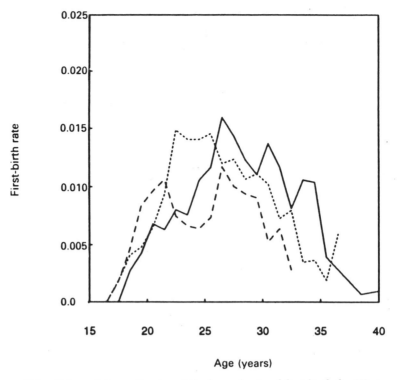

Figure 7.4   *Nelson-Aalen estimates of the hazard rate of first birth for West German women versus age by birth cohort: 1929–31 cohort (solid), 1939–41 cohort (dot), 1949–51 cohort (dash)*

societies: namely, it rises with age and then declines, becoming very low by age 40. The patterns for these two cohorts, though similar in overall shape, differ in that the 1940 cohort has noticeably higher birth rates in the mid twenties. The pattern for the 1949–51 cohort is very unusual because it is markedly bimodal. I will ignore this scientifically intriguing pattern for the moment, but return to it later.

This same series of procedures – examining plots of survivor functions, integrated hazard rates, and hazard rates – can be done for subsequent events as well. For example, Figure 7.5 shows the survivor function for the second birth of German men and women born in 1949–51. Note that the curves look fairly similar to those in Figure 7.2, except that they are shifted farther to the right and the values at the last observed ages are higher. One wonders whether these curves merely reflect differences in the timing of the first birth. A natural follow-up consists of examining the survivor function for the second birth conditional on the length of time since the first birth, or more informatively, the hazard rate of second birth versus the duration since the first birth. The latter is displayed in Figure 7.6 for women in different cohorts. Note that the patterns for women in different cohorts are very similar when viewed in this way. If plots for men are superimposed

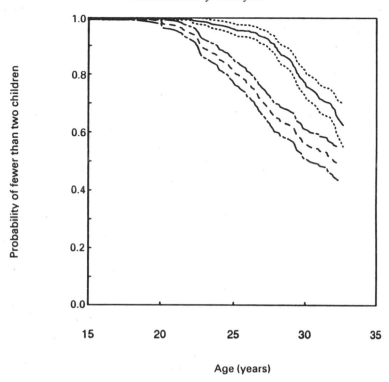

Figure 7.5 *Kaplan-Meier estimates of the survivor function for the second birth of West Germans born in 1949–51 versus age by gender: men (solid), men 95 per cent confidence interval (dot), women (dash), women 95 per cent confidence interval (long dash)*

(results not shown), one sees no marked, systematic differences. Hence, it appears that differences in the timing of the second birth mainly reflect differences in the timing of the first birth. My point here is primarily to suggest how techniques for examining the first event can be extended to study subsequent events.

When there are several possible outcomes (competing risks), one can estimate the conditional probability $m_k(t)$ in essentially the same way as other probabilities – for example, as the relative frequency of outcome k among all events occurring at (or around) time t. Estimation of the transition rate $r_k(t)$ is very similar to estimation of the hazard rate, except that $d_{(i)}$ refers only to the events consisting of a transition to the particular outcome of interest (that is, k).

Multivariate methods

I now want to shift gears and switch to another major area of event history analysis. Earlier I noted that descriptive analyses of event history data like

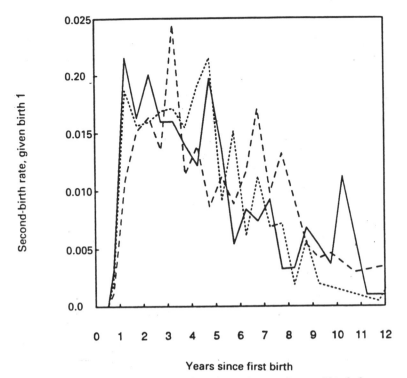

Figure 7.6   *Nelson-Aalen estimates of the hazard rate of second birth for West German women versus years since first birth by birth cohort: 1929–31 cohort (solid), 1939–41 cohort (dot), 1949–51 cohort (dash)*

those I have shown, though sometimes the ultimate goal, more often help in preparing for analyses designed to examine the effects of various explanatory variables on the outcome studied. Such studies are the primary objective of most social scientists using event history analysis. The previous discussion provides a good foundation for this new topic because analyses of effects of explanatory variables often make assumptions about the underlying pattern of time variation in the hazard rate of the event, and then try to estimate how the basic pattern is modified by the level of various explanatory variables.

Proportional hazards models

This method of analysis typically begins by postulating some model of the hazard rate. A common assumption in hazard rate models is that

$$h(t, \mathbf{x}) = \theta(\mathbf{x}) \, q(t)$$

where $\mathbf{x}$ is a vector of explanatory variables. This is called a *proportional hazards model* because the function of the vector of explanatory variables $\theta(\mathbf{x})$ simply multiplies some time-varying baseline hazard rate $q(t)$, so that hazard rates for two different values of **x** are functions only of **x** and not of $q(t)$. (A non-proportional specification of the hazard rate may also be proposed, as I indicate later.)

Two questions follow from this specification. First, what is $\theta(\mathbf{x})$? Second, what is $q(t)$? Ideally, the answers to these questions come from our scientific theories, but unfortunately this is rarely the case. Instead, answers tend to be made on the basis of convenience and fit.

Specification of the function of explanatory variables   Consider first the question of $\theta(\mathbf{x})$. Since $h(t)$ is non-negative for all possible values of t and **x** by definition, $\theta(\mathbf{x})$ should be some function that is non-negative for all xs. This requirement has meant that a linear regression specification

$$\theta(\mathbf{x}) = \lambda_0 + \lambda_1 x_1 + \lambda_2 x_2 + \ldots$$

$$= \boldsymbol{\lambda}'\mathbf{x} \qquad \text{(in vector notation)}$$

is rarely used, although it can be if the parameters $\boldsymbol{\lambda}$ are constrained so that $\theta(\mathbf{x}) > 0$. Instead, by far the most popular specification is

$$\theta(\mathbf{x}) = \exp(\boldsymbol{\lambda}'\mathbf{x}) = \prod_j v_j^{x_j}$$

where $v_j = \exp(\lambda_j)$, or equivalently $\log \theta(\mathbf{x}) = \boldsymbol{\lambda}'\mathbf{x}$. Thus, in this specification, a variable x_j has a multiplicative effect on the hazard rate and an additive effect on the log hazard rate.

Note, for example, that 'no effect of x_j' means that $\lambda_j = 0$ and that $v_j = 1$. Similarly, if $\lambda_j = 0.2$, then $v_j = \exp(0.20) = 1.22$. An interpretation sometimes given to such a result is that a unit increase in x_j increases the hazard rate by 22 per cent $= 100\% \times (1.22 - 1)$. If $\lambda_j = -0.2$, then $v_j = \exp(-0.20) = 0.82$. An interpretation sometimes given to this sort of result is that a unit increase in x_j decreases the hazard rate by 18 per cent $= 100\% \times (0.82 - 1)$.

Specification of the function of time   Next consider the question of $q(t)$. The simplest assumption is that $q(t)$ is a constant. This implies that, conditional on a set of xs, T has an exponential distribution. But there are many other possibilities. Table 7.1 gives many of the common postulates for $q(t)$ and its integral. These mathematical forms are associated with various characteristic patterns of variation over time in the hazard rate and in other fundamental quantities, such as the mean of T. A basic distinction is whether the hazard rate is a *monotonic* function of time (that is, it either decreases or increases steadily over time) or a *non-monotonic* function (that is, sometimes it increases and sometimes it decreases).

Two that are often proposed when a hazard rate has a non-monotonic pattern like that observed for the hazard rates of first birth of German

Table 7.1 *Some common specifications of $q(t)$ and its integral in terms of time $t, t_0 = 0$, and parameters (denoted by Greek letters) chosen so that $q(t) \geq 0$*

Name	$q(t)$	$Q(t) = \int_0^t q(u)du$
Monotonic		
Gamma[1]	$\dfrac{\alpha(\alpha t)^{\beta-1} e^{-\alpha t}}{\Gamma(\beta) - \alpha \int_0^t (\alpha u)^{\beta-1} e^{-\alpha u} du}$	$-\log\left[\dfrac{\alpha}{\Gamma(\beta)} \int_t^\infty (\alpha u)^{\beta-1} e^{-\alpha u} du\right]$
Gompertz-Makeham	$\alpha + \beta e^{\gamma t}$	$\alpha t + \dfrac{\beta}{\gamma}(e^{\gamma t} - 1)$
Rayleigh	$\alpha + \beta t$	$\alpha t + \beta t^2/2$
Pareto	$\alpha/(t + \beta)$	$\alpha[\log(t + \beta) - \log \beta]$
Weibull	$\beta(t + \delta)^\gamma$	$\dfrac{\beta}{\gamma + 1}[(t + \delta)^{\gamma+1} - \delta^{\gamma+1}]$
Non-monotonic		
Generalized Rayleigh	$\alpha + \beta t + \gamma t^2 + \cdots$	$\alpha t + \dfrac{\beta}{2} t^2 + \dfrac{\gamma}{3} t^3 + \cdots$
Inverse Gaussian[2,3]	$\dfrac{\dfrac{\alpha}{\sqrt{(2\pi t^3)}} \exp\left[-\dfrac{(\beta t + \alpha)^2}{2t}\right]}{\Phi\left(\dfrac{\beta t+\alpha}{\sqrt t}\right) - e^{-2\alpha\beta}\,\Phi\left(\dfrac{\beta t-\alpha}{\sqrt t}\right)}$	$-\log\left[\Phi\left(\dfrac{\beta t + \alpha}{\sqrt t}\right) - e^{-2\alpha\beta}\,\Phi\left(\dfrac{\beta t - \alpha}{\sqrt t}\right)\right]$
Log-logistic	$\alpha t^{\gamma-1} \left/ \left(1 + \dfrac{\alpha t^\gamma}{\gamma}\right)\right.$	$\log\left(1 + \dfrac{\alpha}{\gamma} t^\gamma\right)$
Log-Gaussian[2]	$\dfrac{\dfrac{1}{\sigma t \sqrt{2\pi}} \exp\left[-\dfrac{(\log t - \mu)^2}{2\sigma^2}\right]}{1 - \Phi\left(\dfrac{\log t - \mu}{\sigma}\right)}$	$-\log\left[1 - \Phi\left(\dfrac{\log t - \mu}{\sigma}\right)\right]$
Sickle[4]	$\beta t\, e^{\gamma t}$	$\dfrac{\beta}{\gamma^2}\left[(\gamma t - 1)\, e^{\gamma t} + 1\right]$
Sum of exponentials	$\displaystyle\sum_{m=1}^{M} \beta_m\, e^{\gamma_m t}$	$\displaystyle\sum_{m=1}^{M} \dfrac{\beta_m}{\gamma_m}\left(e^{\gamma_m t} - 1\right)$

[1] $\Gamma(\beta)$ denotes the gamma function, $\int_0^\infty u^{\beta-1} e^{-u} du$.
[2] $\Phi(x)$ denotes the cumulative standard Gaussian distribution function, $\int_{-\infty}^x \dfrac{1}{\sqrt{(2\pi)}} \exp(-u^2/2)\, du$.
[3] See Romanow (1983).
[4] See Diekmann and Mitter (1983).

women born in the 1929–31 and 1939–41 cohorts (see Figure 7.4) are the log-logistic and log-Gaussian models. We can evaluate whether one of these models fits the data using extensions of the graphical methods already described (for a discussion, see Wu, 1990). For example, $S(t)$ for the log-logistic model (see Table 7.1) is

$$S_t \equiv S(t) = \exp[-Q(t)] = \frac{1}{1 + \alpha t^\gamma/\gamma}$$

implying

$$W(S_t) \equiv \log(S_t^{-1} - 1) = \gamma \log t + \log \alpha - \log \gamma$$

Hence, a plot of $W(\hat{S}_t)$ versus $\log t$ (the natural logarithm of t) should be linear if a log-logistic model fits the data. For the log-Gaussian model, a plot of $W(\hat{S}_t) \equiv \Phi^{-1}(1 - \hat{S}_t)$ versus $\log t$ should be linear.

Figure 7.7 displays a plot of $W(\hat{S}_t)$ versus $\log t$ for the log-logistic and log-Gaussian models of the first-birth rate of German women born in 1949–51. Neither of the two curves is linear in my opinion, but of the two, the curve for the log-logistic model exhibits more curvature and seems less appropriate.

I should note that I have shown this plot to several people especially fond of these specifications of $q(t)$, and not all of them think that the deviations from non-linearity are marked. Or, at least, some argue that the deviations are not so great as to affect conclusions based on one of these models. This is an open question. The answer may depend partly on just what sort of inferences one wishes to make. For example, it is possible that the deviations are not great enough to affect tests of significance about the effect of some variable x on the hazard rate, but are large enough to affect population-level forecasts that one might want to make. The degree of sensitivity to this type of model misspecification is an area in which further research needs to be done. It is also true that comparable plots within homogeneous subpopulations might deviate less from linearity since time dependence is confounded with population heterogeneity in plots like this one.

Estimation of a proportional hazards model

Suppose that one of these common specifications fits these data or that the deviations from linearity are negligible. To be concrete, suppose the log-logistic model is chosen. How would the analyst proceed? Putting the common specification for $\theta(\mathbf{x}) = \exp(\boldsymbol{\lambda}'\mathbf{x})$ together with the log-logistic specification for $q(t)$ yields the following model of the hazard rate:

$$h(t, \mathbf{x}) = \exp(\boldsymbol{\lambda}'\mathbf{x}) \left[\frac{\alpha\gamma t^{\gamma-1}}{\gamma + \alpha t^\gamma}\right]$$

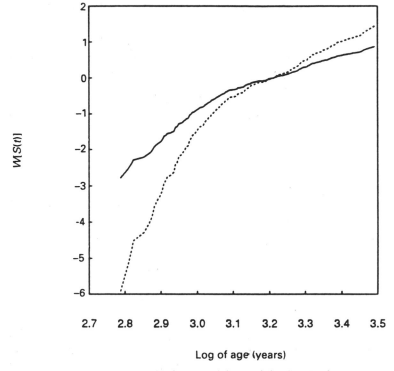

Figure 7.7 *W[S(t)] to assess the functional form of the first-birth rate of West German women born in 1949–51: log-Gaussian (solid), log-logistic (dot)*

which implies that the survivor function is

$$S(t, \mathbf{x}) = \left[\frac{1}{1 + \alpha t^{\gamma}/\gamma} \right]^{\exp(\lambda' \mathbf{x})}$$

Assuming a simple random sample of size I, the likelihood is

$$\mathcal{L} = \prod_{i=1}^{I} h(t_i, \mathbf{x}_i)^{(1 - c_i)} S(t_i, \mathbf{x}_i)$$

where c_i is 1 if case i is censored and 0 if it is uncensored; $\mathbf{x}_i$ is case i's values on the explanatory variables included in the model; and t_i is the time of the event for uncensored cases and the end of the observation period for censored cases. Choosing parameters to maximize the likelihood (a fairly routine procedure with modern computers) yields *maximum likelihood estimates*, which have desirable statistical properties. Moreover, one can perform likelihood ratio tests on nested models, estimate the asymptotic standard errors of parameters, and the like. I have not actually estimated the log-logistic (or log-Gaussian) model from these data, however, because the non-linearity apparent in Figure 7.7 makes me sceptical about the suitability of these two models.

An alternative is available that does not require any particular assumption about the functional form of $q(t)$. David R. Cox (1972; 1975) proposed a method of estimation, which he named *partial likelihood*, in which one can estimate the coefficients of the explanatory variables in the function $\theta(\mathbf{x})$ without specifying the functional form of $q(t)$. The partial likelihood is

$$\mathcal{L}_p = \prod_{i=1}^{I^*} \frac{\theta(\mathbf{x}_{(i)})}{\sum_{\nu \in R_{(i)}} \theta(\mathbf{x}_\nu)}$$

where I^* is the number of events and the risk set $R(t)$ is defined to be the set of cases at risk of an event at a given time t. Usually $\theta(\mathbf{x})$ is assumed to be $\exp(\boldsymbol{\lambda}'\mathbf{x})$, as I mentioned earlier. Although the above expression is written as if the vector of explanatory variables $\mathbf{x}$ does not vary over time, this simplification is not required. The explanatory variables may be time-varying; one just replaces $\mathbf{x}$ with $\mathbf{x}(t)$ in the above expression.

Partial likelihood estimators have been shown to be consistent and efficient under fairly general conditions, and a Monte Carlo study of the properties in small to medium samples found that their efficiency relative to maximum likelihood estimators for the true model was surprisingly high (Tuma and Hannan, 1984). Consequently, in applications in which one is uninterested in time dependence and is confident of the validity of the proportionality assumption, partial likelihood estimation of a proportional hazards model has much to recommend it.

Illustrative application

Since neither of the commonly proposed parametric specifications for a non-monotonic hazard rate seems to fit these data, I chose to use Cox's model and estimation method as a first step in studying the effects of explanatory variables on the hazard rate of first birth of German women. Table 7.2 gives some selected, illustrative results.

Model A includes four background variables. The likelihood ratio χ^2 value compares model A against a null hypothesis that the effects of these four variables are zero; the null hypothesis can clearly be rejected. More specifically, the results indicate that German women with more siblings tend to have a higher hazard rate of first birth, that is, that they tend to have the first child at a younger age. (It need not imply that such women have more children. To decide, we would need to examine the hazard rates of the birth of second and third children, and so forth.) Moreover, the magnitude of this effect seems to be larger for more recent birth cohorts. In addition the older a woman's mother at the birth of her first child, the lower the hazard rate of first birth in these cohorts, though the estimated effect is statistically significant only for the 1929–31 cohort. The magnitude of this effect appears to

Table 7.2   *Partial likelihood estimates of effects of selected covariates on the hazard rate of first birth of German women by birth cohort*

	1929–31	1939–41	1949–51
Model A			
Number of siblings	0.004	0.092[3]	0.111[3]
Age of R's mother			
at first birth (years)	−0.023[1]	−0.014	−0.015
Highest educational degree			
mittlere Reife	−0.300[1]	−0.388[1]	−0.502[2]
Abitur (or higher)	−0.370	−0.588[1]	−1.169[3]
Test of A vs null, χ^2 (4 DF)	10.24[1]	28.77[3]	53.36[3]
Model B			
In school	−6.558	−7.004	−2.311[1]
In training	−2.808[2]	−2.240[3]	−2.634[3]
Test of B vs null, χ^2 (2 DF)	27.23[3]	49.64[3]	77.19[3]
Model C			
Number of siblings	0.006	0.090[2]	0.101[3]
Age of R's mother			
at first birth (years)	−0.020	−0.013	0.000
Highest educational degree			
mittlere Reife	−0.229	−0.207	−0.370[1]
Abitur (or higher)	−0.041	−0.094	−0.442[1]
In school	−5.557	−6.001	−1.924[1]
In training	−2.725[2]	−2.188[3]	−2.393[3]
Test of C vs null, χ^2 (6 DF)	32.82[3]	65.35[3]	96.03[3]
Test of C vs A, χ^2 (4 DF)	22.58[3]	36.57[3]	42.66[3]
Test of C vs B, χ^2 (2 DF)	5.60[3]	15.71[2]	18.84[3]
Number of events	323	316	282
Number of women	361	355	368

[1] Significant at the 0.10 level.
[2] Significant at the 0.01 level.
[3] Significant at the 0.001 level.

have declined across the cohorts. The results for both variables suggest the existence of intergenerational transmission of fertility patterns.

Results for model A also suggest that a woman's own early life experiences affect timing of the first birth. More educated women have a significantly lower hazard rate, and the magnitudes of educational effects seem greater for the more recent cohorts. The expansion of career opportunities for women in recent years may explain the change in the magnitude of these effects across the cohorts.

Another explanation runs as follows. More educated women stay in school longer. Perhaps all women in school tend to have lower birth rates, but once women leave school, birth rates may not differ by educational level. Similarly, women in vocational training (a common practice in Germany) may also have lower birth rates until their training is completed. To test these hypotheses, I defined a dichotomous variable that equals 1 if a woman is currently in school, and is 0 otherwise, and another that equals 1 if she is currently in a training programme, and is 0 otherwise. These variables vary over time for any given woman. Thus, they are time-varying explanatory variables, in contrast to the background variables in model A. Social scientists may understandably ask whether being in school or in training lowers birth rates or whether having a child causes women to drop out of school or a training programme. Putting aside this question (German social scientists believe firmly that being in school and training lower fertility rather than the opposite), we can estimate the effect of time-varying explanatory variables using Cox's model and method, as I noted when I gave the expression for the partial likelihood. (Various other models also let one do this.)

Results for model B, which includes these two time-varying explanatory variables, indicate that the hazard rate of first birth is lowered by both. Note that the effect of being in school is larger in magnitude, but that the effect of being in training is statistically significant more often. This may seem puzzling. It probably reflects the extreme rarity of births among young women in school, which causes the estimated effect of being in schooling to be very imprecise and hence statistically insignificant.

Model C includes both background variables (which do not change over time) and the two time-varying explanatory variables. The likelihood ratio χ^2 values indicate that model C improves significantly upon models A and B, as well as the null model. The estimated effects for educational levels have diminished considerably and are statistically significant only in the 1949–51 cohort. In this combined model, the variables that are consistently most important (as indicated by statistical significance) are number of siblings and being in training.

It is possible that the effects of educational levels are largest when women are young and trying to establish their careers. Note that this hypothesis rests on the idea of effects that are time-varying (that is, non-proportional), contrary to the assumption made earlier. The hypothesis of non-proportionality can be tested in ways outlined below.

Non-proportional hazard rates

Recall that a proportional hazards model assumes that the underlying variation in the hazard rate over time, $q(t)$, is identical for all members of the population and that the effects of different combinations of explanatory variables act on $q(t)$ only multiplicatively. Is this assumption valid?

Again, there are various ways to investigate this issue. A graphical plot of the hazard rate for different groups can be highly informative. Figure 7.8 displays estimates of the hazard rate of first birth of women with low and high levels of education. The hazard rates for the two groups are markedly non-proportional: indeed, the shapes are not even very similar. The group with less education has a bimodal rate, whereas the group with more education has a unimodal rate. The proportional hazards model appears inappropriate for the first-birth rate of women in 1949–51. Naturally one needs to perform similar checks for other variables and for the other cohorts, too.

I am unable to pursue this thoroughly here, but one way to proceed is to estimate piecewise hazard rate models. Such piecewise models make parametric assumptions about hazard rates in specified time intervals and provide a useful way of letting hazard rates both vary with time in a fairly flexible way and also vary non-proportionally with explanatory variables. In a piecewise constant hazard model (see Holford, 1976; Tuma et al., 1979), which is the most common piecewise hazard model, the hazard rate is assumed to be time-invariant in some specified time interval, but may be allowed to depend on explanatory variables **x** in ways that may vary from one time interval to another. Indeed, the explanatory variables do not even need to be the same in different time intervals. For example, analyses of the hazard rate of the first birth of German women suggest that a high level of

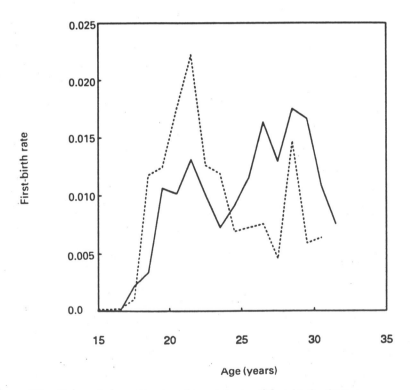

Figure 7.8 *Nelson-Aalen estimates of hazard rate of first birth of West German women without the Hauptabschluss born in 1949–51 versus age by educational level: vocational training (solid), no vocational training (dot)*

education lowers this rate for women in their early twenties, has no effect for those in their mid twenties, and raises this rate for those in their thirties (Huinink and Tuma, 1988). This result seems very plausible. More pertinent to the present discussion, it illustrates one way of studying non-proportional hazard rates.[2]

Multiple and repeatable events

To this point, I have concentrated on the first event, though I have mentioned that there may be competing events or a series of events, or both. At its simplest, switching to these more complex situations involves fairly direct extensions of the techniques that I have been describing. But there are also new possibilities and complications.

With successive events, there are *multiple time scales* (or 'clocks') that may be relevant to the future unfolding of the process being studied. For example, it has been hypothesized that the rate of break-up of a person's *n*th marriage depends not only on the person's age, duration in the *n*th marriage, and historical time, but also on the ages of children born in the marriage. The models and methods outlined above can be extended to test such hypotheses.

In addition, as I indicated previously, there may be *competing risks*. A marriage may end because either the person or his spouse dies, or because they obtain a divorce. The causal factors affecting these different risks and the nature of the time variation in the likelihood of these competing risks are apt to be very different, especially when divorce is contrasted with widowhood. There also may be *history dependence*; that is, the hazard rate of later events may depend on the timing and/or order of previous events. for example, it is sometimes argued that remarriage rates depend on the age of entering the first marriage, or the duration of the first marriage, or both.

I hope that my brief mention of these possibilities suffices to suggest some of the many kinds of questions that event history analysts address. The range of the *kinds* of questions that may be asked is really enormous. And, the fact that such questions can be addressed empirically has led researchers to raise many questions that they never bothered to ask in the past. To me, this is *the* major contribution of event history analysis.

My overview of the fundamentals of event history analysis in current use stops here because I want to discuss a few complications that call for either new statistical developments or improved data.

Complications

The statistical models and methods available for analyzing event history data largely assume that we have data on exactly what we want to study. In my experience, this is rarely true. In this section I indicate some common ways that data deviate from model assumptions.

First, there are problems pertaining to the measurement of the outcome being studied. I have already mentioned that changes in marital status can be conceptualized in various ways. For example, one might argue that cohabitation and separation are important, conceptually distinct statuses that should be included in a study of changes in marital status. Data on these statuses are rarely available. Social scientists typically proceed to analyze marital histories as if cohabitation and separation do not exist or are unimportant, which they rarely believe. In short, the statuses on which we have data are often aggregations of conceptually more basic statuses. Should we modify our models to account for this aggregation? If so, how?

Even when the categories measured in the data match our conceptualization of the process we are studying, other problems often occur. For example, it is widely ignored that the times of events are measured inaccurately (for an exception, see Hill and Hill, 1986). Sometimes inaccuracy is due to simple random error, but there is also heaping on favourite numbers and rounding. Moreover, when people are interviewed, accuracy usually depends on the length of time between events, how recently they occurred, the salience of the previous events, and so forth. In short, we need models that incorporate measurement error in dates of events, or at least, we need to know how the kinds of measurement errors in dates that we are likely to encounter affect statistical inferences.

A related problem is that data on the time of the event may be grouped. For example, I was told of one recent longitudinal study of a large sample of West Germans that was collecting marriage and fertility histories, which sounded very promising. But, a detailed look at the questionnaire revealed that only the year of birth of children and the year of marital status changes were being collected. Since the spacing between births is less than three years in roughly three-fourths of all births, year of birth gives an extremely imprecise measurement of birth spacing. Moreover, timing of first marriage and of first birth often occur fairly close together – yet one would like to know the order of these events. Clearly, either the data collectors need to measure dates more accurately, or statisticians need to think harder about estimating models from grouped data. (Of course, both would be desirable).

More worrisome yet is that some events may not be recorded when events occur too closely together. To my ongoing surprise and dismay, this is sometimes an intentional feature of the observation schemes developed by survey researchers. For example, surveys on length of unemployment usually ask respondents to report only spells of unemployment lasting longer than some minimum, which may be a week, but more often is a month. The statistical consequences of this data collection scheme can be serious. For illustrative purposes, suppose that the hazard rate of leaving unemployment is a constant h, implying that the length of unemployment spells is exponentially distributed. This implies that the mean length of unemployment spells is $1/h$. In the United States a mean length of one to three months is plausible under ordinary economic circumstances. A mean of two months, for example, implies that $h = 0.5$, but this implies that roughly 40 per cent of all employment spells are less than a month long. If respondents dutifully follow the instructions of those collecting data (of course, that does not always happen), unemployment will be tremendously underreported. And it will not be random but will be concentrated entirely on the short failure times. This is similar to left censoring – the situation in which we know one or more events occurred before τ_1, but not exactly how many or when. But, it is much worse because many events are simply not recorded at all.

Left censoring is a well-known but thorny problem. I will not discuss it here except to say that it has received much less attention than it deserves (for one discussion, see Tuma and Hannan, 1984: 128–35). This may be because statisticians have largely been responsive to the needs of medical researchers and engineers, for whom left censoring rarely occurs. But social scientists face it frequently, or more accurately they often have the problem in their data, though they usually ignore it in their analyses.

Related and even more difficult problems arise when one studies a series of events rather than the first and only event. For example, those collecting employment histories often decide to begin collecting them only when people achieve a certain 'suitable' age, for example 16 or 18. This almost always screens out some people who behave 'unsuitably', giving a biased picture of the world.

A similar practice involves gathering event histories for sample members currently in *selected* states of the outcome, but not all. An example will clarify this problem. In the Panel Study of Income Dynamics (PSID), in which roughly 5,000 American families have been interviewed annually for over 20 years, retrospective information on movements into and out of the three most recent spells of unemployment was collected during 1981–3 for people currently working and for those currently unemployed – but *not* for those currently out of the labour force. Thus, if the inability to find a job caused some people to become discouraged and leave the labour force, data recording these events were not collected. This scheme not only ignored a phenomenon of some policy interest (the 'discouraged' worker), but also probably yields biased estimates of the rate of leaving unemployment since those who become discouraged and drop out of the labour force are likely to have longer than average spells of unemployment. This defect in the data was eventually recognized, and since 1985 the PSID has collected information on unemployment spells for all husbands and wives, whatever their current employment status.

Or, those designing prospective longitudinal studies may collect information on people's current statuses and then follow them forward, but obtain only limited information on previous events. Previous employment experiences may affect the hazard rate of leaving a job, of getting promoted, and so forth, but one often lacks the data to investigate such hypotheses.

Let me be concrete. It is often argued that divorce rates for first marriages differ from those for second and subsequent marriages. Some years ago I participated in an experimental study of the effects of social welfare programmes on marital stability of low-income couples. A key question was: did these programmes stabilize marriages, break them up, or have no effect? We did our best, given the available data and what we knew about event history analysis at the time. But some doubts remain, and these mainly stem from limitations due to the observation scheme and study design. For one thing, those who designed the data collection instruments did not ask how many times the subjects had been married, only when they had entered their current marriage. For another, treatments were not assigned in a simple random way: poorer couples (who are more likely to have been married more than once) were more likely to be given certain treatments than others. It turned out that these treatments had the biggest effects. Could it be that these treatments had different effects on second marriages than on first marriages? There are still other problematic issues of analysis due to the kind of data that were collected in this particular study, but this question is enough to illustrate my point about the importance of collecting the *complete* history.

I have been focusing on deviations between common statistical assumptions and the data actually collected on the *outcome* being studied. A related and classical problem concerns errors in explanatory variables hypothesized to affect the outcome. Simple random measurement error comes immediately to mind. In linear models, conclusions about the effects of explanatory variables are biased only when random errors are correlated with measured variables included in the model. Unfortunately, the situation is known to be more complex in event history models. Even simple measurement error that is uncorrelated with any measured explanatory variable tends to bias estimates of the effects of explanatory variables on the hazard rate and also to bias estimates of the nature of time variation in the hazard rate. In recent years there has been extensive research on the general topic of *unobserved heterogeneity* that affects hazard rates, and there has been considerable progress on statistical techniques to correct for the problem (for example, see Heckman and Singer, 1984; Trussell and Richards, 1985; Tuma, 1985; Yamaguchi, 1986 and Chapter 2 of this volume). But the solutions require strong assumptions. Moreover, more complex types of random errors – errors that are stable across a series of events occurring to a given sample member, or errors that vary over time in various ways, or errors that are correlated across sample members (such as a husband and wife) – have received very little attention to date. Much more work remains to be done in this area.

Another complication on which work is needed involves what are sometimes called *contextual variables*. Suppose, for example, that the level of unemployment in a community affects the hazard rate of out-migration of those residing in this place. The community's level of unemployment is often measured, but imperfectly. If we include the measured level of unemployment in a model of out-migration rates of individuals, then the unmeasured error in this variable affects everyone residing in the community. These errors will, of course, be correlated across individuals. What impact does this have on estimated effects of individual-level explanatory variables or of the contextual variable? To my knowledge, this question has not yet been addressed within the context of event history models.[3]

Other complexities are introduced by the existence of time-varying explanatory variables. To date, event history analysts have shown at least moderate concern for the completeness of information on the outcome – for example, the marital or fertility histories of the people they are studying. There has, however, been considerable nonchalance with regard to the completeness of the available information on the explanatory variables thought to explain or predict the outcome. Explanatory variables that change over time are necessarily measured intermittently, not continuously. Investigators often use the most recent value of an explanatory variable, and hope that this is good enough. Is it? We do not know.

It is also true that almost no thought has yet been given concerning how best to draw a sample that is to be used for event history analysis. The occurrence of the event – for example, an illegitimate birth or death from AIDS – may be known to be rarer in some populations than in others. In view of this, what sample design is optimal? It is tempting to oversample subpopulations who have had the event, but this can bias results. It may be desirable to oversample subpopulations expected to have a high risk of the event, especially if these groups are a small fraction of the whole population. Events may also be more likely in some time intervals than in others (for example, marriages are more common under age 30 than above), in which case it may be optimal to oversample certain individuals in certain time intervals (for example, never-married individuals over age 30). These suggestions seem plausible to me, but the statistical foundation for them has not yet been developed. Given the expense and time involved in collecting event histories, the value of scientific investments targeted on devising optimal sample designs for event history analysis should be obvious.

The length of my list of problems to solve in the area of event history analysis may be daunting, so I will stop here. I hope, however, that my first sections have illustrated both the promise and the practice of event history analysis and that this section has aroused interest in solving the methodological problems that remain.

Appendix: statistical software for event history analysis

The statistical software listed below can be used to perform various aspects of event history analysis. Blossfeld et al. (1989) give examples of ways to use software preceded by a dagger (†); they focus on software designed for mainframe computers. Goldstein et al. (1989) review those preceded by an asterisk (*); they focus on software designed to run on a personal computer under MS-DOS.

†*BMDP: BMDP Statistical Software, 1440 Sepulveda Blvd, Los Angeles, CA 90025.
CSS: Stat Soft, 2325 E 13th St., Tulsa, OK 74104.
CTM: ERC/NORC, 1155 E 60th St., University of Chicago, Chicago, IL 60637.
*EGRET 1.0: Statistics and Epidemiology Research Corp., 909 NE 43rd, Suite 310, Seattle, WA 98105.
*EPILOG PLUS 2.0: Epicenter Software, PO Box 90073, Pasadena, CA 91109.
*GAPM 1.0: Recurrent Statistics, RD 1, Box 103, Niverville, NY 12130.
GAUSS: Aptech Systems Inc., 26250 SE 196th Pl., Kent, WA 98042;

GLIM: Numerical Algorithms Group, Wilkinson House, Jordan Hill Rd., Oxford OX2 8D2, UK.
*KWIKSTAT 2.0: TexaSoft, PO Box 1169, Cedar Hill, TX 75104.
*LIMDEP 5.1: Econometric Software Inc., PO Box 3526, Church St. Station, New York, NY 10008-3526.
*MINITAB 7.1: MINITAB, Inc., 3081 Enterprise Drive, State College, PA 16801.
*NCSS 5.5: 865 E 400 North, Kaysville, UT 84037.
†RATE: DMA Corporation, PO Box 881, Palo Alto, CA 94302.
†*SAS 6.03: SAS Institute, Inc., Cary, NC 27512-8000.
SPIDA 5.25: Statistical Laboratory, Macquarie University, New South Wales 2109, Australia.
†SPSS^x: 444 N Michigan Ave., Chicago, IL 60611.
*STATA: Computing Resource Center, 10801 National Blvd, Los Angeles, CA 90064.
*SURVCALC 1.0: John Wiley & Sons, Inc., 605 Third Ave., New York, NY 10158.
*SURVIVAL 4.1 (Module of SYSTAT): Systat, Inc., 1800 Sherman Ave., Evanston, IL 60201.
*SURVPAK 3.0: Johns Hopkins Oncology Center, Oncology Information Systems, c/o Judy Fields, Room 118, 600 N Wolfe St., Baltimore, MD 21205.
*TRUE EPISTAT 3.0: Epistat Services, 2011 Cap Rock Circle, Richardson, TX 75080-3417.
*yMED 1.08: Ming Telecomputing Inc., PO Box 101, Lincoln Center, MA 01773-6101.

Notes

Yongchuan Liu, Ray Mirikitani, Kathryn Tuma, and Stephen Van Rompaey provided expert research assistance. This research was supported by the National Institute of Child Health and Human Development (HD 21738) and by the National Science Foundation (SES 89-11666). Additional research support and facilities were provided by the Hoover Institution on War, Revolution, and Peace. Editorial changes were supported partly by the Center for Advanced Study in the Behavioural Sciences with funds from the National Science Foundation (BNS87-00864). Empirical examples based on analyses of the German Life History Study are drawn from work done in collaboration with Johannes J. Huinink of the Max-Planck-Institut für Bildungsforschung in Berlin.

1 The Appendix gives a partial list of statistical software that performs some form of event history analysis on either a mainframe or a personal computer.

2 Another way is to let parameters in models of $q(t)$ (see Table 7.1) be functions of covariates. For example, rather than multiplying $q(t)$ for the log-logistic model by $\theta(\mathbf{x}) = \exp(\boldsymbol{\lambda}'\mathbf{x})$ as I indicated earlier, one could let α and/or γ in the expression for $q(t)$ for the log-logistic model be functions of $\mathbf{x}$. Estimation of a non-proportional hazards model is similar to that for a parametric proportional hazards model, though usually more complex computationally.

3 Blossfeld (1986) is one of the few who have incorporated contextual variables in event history models.

References

Aalen, Odd O. (1978) 'Nonparametric inference for a family of counting processes', *Annals of Statistics*, 6(4): 701–26.
Barnett, William P. (1990) 'The organizational ecology of a technical system', *Administrative Science Quarterly*, 35: 31–60.
Bienen, Henry and Van de Walle, Nicolas (1989) 'Time and power in Africa', *American Political Science Review*, 83(1): 19–34.
Blossfeld, Hans-Peter (1986) 'Career opportunities in the Federal Republic of Germany: a dynamic approach to study of life-course, cohort, and period effects', *European Sociological Review*, 2: 208–25.

Blossfeld, Hans-Peter, Hammerle, Alfred and Mayer, Karl Ulrich (1989) *Event History Analysis: Statistical Theory and Application in the Social Sciences.* Hillsdale, NJ: Lawrence Erlbaum.

Carroll, Glenn R. and Hannan, Michael T. (1981) 'Dynamics of formal political structure: an event-history analysis', *American Sociological Review*, 46(1): 19–35.

Carroll, Glenn R. and Hannan, Michael T. (1989) 'Density delay in the evolution of organizational populations: a model and five empirical tests', *Administrative Science Quarterly*, 34: 4111–30.

Cox, David R. (1972) 'Regression models and life tables (with discussion)', *Journal of the Royal Statistical Society, Series B*, 34(2): 187–220.

Cox, David R. (1975) 'Partial likelihood', *Biometrika*, 62(2): 269–76.

Cox, David R. and Oakes, D. (1984) *Analysis of Survival Data*. London: Chapman and Hall.

Diekmann, Andreas and Mitter, Peter (1983) 'The "sickle hypothesis": a time dependent Poisson model with applications to deviant behaviour and occupational mobility', *Journal of Mathematical Sociology*, 9: 85–101.

Drass, Kriss A. (1986) 'The effect of gender identity on conversation', *Social Psychology Quarterly*, 49: 294–301.

Edelman, Lauren B. (1990) 'Legal environments and organizational governance: the expansion of due process in the American workplace', *American Journal of Sociology*, 95(6): 1401–40.

Felmlee, Diane H., Sprecher, Susan and Bassin, Edward (1990) 'The dissolution of intimate relationships: a hazard model', *Social Psychology Quarterly*, 53(1): 13–30.

Goldstein, Richard, Anderson, Jennifer, Ash, Arlene, Craig, Ben, Harrington, David and Pagano, Marcello (1989) 'Survival analysis software on MS/PC-DOS computers', *Journal of Applied Econometrics*, 4: 393–414.

Griffin, William A. and Gardner, William (1989) 'Analysis of behavioural durations in observational studies of social interaction', *Psychological Bulletin*, 106(3): 497–502.

Halliday, Terence C., Powell, Michael J. and Granfors, Mark W. (1987) 'Minimalist organizations: vital events in state bar associations, 1870–1930', *American Sociological Review*, 52(4): 456–71.

Hall, W.J. and Wellner, Jon A. (1980) 'Confidence bands for a survival curve from censored data', *Biometrika*, 67(1): 133–43.

Heckman, James J. and Singer, Burton (1984) 'A method for minimizing the impact of distributional assumptions in econometric models for duration data', *Econometrica*, 52(2): 271–320.

Hill, Martha S. and Hill, Daniel H. (1986) 'Labor force transitions: a comparison of unemployment estimates from two longitudinal surveys', in *American Statistical Association 1986: Proceedings of the Section on Survey Research Methods*. Washington, DC: American Statistical Association. pp. 220–5.

Hobcraft, John and Murphy, Mike (1986) 'Demographic event history analysis: a selective review', *Population Index*, 52(1): 3–27.

Holford, T.R. (1976) 'Life tables with concomitant information', *Biometrics*, 32: 587–97.

Huinink, Johannes J. and Tuma, Nancy Brandon (1988) 'An intercohort comparison of postwar patterns of family formation in the Federal Republic of Germany', paper presented at the Annual Meetings of the American Sociological Association, Atlanta, August.

Kalbfleisch, John D. and Prentice, Ross L. (1980) *The Statistical Analysis of Failure Time Data*. New York: Wiley.

Kaplan, E.L. and Meier, Paul (1958) 'Nonparametric estimation from incomplete observations', *Journal of the American Statistical Association*, 53(282): 437–81.

Knoke, David (1982) 'The spread of municipal reform: temporal, spatial, and social dynamics', *American Journal of Sociology*, 87(6): 1314–39.

Marsden, Peter V. and Podolny, Joel (1990) 'Dynamic analysis of network diffusion', in Henk Flap and Jeroen Weesie (eds), *Social Networks Through Time*. Utrecht: Rijksuniversiteit Utrecht.

Mayer, Karl Ulrich and Tuma, Nancy Brandon (1990) *Event History Analysis in Life Course Research*. Madison: University of Wisconsin Press.

Miller, Rupert G. (1981) *Survival Analysis*. New York: Wiley.

Nair, Vijayan N. (1984) 'Confidence bands for survival functions with censored data: a comparative study', *Technometrics*, 26(3): 265–75.

Nelson, Wayne (1972) 'Theory and applications of hazard plotting for censored failure data', *Technometrics*, 14(4): 945–66.

Olzak, Susan (1987) 'Causes of ethnic conflict and protest in urban America, 1877–1889', *Social Science Research*, 16: 185–210.

Olzak, Susan (1989a) 'Analysis of events in the study of collective action', *Annual Review of Sociology*, 15: 119–41.

Olzak, Susan (1989b) 'Labor unrest, immigration, and ethnic conflict in urban America, 1880–1914', *American Journal of Sociology*, 94(6): 1303–33.

Robinson, Dawn and Smith-Lovin, Lynn (1990) 'Timing of interruptions in group discussions', *Advances in Group Processes*, 7: 45–73.

Romanow, Allyn Lea (1983) 'Performance and promotion: a stochastic model of decision making by performance evaluation'. PhD dissertation, Stanford University.

Strang, David (1990) 'From dependency to sovereignty: an event history analysis of decolonization 1870–1987', *American Sociological Review*, 55: 846–60.

Strang, David and Tuma, Nancy Brandon (1993) 'Spatial and temporal heterogeneity in diffusion', *American Journal of Sociology*, (99): 614–39.

Sutton, John R. (1988) *Stubborn Children: controlling Delinquency in the United States, 1640–1981*. Berkeley: University of California Press.

Trussell, James and Richards, Toni (1985) 'Correcting for unobserved heterogeneity in hazard models using the Heckman-Singer procedure', in Nancy Brandon Tuma (ed.), *Sociological Methodology 1985*. San Francisco: Jossey-Bass. pp. 242–76.

Tuma, Nancy Brandon (1985) 'Effects of labor market structure on job-shift patterns', in James J. Heckman and Burton Singer (eds), *Longitudinal Analysis of Labor Market Data*. Cambridge: Cambridge University Press. pp. 327–63.

Tuma, Nancy Brandon and Hannan, Michael T. (1984) *Social Dynamics: Models and Methods*. Orlando: Academic Press.

Tuma, Nancy Brandon, Hannan, Michael T. and Groeneveld, Lyle P. (1979) 'Dynamic analysis of event histories', *American Journal of Sociology*, 84: 820–54.

Wu, Lawrence L. (1989) 'Issues in smoothing empirical hazard rates', in Clifford C. Clogg (ed.), *Sociological Methodology 1989*. Oxford: Basil Blackwell. pp. 127–59.

Wu, Lawrence L. (1990) 'Simple graphical goodness-of-fit tests for hazard rate models', in Karl Ulrich Mayer and Nancy Brandon Tuma (eds), *Event History Analysis in Life Course Research*. Madison: University of Wisconsin Press. pp. 184–99.

Yamaguchi, Kazuo (1986) 'Alternative approaches to unobserved heterogeneity in the analysis of repeatable events', in Nancy Brandon Tuma (ed.), *Sociological Methodology 1986*. San Francisco: Jossey-Bass. pp. 213–49.

8

Discrete-Time Mixed Markov Latent Class Models

Editors' introduction

Markov methods are used to analyze movements between states. In a social science context, these states are typically categories of an individual-level response variable such as marital status, voting intention or social class. The two illustrative examples in this chapter relate to choice of brand in purchasing a particular product and states of self-assessed work disability at successive time points. However, applications of Markov methods are not confined to individual or household behaviour and have included land-use change, industrial relocation, and settlement size. The main point is that Markov methods have been developed specifically for the analysis of longitudinal data and are relevant to the categorical and qualitative variables which are so common in social science research. In addition, by focusing upon the type of outcome on successive occasions, they are complementary to the methods for analysis of event history data discussed in the previous chapter. Indeed, Markov and duration models may be combined in sophisticated formulations (variously termed semi-Markov and competing risk methods) which permit the simultaneous analysis of incidence and outcome together with the interrelationship between the two. Such formulations are beyond the scope of an introductory volume but serve to emphasize the importance of Markov methods.

The basic features of Markov methods are conceptually straightforward and may be illustrated by a simple matrix of transition probabilities:

| | | Time $t + 1$ | |
		State 1	State 2
	State 1	p	$1-p$
Time t			
	State 2	$1-q$	q

where, for example, p is the probability of an individual being in state 1 at time $t + 1$ if he is in state 1 at time t. This matrix defines a Markov chain for movement between two states over discrete time intervals: the probability of being in any specific state at time $t + 1$ depends upon the state occupied at the previous time. More precisely, this is a *first-order* Markov chain to distinguish it from an nth-order chain in which the probability of being in any specific state depends upon the states occupied at the previous *n* times.

At one extreme, both the probabilities *p* and *q* are equal to 1 (Langeheine and van de Pol refer to this as the *identity matrix*) and there is perfect stability with no one switching states. At another extreme, $p = 1-q$ and any stability is due solely to chance; state at time *t*+1 is independent of state at time *t*. This defines a *zero-order* or *independence* model. More generally the Markov chain provides a probabilistic representation of different levels of continuity in behaviour over discrete time intervals. The time intervals are not necessarily of uniform length and, depending upon the substantive context, do not even have to be synchronous over the population; in Langeheine and van de Pol's brand choice example, the intervals between purchases will vary both between and within individual brand choice sequences.

Perhaps not surprisingly, empirical experience has shown that social processes do not conform, even approximately, to the simple Markov chain model. But the Markov chain formulation is readily generalized, and Langeheine and van de Pol provide an introduction to the disparate and often complex methods which are based upon the Markov chain and which have received attention in the social science literature. It is recognized that many readers will have little or no previous knowledge of Markov methods because applications have tended to be marginalized to the more quantitative publications; their complexity, or perhaps their dissimilarity to conventional statistical methods, has hindered their adoption. To simplify subsequent exposition Langeheine and van de Pol establish at the outset of the chapter a consistent notation and a unifying framework for the different methods discussed.

If this initial section seems daunting, skip to the second section which begins by introducing the simplest model before proceeding with successively more complex formulations. This progression is divided into two parts. The first considers models formulated on the recorded (manifest) data and includes non-stationarity (variation in the transition probabilities over time – also termed *time heterogeneity*) and mixed models in which the behaviour of different groups in the population conforms to different Markov chains (population heterogeneity). Patterns of stability and change in mixed models are allowed to vary within the population, and this variation is described probabilistically rather than by identifying the individuals in each group. Readers having difficulty with the technical details of Markov chains may wish to concentrate initially on this first part. The second part reviews latent class formulations, with and without allowance for measurement error. Although the latent variables in these models are categorical rather then continuous, there are evident similarities with structural equation modelling (see Bynner's contribution in Chapter 5). For example, the underestimation of continuity or stability over time if measurement error is ignored in a Markov model corresponds to the attenuation of parameter estimates in structural equation modelling.

The third section covers disaggregation into subpopulations to allow the measures of stability and change incorporated into the model to vary with the values of explanatory variables. As with mixture models, this enables different patterns of behaviour to be estimated for different groups in the population. However, in this case the groups are identified explicitly on the basis of concomitant information (the explanatory variables). Formally, the distinction is between observed and unobserved population heterogeneity.

Discrete-Time Mixed Markov Latent Class Models

Rolf Langeheine and Frank van de Pol

This chapter deals with the situation where one discrete (or categorical) variable x, which may refer to attitudes, voting intentions, employment status or the occurrence of some sort of behaviour like buying, is measured at several (T) consecutive occasions, x_1, x_2, ... x_T, with realizations i, j, ... , m. In general T is rather small (say from three to six) and the sample size is rather large. In principle, x may be polytomous, but for ease of exposition we will consider dichotomous variables only. Such data, which may be compiled in contingency table form, may be available for one population only (see Table 8.1) or for several subpopulations (see Table 8.9). Analysis with Markov models presented in this chapter focuses on the types of change and stability that exist in these subpopulations.

These models are specifically tailored for the data at hand, taking into consideration the discreteness of both space and time. They may be formulated on the manifest level or extended to the latent level either by postulating several (unknown) types of change for a (sub)population or by incorporating measurement error. First developments in the field are mainly due to Wiggins (1955), a dissertation that later appeared in book form (Wiggins, 1973). Although conceptually appealing, Wiggins's work was plagued by several problems, most of which were tied to inefficient methods of parameter estimation. These problems were surmounted by Poulsen (1982) who showed how to perform maximum likelihood (ML) estimation of the parameters of the mixed Markov model (see below) and the latent Markov model (see below) by use of the expectation maximization (EM) algorithm of Dempster et al. (1977). In a parallel development Davies and Crouchley (1986) also described the mixed Markov model, restricting a continuous distribution to a set of latent classes.

Exogenous variables may be modelled by analyzing several subpopulations simultaneously (van de Pol and Langeheine, 1990). Spilerman (1972) may have been the first to analyze the effect of exogenous variables on a single Markov chain. He used a regression framework, which has been refined by Kelton and Smith (1991). Davies and Crouchley (1985), building on the econometric literature of discrete-choice models, included several exogenous variables and also modelled unobserved heterogeneity, but not with latent classes. Another difference with the approach that is adopted in the present chapter is that their model has no parameters for response uncertainty.

Our exposition will start with the most general model, the latent mixed Markov model for several subpopulations. From a didactic point of view it may not be optimal to start top-down with this model. However, we considerably simplify the notation used in the subsequent sections in doing so. Subsequently, we proceed bottom-up by starting with the simplest Markov model and ending with the most general model in the penultimate section. This enables us to focus on the strengths and weaknesses of the various models considered. Readers who feel the most general model to be too complicated should just try to get a cursory understanding and then continue with the simple Markov model in the next section.

The general latent mixed Markov model for several populations

Assume that repeated measurements of some discrete variable x are available for several (T) points in time for several (H) subpopulations. An example is given in Table 8.9. There we have $H=2$ subpopulations (males/females), x has $J=2$ categories (disabled/not disabled), and $T=3$ (1971,1972,1974). The data are thus given by an $H \times J^T$ table. The general latent mixed Markov model for several subpopulations (LMMS, where S stands for several subpopulations that are defined by additional external variables, like gender in Table 8.9) is in the case of three occasions given by

$$P_{hijk} = \gamma_h \sum_{s=1}^{S} \sum_{a=1}^{A} \sum_{b=1}^{B} \sum_{c=1}^{C} \pi_{s|h} \; \delta^1_{a|sh} \; \rho^1_{i|ash} \; \tau^{21}_{b|ash} \; \rho^2_{j|bsh} \; \tau^{32}_{c|bsh} \; \rho^3_{k|csh} \qquad (8.1)$$

with P_{hijk} the proportion in the population in cell (h,i,j,k). The model assumes that each subject belongs to one of one or more subpopulations. Membership of subpopulation h ($h=1, \ldots , H$) remains unchanged for all occasions. The proportion that belongs to subpopulation h is denoted by γ_h. All other parameters that will be described below are considered conditional on subpopulation h.

Each member of subpopulation h can belong to one of one or more (manifest or latent) Markov chains, i.e. parts of the (sub)population that have the same dynamics. A proportion $\pi_{s|h}$ in subpopulation h belongs to chain s ($s = 1, \ldots , S$). Hence the proportion in subpopulation h and chain s is $\gamma_h \pi_{s|h}$.

A member of subpopulation h and chain s is assumed to belong to one of A latent classes. The proportion in class a ($a = 1, \ldots , A$) at occasion 1, for subpopulation h and chain s, is denoted by $\delta^1_{a|sh}$. Hence the proportion in subpopulation h, chain s, and class a at occasion 1 is $\gamma_h \pi_{s|h} \delta^1_{a|sh}$.

The probability $\rho^1_{i|ash}$ of response i on occasion 1, given h, s and a, is assumed the same for all subjects in subpopulation h, chain s and class a. Hence, the proportion in subpopulation h, chain s, class a and category i at occasion 1 is $\gamma_h \pi_{s|h} \delta^1_{a|sh} \rho^1_{i|ash}$. If the model is manifest, the latent classes (indexed by a for occasion 1, b for occasion 2, etc.) and the manifest categories (i for occasion 1, j for occasion 2, etc.) are identical. Therefore, the response probabilities $\rho^1_{i|ash}$ are superfluous in a manifest model.

If the model applies to more than one occasion then, for subpopulation h, each member of chain s is assumed to behave according to the same transition probabilities, $\tau^{21}_{b|ash}$, from latent class a at time 1 to latent class b at time 2. As on occasion 1, the probability $\rho^2_{j|bsh}$ of response j on occasion 2, given h, s and b, is assumed to be the same for all subjects in subpopulation h, chain s and class b. Hence, the proportion in subpopulation h, chain s, class a and category i at occasion 1, and class b and category j at occasion 2, is $\gamma_h \, \pi_{s|h} \, \delta^1_{a|sh} \, \rho^1_{i|ash} \, \tau^{21}_{b|ash} \, \rho^2_{j|bsh}$.

Extension to more occasions is straightforward. Summing over chains and latent classes we obtain the proportion of subjects P_{hijk} in subpopulation h, category i at occasion 1, category j at occasion 2, and category k at occasion 3.

A sample gives an estimate of the P_{hijk} from which the γ, π, δ, ρ, and τ parameters may be estimated. Special cases of the general LMMS model considered in the subsequent sections have been estimated using the TURBO PASCAL™ program PANMARK (van de Pol et al., 1989). It computes maximum likelihood (ML) parameter estimates using a version of the EM algorithm and standard errors of the parameters by numerical differentiation of the likelihood (for details, see also van de Pol and de Leeuw, 1986; van de Pol and Langeheine, 1989; van de Pol and Langeheine, 1990).

For completeness, we note that in order to be uniquely defined all sets of parameters have to sum to unity, given any combination of variables that is conditioned on (e.g. $\Sigma_h \, \gamma_h = \Sigma_s \, \pi_{s|h} = \Sigma_a \, \delta^1_{a|sh} = \Sigma_i \, \rho^1_{i|ash} = \Sigma_b \, \tau^{21}_{b|ash} = 1$).

Models for one population

In order to demonstrate the advantages and disadvantages of several models we will first use a data set from a single population. The data, which are taken from Aaker (1970), are reproduced in Table 8.1. These data provide a record of family brand purchases over time. Each purchase is coded 2 if brand B is purchased, and 1 if another brand in the product class is purchased. Data are available for $T = 5$ occasions (or waves) for a sample of 988 families.

The simple Markov model

In order to pinpoint stability and change, data such as in Table 8.1 are often first analyzed using the simple Markov (M) model:

$$P_{ijk} = \delta^1_i \, \tau^{21}_{j|i} \, \tau^{32}_{k|j} \tag{8.2}$$

(As in the case of the general LMMS model we will give formulae by including $T = 3$ occasions only throughout. Extension to more occasions is straightforward.)

Table 8.1   *Contingency table[1] of brand purchase data*

t=1	t=2	t=3	t=4	t=5	Observed frequencies
1	1	1	1	1	464
1	1	1	1	2	31
1	1	1	2	1	26
1	1	1	2	2	12
1	1	2	1	1	28
1	1	2	1	2	9
1	1	2	2	1	6
1	1	2	2	2	5
1	2	1	1	1	49
1	2	1	1	2	5
1	2	1	2	1	7
1	2	1	2	2	2
1	2	2	1	1	12
1	2	2	1	2	5
1	2	2	2	1	12
1	2	2	2	2	10
2	1	1	1	1	79
2	1	1	1	2	11
2	1	1	2	1	10
2	1	1	2	2	8
2	1	2	1	1	12
2	1	2	1	2	8
2	1	2	2	1	3
2	1	2	2	2	12
2	2	1	1	1	31
2	2	1	1	2	5
2	2	1	2	1	7
2	2	1	2	2	9
2	2	2	1	1	25
2	2	2	1	2	12
2	2	2	2	1	15
2	2	2	2	2	58

[1]Categories: 2, purchase of brand B; 1, purchase of some other brand.
Source: Aaker, 1970

Model M (8.2) is derived from model (8.1) by taking into consideration the following issues. First, since we have one population only, there is no index h. Second, the simple Markov model assumes one chain only. There is therefore no index s. Thirdly, this chain is defined to be a manifest chain. Response probabilities, the ρs, are therefore superfluous, and the latent classes (a, b and c) coincide with the manifest categories (i, j and k). Hence the proportion of subjects with response sequence i, j and k is given by the probability of response i on occasion 1 (δ_i^1), multiplied by the probability of response j on occasion 2 given response i on occasion 1 ($\tau_{j|i}^{21}$), multiplied by the probability of response k on occasion 3 given response j on occasion 2 ($\tau_{k|j}^{32}$).

The simple Markov chain is exceptional because ML parameter estimates can be obtained directly without using an iterative algorithm. Table 8.2

Table 8.2 *Estimation of parameters for the simple Markov model (brand purchase data)*

		$t=2$					
		$j=1$	$j=2$	Total	$\hat{\delta}_i^1$	$\hat{\tau}_{j\|i}^{21}$	
	$i=1$	581	102	683	0.69	0.85	0.15
$t=1$	$i=2$	143	162	305	0.31	0.47	0.53
				988			

		$t=3$			$\hat{\tau}_{k\|j}^{32}$	
		$k=1$	$k=2$	Total		
	$j=1$	641	83	724	0.89	0.11
$t=2$	$j=2$	115	149	264	0.44	0.56

$\hat{\tau}_{j\|i}$

	$j=1$	$j=2$
$i=1$	0.88	0.12
$i=2$	0.45	0.55

		$t=4$			$\hat{\tau}_{l\|k}^{43}$	
		$\ell=1$	$\ell=2$	Total		
	$k=1$	675	81	756	0.89	0.11
$t=3$	$k=2$	111	121	232	0.48	0.52

		$t=5$			$\hat{\tau}_{m\|l}^{54}$	
		$m=1$	$m=2$	Total		
	$\ell=1$	700	86	786	0.89	0.11
$t=4$	$\ell=2$	86	116	202	0.43	0.57

shows in more detail how the (conditional) probabilities are estimated. We have first presented the bivariate distribution at time points 1 and 2. The marginal distribution at $t=1$ shows that brand B ($i=2$) is purchased in 305 out of 988 cases (which is 31 per cent). The rest (683 families or 69 per cent) decided in favour of some other brand. This gives the estimates of the initial distribution at $t=1$ (The $\hat{\delta}$s). How does the purchase sequence continue if a simple Markov model applies? Given that someone did not buy brand B at $t=1$, what purchase is made at $t=2$? We see that out of the 683 families ($t=1$ and $i=1$), 581 or 85 per cent decide against brand B at $t=2$ again, whereas 102 purchasers or 15 per cent switch to brand B. The proportion of those who bought brand B at $t=1$ and stay with it at $t=2$ is 53 per cent (162 out of 305), whereas 47 per cent switch to some other brand. In Markov chain theory these conditional probabilities (the τs) are also called transition probabilities. If we proceed to compute transition probabilities from $t=2$ to $t=3$ and so on from the respective bivariate tables, we end up with the series of $\hat{\tau}$s listed in Table 8.2.

According to the simple Markov model the vector of probabilities at the second occasion, $\hat{\delta}^2 = [0.73\ 0.27]$ in our sample, may be obtained by post-multiplying the initial probabilities, here $\hat{\delta}^1 = [0.69\ 0.31]$, with the matrix of observed transition probabilities,

$$\hat{T}^{21} = \begin{bmatrix} 0.85 & 0.15 \\ 0.47 & 0.53 \end{bmatrix}$$

The distribution at later occasions may be obtained in the same way. Therefore the simple Markov model may be represented by the path diagram of Figure 8.1. For the simple Markov chain $[\delta_1^1 \; \delta_2^1] = [P_{1++} \; P_{2++}]$, $[\delta_1^2 \; \delta_2^2] = [P_{+1+} \; P_{+2+}]$ etc., where $P_{i++} = \Sigma_j \Sigma_k P_{ijk}$ and $P_{+j+} = \Sigma_i \Sigma_k P_{ijk}$.

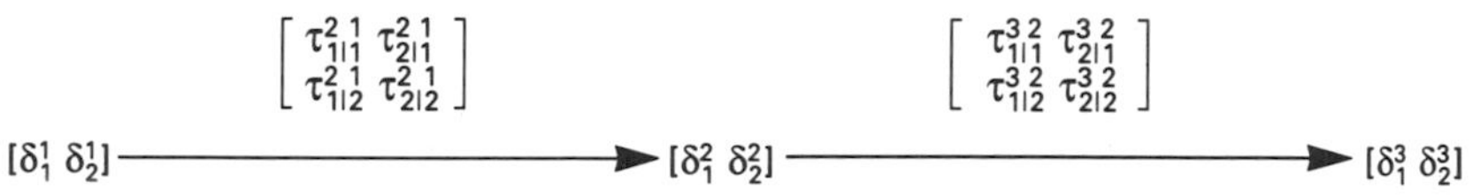

$$[\delta_1^1 \; \delta_2^1] \xrightarrow{\begin{bmatrix} \tau_{1|1}^{2\,1} & \tau_{2|1}^{2\,1} \\ \tau_{1|2}^{2\,1} & \tau_{2|2}^{2\,1} \end{bmatrix}} [\delta_1^2 \; \delta_2^2] \xrightarrow{\begin{bmatrix} \tau_{1|1}^{3\,2} & \tau_{2|1}^{3\,2} \\ \tau_{1|2}^{3\,2} & \tau_{2|2}^{3\,2} \end{bmatrix}} [\delta_1^3 \; \delta_2^3]$$

Figure 8.1 *Path diagram of a simple Markov model: three measurements of a dichotomous variable*

The transition matrices in Table 8.2 reveal a fact that is very often observed with data of this type: they are very similar. In order to save parameters, we may therefore restrict the Markov chain to be stationary, which means that transition probabilities in formula (8.2) are homogeneous (or constant) in time:

$$\tau_{j|i}^{2\,1} = \tau_{j|i}^{3\,2} = \ldots = \tau_{j|i} \tag{8.3}$$

These τs, as given in the right-hand side of Table 8.2, may be estimated by the sum of all corresponding frequencies, divided by the sum of the respective marginal frequencies. In the example we have for instance: $\hat{\tau}_{1|1} = (581+641+675+700) / (683+724+756+786) = 0.88$.

The resulting stationary simple Markov chain model is a very parsimonious model in terms of parameters. Regardless of the number of panel waves, for a binary variable there are just three non-redundant parameters (one δ and 2 τs). However, is it also a good model for our example data? In order to evaluate this we compare the observed frequencies $N \times p_{ijk}$ (where N is the sample size) with the frequencies expected under the model. These are obtained by applying formula (8.2) to the parameter estimates of Table 8.2 (and again multiplying by N). A summary statistic to evaluate the fit of the model is the log of the likelihood ratio (LR) χ^2 statistic, which has convenient properties for the comparison of nested models, but which is less robust than Pearson's χ^2 statistic in the presence of scarce data. A nested model is a restricted version of a more general model. The restriction to nested models is not necessary for some information criterion statistics (Read and Cressie, 1988).

If the model were correct, the LR would be expected to be about equal to the degrees of freedom (DF). For large (random) samples a χ^2_{DF} distribution may be used to test whether the LR is significantly too large. From Table 8.3, which gives LR statistics together with degrees of freedom for various models fitted to the brand B data, we see that the simple stationary Markov model has a bad fit: the LR (= 196.53) is much larger than χ^2_{28} at the 10 per cent level (= 37.92). The poor fit of the simple stationary Markov chain, which will be found for almost every data set in the social sciences, may be due to several reasons:

Table 8.3 *Likelihood ratio (LR) statistics and degrees of freedom for various models fitted to the brand purchase data*

Model	LR	DF
Simple stationary Markov	196.53	28
Simple non-stationary Markov	187.20	22
Simple stationary Markov, second order	47.65	24
Simple non-stationary Markov, second order	42.20	16
Stationary mixed Markov, two chains	49.18	24
Non-stationary mixed Markov, two chains	23.92	12
Stationary mixed Markov, two chains, second order	16.38[1]	16
Stationary mixed Markov, three chains	28.40[1]	20
Stationary mover-stayer	71.07	26
Stationary mover-stayer with two mover chains	39.10	22
Stationary mover-stayer, second order	26.96[1]	22
Stationary independence-stayer	146.00	27
Non-stationary independence-stayer = biased coin black-and-white	123.36	24
Two-class time-homogeneous latent class	150.46	28
Two-class time-heterogeneous latent class	72.02	20
Latent stationary Markov, time-homogeneous ρs	40.13	26
Latent non-stationary Markov, time-homogeneous ρs	34.07	20
Latent stationary Markov, time-heterogeneous ρs	30.23	18
Latent Markov plus random response	20.81[1]	21
Partially latent mover-stayer	22.46[1]	24
One latent, one manifest chain	20.23[1]	22
Mixed Markov with chain turnover	23.93[1]	20
Latent mixed Markov, chain-homogeneous resp. probs.	25.29[1]	22

[1] This model fits at least at the 10 per cent level.

1   The chain is assumed to be stationary. In the present case, allowance for non-stationarity does not result in a significant improvement (the LR difference is 196.53–187.20=9.33 with 6DF).

2   The chain is assumed to be of first order. That is, knowledge of someone's state at $t=2$ is sufficient to predict someone's state at $t=3$. In a second order Markov model, transition probabilities to $t=3$ depend not only upon the state at $t=2$ but also on the state at $t=1$. Second-order Markov chains are not a special case of the LMMS model since transition probabilities in this model are conditional on one previous point in time only. However, they may be applied within this framework by manipulating the cross-table of $x_1, x_2, \ldots, x_T$ (Coleman, 1964; Poulsen, 1982; van de Pol and Langeheine, 1990). Since higher-order models have a rather bad image in the literature (e.g. Coleman, 1964), we will not go into details, but simply give the results of both the stationary and non-stationary version of this model in Table 8.3. As the results show, improvement in fit over the first-order model is impressive. However, the fit of these models is not satisfactory in absolute terms.

3   The model assumes the population to be homogeneous with all individuals conforming to the same process. This assumption may be unrealistic, of course. Instead, the population may be heterogeneous with two or more chains, each of which has its own dynamics. An extension presented in the next subsection develops this theme.

4   The model assumes the data to be free of measurement error. Again, this is often an unrealistic assumption in the social sciences. Below, we will therefore present the latent Markov model that allows corrections for measurement error.

To sum up, the simple Markov model has the advantage of parameter parsimony. In addition, an iterative estimation procedure is unnecessary since the parameters can be estimated directly; only a few seconds of computer time are needed to fit a model. On the other hand, the model is characterized by a series of rather restrictive and unrealistic assumptions that render it inadequate in most situations.

The mixed Markov model

To our knowledge, the first successful attempt to extend the simple Markov model to a mixture of two or more Markov chains is due to Poulsen (1982). The non-stationary mixed Markov (MM) model is given by

$$P_{ijk} = \sum_{s=1}^{S} \pi_s \, \delta_{i|s}^1 \, \tau_{j|is}^{21} \, \tau_{k|ijs}^{32} \tag{8.4}$$

which assumes S (latent) chains, each having its own initial probabilities at $t=1$, $\delta_{i|s}^1$, and transition probabilities, the τs. The proportion of the population which behaves according to chain s is denoted by π_s. A stationarity restriction (formula (8.3)) may be conceived for each chain. A path diagram of a two-chain MM model is given in Figure 8.2. It is emphasized that this is a probabilistic model; the probabilities are estimated simultaneously and the model does not seek to identify which individuals are associated with each chain.

The stationary and the non-stationary two-chain mixed Markov models fit the data considerably better than the simple Markov model. The improvement in fit for the stationary two-chain MM model is about equal to the improvement obtained with the stationary second-order model. Again, however, fit is inadequate in absolute terms. To facilitate understanding of the MM model the estimated parameter values of the two-chain model are given in Table 8.4.

Under the (incorrect) assumption of a two-chain MM model the majority (77 per cent of the population) belongs to chain 1. Most of these people (82.7 per cent) decide against brand B at $t = 1$ and show a high repeat probability of 0.922 to stay with their behaviour at successive points in time. However, of those 17.3 per cent who initially purchased brand B, 77.8 per cent switch to some other brand on each of the successive occasions. Chain 2 depicts a somewhat different dynamic. From the members of this chain

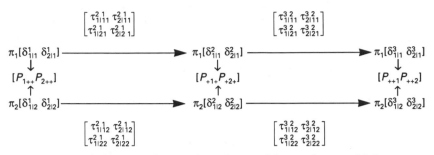

Figure 8.2   *Path diagram of a mixed Markov model: two-chain model for three measurements of a dichotomous variable*

Table 8.4   *Estimated parameter values[1] (and standard errors) for various mixed Markov models fitted to the brand purchase data*

Model	Chain, category	Chain proportion $\hat{\pi}$	Category proportion at $t=1$ $\hat{\delta}$	Transition probabilities $\hat{\tau}$			
				From t to $t+1$		From $t=1$ to $t=5$	
				Other	Brand B	Other	Brand B
Two-chain	Chain 1,	0.770(0.05)					
stationary	other		0.827(0.03)	0.922(0.01)	0.078(0.01)	0.909	0.091
mixed	brand B		0.173(0.03)	0.778(0.06)	0.222(0.06)	0.908	0.092
Markov							
	Chain 2,	0.230(0.05)					
	other		0.237(0.06)	0.475(0.11)	0.525(0.11)	0.340	0.660
	brand B		0.763(0.06)	0.270(0.04)	0.730(0.04)	0.339	0.661
Mover-	Chain 1,	0.614(0.03)					
stayer	other		0.577(0.03)	0.783(0.02)	0.217(0.02)	0.722	0.278
	brand B		0.423(0.93)	0.563(0.02)	0.437(0.02)	0.720	0.280
	Chain 2,	0.386(0.03)					
	other		0.872(0.02)	1	0	1	0
	brand B		0.128(0.02)	0	1	0	1
Independ-	Chain 1,	0.534(0.02)					
ence-stayer	other		0.527(0.02)	0.678(0.01)	0.322(0.01)	0.678	0.322
	brand B		0.473(0.02)	0.678(0.01)	0.322(0.01)	0.678	0.322
	Chain 2,	0.466(0.02)					
	other		0.880(0.01)	1	0	1	0
	brand B		0.120(0.01)	0	1	0	1
Two-class	Chain 1,	0.756(0.02)					
time-homo-	other		0.902(0.01)	0.902(0.01)	0.098(0.01)	0.902	0.098
geneous	brand B		0.098(0.01)	0.902(0.01)	0.098(0.01)	0.902	0.098
latent							
class	Chain 2,	0.244(0.02)					
	other		0.304(0.02)	0.304(0.02)	0.696(0.02)	0.304	0.696
	brand B		0.696(0.02)	0.304(0.02)	0.696(0.02)	0.304	0.696

[1] Parameter values of 0 and 1 are fixed by definition.

76.3 per cent bought brand B initially, and the probability to stay with brand B appears to be comparatively high (0.73). In addition, more than half of those who decided for some other brand at $t=1$ decide in favour of brand B at later points in time.

However, transition probabilities from t to $t+1$ are sometimes misleading. We have therefore also included transition probabilities from the first to the last wave. In the present case, the rows of these matrices are nearly identical within both chains. This simply tells us that the change process has reached a steady state at $t=5$ already. If we compare these probabilities with the initial ones we clearly see that the dynamics of the market are adverse to the newly introduced brand B within both chains (chain 1, 9 per cent versus 17 per cent; chain 2, 66 per cent versus 76 per cent).

In order to end up with an MM model with a potentially satisfactory fit we are left with several alternatives. Owing to lack of space and the availability of some more attractive models to be presented below, we will mention very briefly only two of these alternatives. Just as in the case of the simple Markov model we may specify a two-chain stationary *second-order* MM model. This model not only results in an acceptable fit (LR = 16.38, DF = 16), but also significantly improves on fit as compared with both the one-chain second-order model and the two-chain first-order MM.

Another possibility is to extend the first-order MM model from two to three chains. Again, the fit is acceptable (LR = 28.40 with 20 DF) and this model fares significantly better than the two-chain MM model. However, this model has two outliers (rather badly fitted cells).

Alternatively, the two-chain MM model may be restricted in several ways. We will comment on some special cases which are well known in the literature, although most of them do not fit well for the present data set. At the same time, this enables us to introduce some new concepts such as 'no change', 'independence' and 'random response'.

The mover-stayer model The first attempt to incorporate unobserved heterogeneity into the Markov model is due to Blumen et al. (1955). These authors proposed a mixture of two Markov chains, where movers are characterized by an ordinary stationary Markov chain, whereas stayers (the second chain, $s=2$) stay in their initial category with probability one across time. That is, the latter transition probabilities are restricted to be

$$\tau_{j|is} = 1 \quad \text{for } i=j \quad \text{and} \quad \tau_{j|is} = 0 \quad \text{otherwise} \tag{8.5}$$

Arranged in a matrix, these stayer or no-change probabilities constitute the identity matrix, as shown in Table 8.4. If the mover-stayer (MS) model does not fit, it may be extended with a second mover chain. Although the MS model with two mover chains does not fit adequately, there is considerable improvement upon the classical MS model as well as the two-chain MM model.

Another extension would be to make the mover chain second-order. This model fits well and is not significantly worse than the more general two-chain stationary second-order MM model (LR = 10.58 with 6 DF, whereas χ_6^2 is 10.64 at the 10 per cent level).

The independence-stayer model If the mover-stayer model fits, it may be advisable to look for more parsimonious models. One such candidate is the independence-stayer (IpS) model. It assumes that the probability of changing from time t to time $t+1$ does not depend on the category to which a person belonged at time t. All rows of the transition matrix of the movers are therefore restricted to be equal (chain 1 of IpS in Table 8.4):

$$\tau_{j|11} = \tau_{j|21} = \ldots \tau_{j|J1} \tag{8.6}$$

If the transition probabilities are also assumed to be non-stationary, we get the Converse (1974) version of the black-and-white model. This model, which has been proposed to evaluate attitude stability, postulates a dichotomy within the population: one part behaves perfectly stably over time, whereas members of the other part respond as though flipping a biased coin (maybe a different one on each occasion).

Converse (1964) originally proposed an even more restrictive version of this model, where people were assumed to flip an unbiased coin at every occasion, i.e. to respond randomly. This model would require the following restrictions for the random response chain: $\delta_{j|1}^1 = 1/J$; $\tau_{j|i1} = 1/J$.

The classical latent class model Consider the S-chain non-stationary MM model discussed earlier. This model says that the probability of being in category j at some time $t+1$ depends not only on the category i at the previous occasion but also on chain membership. If we drop the local dependence assumption within every transition matrix (that is, formula (8.6) holds) the result is a model with S independence chains which is Lazarsfeld's (1950) classical latent class (LC) model:

$$P_{ijk} = \sum_{s=1}^{S} \pi_s \, \delta_{i|s}^1 \, \delta_{j|s}^2 \, \delta_{k|s}^3 \tag{8.7}$$

given here for three measurements of one variable. The classical latent class model may be interpreted as a heterogeneity model: the S latent classes in the population are assumed to have different distributions, $\delta_{i|1}^1, \ldots, \delta_{i|S}^1$ for occasion (indicator) 1, $\delta_{j|1}^2, \ldots, \delta_{j|S}^2$ for occasion 2, and so on. The observed distribution is a mixture, or average, of these distributions with weights π_s. Equation (8.7) is the time-heterogeneous version of this model. Of course, time homogeneity may be assumed by imposing restrictions $\delta_{i|s}^1 = \delta_{i|s}^2 = \delta_{i|s}^3$. For illustrative purposes, parameter estimates of the latter version are included in Table 8.4 in terms of a restricted MM model, the two-class time-homogeneous LC model.

To sum up, the mixed Markov model turns out to be rather general. Not only does it explicitly take into account unobserved population heterogeneity, but it also contains a variety of models well known in the literature as special cases, such as the simple Markov model (which is MM with $S=1$), the mover-stayer model, the black-and-white models and the classical latent class model. In addition, many other models (such as mover-independence, mover random response etc.) may be devised (van de Pol and Langeheine, 1990). Just as LC models are sometimes called local independence models, so MM models may be conceptualized as local dependence LC models. These models are latent because an unobserved variable with S categories is introduced in addition to the manifest xs.

A restrictive aspect of MM models, however, is that membership in chain s is permanent across time, i.e. there is no turnover between chains. Another drawback is that (with the exception of LC versions) MM models may not be given an error in measurement interpretation, which is a special feature of the latent Markov model that will be presented in the next section.

Finally, all of the MM models mentioned so far may be estimated using the PANMARK program. Since estimation is done iteratively, a solution with a local (though not global) maximum of the log-likelihood may be found. Poulsen (1982) reports such a solution (LR = 69.03 instead of our 49.18) for the two-chain stationary MM model. We therefore urge users not to rely on results obtained from a single set of starting values (PANMARK allows for default or user-specified starting values). In addition, identifiability of a specific model should be checked carefully. Again, PANMARK provides several ways in which this may be done. Both of these issues are addressed in detail by van de Pol and Langeheine (1989).

The latent Markov model

The latent Markov (LM) model considered in this section is due to Wiggins (1955; 1973):

$$P_{ijk} = \sum_{a=1}^{A} \sum_{b=1}^{B} \sum_{c=1}^{C} \delta_a^1 \, \rho_{i|a}^1 \, \tau_{b|a}^{2\,1} \, \rho_{j|b}^2 \, \tau_{c|b}^{3\,2} \, \rho_{k|c}^3 \tag{8.8}$$

This model assumes that the whole population changes according to one Markov chain, but measurement error causes the observed cross-table to diverge from what would be observed if reliability was perfect. The model thus allocates a subject into one of A latent classes at $t=1$ which are characterized by response probabilities ($\rho_{i|a}^1$). For panel data the number of latent classes, A, is usually assumed to be equal to the number of manifest response categories, J. Moreover, latent classes are ordered so that we get high values for the diagonal elements $\rho_{i|a}^1$ (with $a=i$) in the $A \times J$ matrix of response probabilities **R**. Change from one point in time to the next is captured by latent transitions, the τs. That is, someone may stay in a class ($b=a$) or switch to some other class ($b \neq a$). A path diagram is given in Figure 8.3.

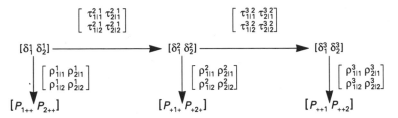

Figure 8.3   *Path diagram of a latent Markov model: three measurements of a dichotomous variable*

As with MM models, time homogeneity may be assumed for transition probabilities τ, giving a latent stationary Markov chain. Moreover, in the LM model, time homogeneity may also be assumed for response probabilities. In general, time heterogeneity of the τs does not cause any problems, but, for three waves only, the ρs have to be time homogeneous in order to render a model identifiable.

For the brand B data the latent variable may be labelled 'brand loyalty', buying behaviour being a fallible indicator. None of various two-class LM models fits (see Table 8.3). The LM model with both time-heterogeneous ρs and τs is not identified. Just as with MM models, relaxing time homogeneity in one way or another does not significantly improve the fit.

Nevertheless, we have included estimated parameter values of the stationary LM model in Table 8.5 for illustrative purposes. Comparison with the results of the simple Markov model reveals some interesting features of the LM model. First, extension by two parameters only (the ρs) results in a dramatic improvement in fit (from 196.53 to 40.13: see Table 8.3). Second, response probabilities indicate that the implicit assumption of perfect reliability in the simple Markov model (model M) is incorrect; the class 1 → other and class 2 → brand B probabilities are each significantly less than unity. Third, this results in overestimation of change by model M; the off-diagonal transitional probabilities for model M (see Table 8.2) are larger than the off-diagonal transitional probabilities for the LM model.

If the LM model fits, the conclusion may be that some real change takes place. However, before accepting this hypothesis, the LM model should be confronted with the rival hypothesis of no latent change. This hypothesis requires the transition matrix to be the identity matrix (or a latent stayer matrix). In this case, we have one latent variable with A categories only, and the τs are dropped from formula (8.8), which reduces to

$$P_{ijk} = \sum_{a=1}^{A} \delta_a \, \rho^1_{i|a} \, \rho^2_{j|a} \, \rho^3_{k|a} \tag{8.9}$$

which, again, is the same as the classical latent class model in equation (8.7). The present notation, however, suggests a measurement error interpretation

Table 8.5 *Estimated parameter values[1] (and standard errors[2]) for two latent Markov models[3] fitted to the brand purchase data*

Model	Class	Class proportions δ̂	Response probabilities ρ̂		Latent transition probabilities τ̂ From t to t+1			From t=1 to t=5		
			Other	Brand B	Class 1	Class 2	Class 3	Class 1	Class 2	Class 3
Latent Markov	1	0.667(0.02)	0.936(0.01)	0.064(0.01)	0.982(0.01)	0.018(0.01)	-	0.949	0.051	-
	2	0.333(0.02)	0.213(0.03)	0.787(0.03)	0.187(0.02)	0.813(0.02)	-	0.548	0.452	-
Latent Markov with random response class	1	0.535(0.05)	0.966(0.02)	0.034(0.02)	0.968(0.04)	0.002(0.02)	0.030(0.06)	0.915	0.008	0.077
	2	0.138(0.05)	0.100(0.08)	0.900(0.08)	0.089(0.16)	0.900(0.14)	0.011(0.28)	0.305	0.656	0.039
	3	0.327(0.09)	0.5	0.5	0.237(0.09)	0.004(0.10)	0.759(0.17)	0.628	0.011	0.361

[1] Parameter values of 0.5 are fixed by definition.
[2] Standard errors are obtained from the information matrix.
[3] Both models assume time-homogeneous ρs and τs.

of the classical LC model, with only one latent distribution, δ_a, which is unreliably measured at three occasions (or with three indicators). Latent Markov models may therefore also be called latent class models with latent change.

Since the LM model with $A=J$ classes did not fit the brand B data, we will consider two extensions. Poulsen (1982) reports a satisfactory fit for the three-class unrestricted stationary LM model (LR = 20.58, DF = 20). Re-estimation with the PANMARK program revealed that this model is not identified. Poulsen's results suggest, however, that we estimate a model with the third class consisting of people who respond randomly, or who buy both brand B and other brands simultaneously. That is, we fix the response probabilities of this class at 0.5. The fit of this model is excellent, but transition probabilities are estimated with large standard errors (Table 8.5) (latent Markov with random response: LMRr).

Probably the most surprising result is that about one-third of the population is classified as giving random response (or buying both brand B and other brands) at $t=1$. Measurement is almost perfect for class 1 which contains buyers of all other brands. As compared with the LM model, brand B purchasers (class 2) are also measured more reliably now. Both sets of transition probabilities (from one point in time to the next and from the first to the last wave) reveal that there is considerable change over time in favour of switching to some other brand. Nearly one-third of the brand B buyers at $t=1$ do not show brand loyalty at $t=5$. Nearly two-thirds of those initially classified random respondents switch to some other brand at $t=5$. The latent distribution at $t=5$ (the vector of estimates is $\hat{\delta}^5 = [0.736 \ 0.099 \ 0.165]$) shows total net latent change to be 20.1 per cent in favour of some other brand. Note that this is mostly due to those who gave random response (or bought both brand B and other brands) at the first wave.

To sum up, the main feature of the latent Markov model, which postulates one latent chain to hold for the entire population, is to correct manifest responses for measurement error. Consequently, transition probabilities are latent and allow for turnover from one latent class to another across time. In general, comparison with the simple (manifest) Markov model shows that the latter overestimates both reliability and change. We will return to this issue below. Again, the LM model contains the classical latent class model as a special case which is LM with the transition matrix restricted to be the identity matrix.

As long as the number of classes is specified to be equal to the number of manifest response categories, we have never encountered any identifiability problems, not even with a non-stationary latent Markov chain. However, these may occur with time-heterogeneous response probabilities or if the number of classes is allowed to be greater than the number of response categories.

Of course, latent Markov chains can also be measured via multiple indicators. Consider for a moment a latent Markov model for one indicator and six occasions with non-stationary transition probabilities. A path diagram of this model is given in Figure 8.4a with matrices of transition probabili-

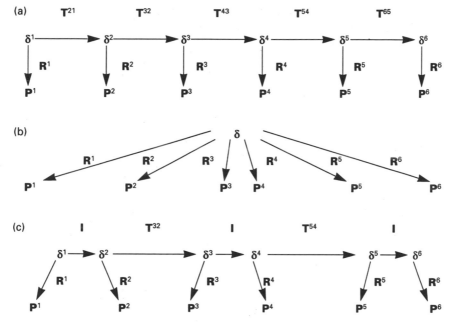

Figure 8.4. *Path diagrams for (a) a latent Markov model (one indicator, six occasions) (b) a classical latent class model (c) a multiple-indicator latent Markov model (two indicators, three occasions)*

ties from time $t-1$ to time t designated by $\mathbf{T}^{t,t-1}$, matrices of response probabilities at time t designated by $\mathbf{R}^t$, and with $\mathbf{P}^t$ designating the observable distribution vector at time t. If all $\mathbf{T}^{t,t-1}$ are restricted to be the identity matrix $\mathbf{I}$ (i.e. with diagonal elements equal to 1 and other elements 0), the latent Markov model reduces to a classical latent class model (formula (8.9)) with one latent variable that does not change over time. The respective path diagram in Figure 8.4b shows that variables at all time points are considered as (fallible) indicators of one latent variable. Now think of a situation where we have two indicators of one latent variable for three occasions. This can be modelled as a latent non-stationary Markov chain by using one latent variable for each indicator and restricting some of the matrices of transition probabilities between these latent variables to be the identity matrix, as shown in Figure 8.4c. Parameter estimates will be less sensitive to departures from the Markov assumption if multiple indicators are used.

The latent mixed Markov model

Model enthusiasts might be interested in whether there is an even more general model that contains both the mixed Markov and the latent Markov model as special cases. In fact, there are several ways to derive such a model. The version we prefer, the latent mixed Markov (LMM) model in Langeheine and van de Pol (1990), is given by

$$P_{ijk} = \sum_{s=1}^{S} \sum_{a=1}^{A} \sum_{b=1}^{B} \sum_{c=1}^{C} \pi_s \, \delta_{a|s}^1 \, \rho_{i|as}^1 \, \tau_{b|as}^{21} \, \rho_{j|bs}^2 \, \tau_{c|bs}^{32} \, \rho_{k|cs}^3 \qquad (8.10)$$

This extends the single-chain LM model to a mixture of S latent chains, having one additional set of parameters, the πs, which are the proportions of the S chains. Within each chain, the chain variable (with index s) is added as a conditioning variable to the rest of the parameters. A path diagram of the LMM model would look like Figure 8.2, with matrices of response probabilities added on the arrows from δs to Ps, as in Figure 8.3.

As Table 8.6 shows, any S-chain A-class LMM model may be formulated as a one-chain LM model with $A' = S \times A$ classes with certain transition probabilities defined to be structural zeros.

All models considered above are special cases of the LMM model. This is quite obvious for the LM model, which is LMM with $S=1$. The MM model is obtained by specifying perfect measurement within all classes (e.g. $\rho_{i|a} = 1$ if $a=i$ and $\rho_{i|a} = 0$ otherwise).

In principle, the LMM model opens a wide avenue for specifying new models unknown in the literature so far. However, this generality comes at a price. That is, an LMM model may not be identified unless some restrictions are imposed on the general version. First experience from a few data sets has shown that measurements from at least six waves are necessary for the general version to be identified. Identification problems can be overcome by using more than one indicator for each occasion.

For the five-wave brand B data several two-chain two-class models have been considered. The general version is not identified in this case, nor is a model that restricts the transition matrix of one of these chains to be the identity matrix. Note that this model may be called a latent mover-stayer model owing to incorporation of measurement error into both chains, as opposed to the classical mover-stayer model. We therefore decided to specify perfect measurement for the stayers, which reduces the latent mover-stayer model to a partially latent model with latent movers but manifest stayers. This model fits extremely well and significantly better than the one-chain

Table 8.6 *Latent transition parameters[1] in a two-chain two-class latent Markov model in terms of $A' = 2 \times 2$ classes*

				Time $t + 1$				
			$b'(t+1)$	1	2	3	4	Total
			Chain s	1	1	2	2	
	$a'(t)$	Chain s	Class a	Class b	1	2	1	2	
	1	1	1		$\tau_{1|11}$	$\tau_{2|11}$	0	0	1
	2	1	2		$\tau_{1|21}$	$\tau_{2|21}$	0	0	1
Time t	3	2	1		0	0	$\tau_{1|12}$	$\tau_{2|12}$	1
	4	2	2		0	0	$\tau_{1|22}$	$\tau_{2|22}$	1

[1] Structural zeros are fixed by definition.

Source: adapted from Langeheine and van de Pol, 1990

Table 8.7 Estimated parameter values[1] (and standard errors) for the partially latent mover-stayer model (brand purchase data)

Chain	Class	Chain proportions $\hat{\pi}$	Class proportions $\hat{\delta}$	Response probabilities $\hat{\rho}$		Latent transition probabilities $\hat{\tau}$			
						From t to $t+1$		From $t=1$ to $t=5$	
				Other	Brand B	Class 1	Class 2	Class 1	Class 2
1		0.824(0.11)							
	1		0.587(0.05)	0.932(0.03)	0.068(0.03)	0.972(0.01)	0.028(0.01)	0.924	0.076
	2		0.413(0.05)	0.308(0.05)	0.692(0.05)	0.233(0.03)	0.767(0.03)	0.626	0.374
2		0.176(0.11)							
	1		0.778(0.15)	1	0	1	0	1	0
	2		0.222(0.15)	0	1	0	1	0	1

[1] Parameter values of 1 and 0 are fixed by definition.

two-class LM model which is extended by the two additional parameters for perfectly stable stayers (see Tables 8.5 and 8.7). The model also fits significantly better than the classical mover-stayer model to which it adds two parameters to capture measurement error in the mover chain.

The estimated parameter values for the partially latent mover-stayer model are given in Table 8.7. According to this model, perfectly stable stayers of all other brands ($17.6 \times 0.778 = 13.7$ per cent) and perfectly stable brand B purchasers ($17.6 \times 0.222 = 3.9$ per cent) add up to 17.6 per cent. All blame for measurement error now goes to chain 1. This is the reason for the somewhat lower reliabilities as compared with the respective values for the LM and LMRr models (see Table 8.5). Again, both sets of transition probabilities show change over time towards being adverse to brand B. The latent distribution at the last wave is δ^5: [0.659 0.164 0.137 0.039]. This model thus says that there is a total net loss of $0.659 - 0.484 = 17.5$ per cent of brand B market share during the observation period. There is no steady state at $t=5$. The model thus predicts that loss of brand B market share will continue.

Before concluding this section we shall briefly mention some additional models, all of which are LMM with some restrictions added. One such candidate is a mixture of one latent and one manifest chain. This model simply removes the no-change restriction of the partially latent mover-stayer model. But the two parameters added to the latter model do not significantly increase the fit for the brand purchase data.

In commenting on the mixed Markov model we mentioned the restrictive aspect of constant chain membership across time. Now that we can formulate an MM model as an LMM model, it is easy to incorporate turnover between chains into the MM model by removing (some of the) zero restrictions for transition probabilities in Table 8.6 (while fixing response probabilities at zero and one). For the two-chain MM model with chain turnover listed in Table 8.3 we removed four zero restrictions on the transitions, i.e. the transition matrix looks like

$$\begin{bmatrix} \tau & \tau & 0 & \tau \\ \tau & \tau & \tau & 0 \\ 0 & \tau & \tau & \tau \\ \tau & 0 & \tau & \tau \end{bmatrix}$$

Moreover, in this four-class latent Markov model the response probability matrices are restricted to

$$\begin{bmatrix} 1 & 0 \\ 0 & 1 \\ 1 & 0 \\ 0 & 1 \end{bmatrix}$$

This model also fits quite well and significantly improves on the fit of the traditional MM model, to which it adds four parameters.

Another possibility is to assume the response probabilities of one chain to be equal to the corresponding response probabilities of the other chain, without imposing such equality restrictions on transition probabilities. We found this model to fit well for the brand purchase data. Likewise, we may specify transitions to be chain homogeneous without imposing such restrictions on response probabilities. The latter model is not identified for the brand purchase data, however.

In conclusion, it should have become evident that, though simple in principle, the LMM model allows for complex extensions of both MM and LM models. However, some models that may be conceptually valid may not be identifiable for one indicator per occasion, especially if the number of occasions is small.

Stability and change

Now that we have considered quite a variety of models for the brand purchase data, we will comment briefly on the different types of stability and change implied by these models (for details, see Langeheine and van de Pol, 1990). Table 8.8 gives estimated proportions for some selected models.

First consider models from the simple Markov to the latent class formulation (M to LC) listed across the top of the table. In these models, all change is considered to be manifest (and likewise stability). In comparison with the respective proportions in the data (where the two cells with response patterns 11111 and 22222 indicate stability and the rest correspond to change), models M, MM and LC overestimate manifest change. In mover-stayer models this proportion equals that in the data, because no-change data cells are fitted perfectly. In MS models we distinguish perfect stability for stayers from stability in mover chains. Note that any Markov chain except for a stayer

Table 8.8 *Estimated proportions of stability and change in some selected models (brand purchase data)*

	Data	M	MS	MM	LC	LC'	LM	pLMS
					Model			
Perfect stability			0.386					0.176
Stability	0.528	0.444	0.142	0.513	0.492	0.492	0.766	0.550
true stability						0.491	0.490	0.322
measurement error						0.001	0.276	0.228
Change	0.472	0.556	0.472	0.487	0.508		0.234	0.274
true change							0.116	0.105
measurement error						0.508	0.118	0.169
Total error						0.509	0.394	0.397

M, simple Markov; MS, mover-stayer; MM, stationary two-chain mixed Markov;
LC, two-class time-homogeneous latent class; LC', error of measurements interpretation of LC;
LM, two-class latent stationary Markov with time-homogeneous response probabilities;
pLMS, partially latent mover-stayer.

or random response chain contains a certain amount of stability despite the fact that it may be called a mover chain.

In models that allow for an 'error of measurements' interpretation (the models LC' to pLMS listed across the top of Table 8.8), both stability and change may be broken down into a true and an error proportion. In a latent stayer model (LC') there is no change by definition. Consequently, all change is considered as error in this model. Figures for the latent Markov model as well as the partially latent mover-stayer model both demonstrate the well-known fact that stability is underestimated while change is overestimated if the problem of measurement error is neglected. In both of these models, the proportion of total error sums to nearly 40 per cent with approximately 50 per cent true stability and about 11 per cent true change.

Note that all quantities in Table 8.8 give total proportions. Net change, which refers to change in marginal distributions, should therefore be distinguished from total change.

Models for several subpopulations

Very often multi-way tables of consecutive measurements of one target variable are available not only for a single sample but also for subsamples that are defined by one or more qualitative variables such as gender, age, or education. The additional variables may have been recorded because the subgroups so defined are expected to differ in their dynamics on the target variable. In such cases it is advisable to perform a simultaneous analysis for all subgroups instead of separate analyses for each subgroup or even a single analysis of the total sample pooled across subgroups.

To enable this sort of analysis, the latent mixed Markov model (8.10) is extended by a parameter γ_h that refers to the proportion of each of the H subpopulations, and all other parameters are considered conditional on subpopulation h. This brings us back to the general latent mixed Markov model for several subpopulations which was outlined at the outset of this chapter (equation (8.1)); we have reached the top of the model hierarchy.

This model opens a Pandora's box. All the models considered above may be fitted into this framework. At one extreme, complete heterogeneity of subsamples may be permitted, leaving each subsample with its own parameters. This would be equivalent to fitting a model to each subsample separately. At the other extreme, it is possible to assume homogeneity across subsamples. Between these two extremes many across-group restrictions may be devised that result in partially homogeneous models. In addition, within-group restrictions may be specified with, for example, a mover-stayer model for one subgroup but an independence-stayer model for another. If there are two or more variables defining subgroups, these variables may be combined into one composite variable (for example, two binary variables define $H=4$ subgroups).

However, sample sizes for subpopulations will be smaller, resulting in less accurate parameter estimates (larger standard errors). Put differently, a model with complete across-group heterogeneity requires H times the number of parameters of the corresponding model for the pooled sample (excluding γ_h). More realistic models may therefore require some across group equality restrictions. If theory is lacking, this requirement may be difficult to achieve, especially in view of the multitude of potential models. In van de Pol and Langeheine (1990) we have therefore proposed a procedure for the selection of appropriate equality constraints across subgroups.

A panel analysis on two subpopulations

In this section we will consider a sample of people who reported some work disability in 1971, and who were reinterviewed about self-assessed work disability in 1972 and 1974 (Table 8.9). Bye and Schechter (1986), who proposed another method for estimating the parameters of the latent Markov model, report results for the pooled sample and for males and females considered as separate groups.

Some results[1] are given in Tables 8.10 and 8.11. The models in Table 8.11

Table 8.9   *Contingency tables for males and females having some work disability[1] in 1971*

Time 1971	1972	1974	Males	Sample Females	All cases
1	1	1	79	140	219
1	1	2	7	34	41
1	2	1	8	26	34
1	2	2	13	26	39
2	1	1	14	31	45
2	1	2	1	17	18
2	2	1	23	24	47
2	2	2	69	76	145

[1] Categories: 1, severely disabled; 2, not severely disabled or no longer disabled.

Source: Bye and Schechter, 1986

Table 8.10   *Likelihood ratio statistics (LR) and degrees of freedom (DF) for latent Markov models fitted to the work disability data*

Subgroups	Stationarity	Across-group equality constraints			LR	DF
		Class prob. $\hat{\delta}$	Response prob. $\hat{\rho}$	Transition prob. $\hat{\tau}$		
All cases	Yes	–	–	–	3.05	2
Male/female	Yes	No	No	No	11.54	4
Male/female	Fem. only	No	No	No	0.07	2
Male/female	Fem. only	Yes	No	No	3.01	3
Male/female	Fem. only	No	Yes	No	7.68	4
Male/female	Yes	No	No	Yes	12.37	6
Male/female	Yes	Yes	Yes	Yes	34.16	9

Table 8.11 *Estimated parameter values (and standard errors) for the latent stationary Markov model on work disability*

Subpop., class	Subpop. proportions γ̂	Class proportions δ̂	Response probabilities ρ̂		Latent transition probabilities τ̂			
					From $t=1$ to $t=2$		From $t=1$ to $t=5$	
			Severe	Other	Class 1	Class 2	Class 1	Class 2
All cases								
Class 1		0.574(0.03)	0.914(0.02)	0.086(0.02)	0.911(0.02)	0.089(0.02)	0.843	0.157
Class 2		0.426(0.03)	0.083(0.04)	0.917(0.04)	0.148(0.04)	0.852(0.04)	0.261	0.739
Males	0.364(0.02)							
Class 1		0.501(0.05)	0.967(0.02)	0.033(0.02)	0.902(0.04)	0.098(0.04)	0.831	0.169
Class 2		0.499(0.05)	0.017(0.05)	0.983(0.05)	0.177(0.05)	0.823(0.05)	0.306	0.694
Females	0.636(0.02)							
Class 1		0.637(0.05)	0.875(0.03)	0.125(0.03)	0.925(0.04)	0.075(0.04)	0.863	0.137
Class 2		0.363(0.05)	0.127(0.05)	0.873(0.05)	0.105(0.07)	0.895(0.07)	0.192	0.808

are latent stationary Markov with time-homogeneous response probabilities. If males and females are pooled, the model fits well (Table 8.10: LR = 3.05 with 2 DF). The same parameter estimates are found if males and females are not pooled, but all parameters are set equal for men and women. However, for these non-pooled data the fit of the LM model appears to be very bad (LR = 34.16 with 9 DF). Even if all parameters are assumed different for men and women we find an unsatisfactory fit (LR = 11.54 with 4 DF). Inspection of the standardized residuals for this model shows that the poor fit is due largely to the males subgroup. When the stationarity assumption is relaxed, males' disability status turns out to have changed much more in the first period than in the second, and also more than females' disability status has changed in any period. Therefore a model with time-heterogeneous transition probabilities for males only is chosen, which fits well (LR = 0.07, DF = 2). The stationarity assumption for females is not relaxed because the possible bias caused by this assumption may be outweighed by lower standard errors of the estimates.

There is a clear message from these analyses: pooling of subgroups may obscure heterogeneity which can be detected in a simultaneous analysis of several subpopulations.

Our results are consistent with Bye and Schechter's conclusion that response error is less for males than for females. However, our methodology allows a single likelihood ratio test of this hypothesis by constraining response probabilities to be equal across groups (LR = 7.68–0.07 = 7.61 with 2 DF). In interpreting their results, Bye and Schechter (1986:378) note:

> The difference . . . for males and females might be explained by the work-related nature of the disability questions in the surveys. Given that women are more likely to be marginally attached to the labour force than men, women might have greater difficulty in deciding whether they are unable to work altogether.

Concluding comments

The aim of this chapter is to demonstrate the main features of discrete-space, discrete-time Markov modelling. In so doing, we have decided against the more traditional approach of starting with the theoretical, mathematical and statistical background and ending with the application to a substantive example. Instead, we have followed a bottom-up strategy that starts with the most simple model. The weaknesses of this model may be easily shown by extending it to a mixed Markov model or a latent Markov model, both of which turn out to be special cases of the more general latent mixed Markov model. Finally, we have shown how the latter model may be extended to cope with the situation where several subpopulations instead of a single one are the focus of the analysis. To emphasize that all of these models are latent class models, be it with or without the assumption of local independence, we refer to them as mixed Markov latent class (MMLC) models.

In general, we have tried to keep the reference list short by giving some key references only. This is not to say that Markov models have found little interest so far. Extensive references, both with respect to theory and applications, may be found in Bartholomew (1981), van de Pol and Langeheine (1989; 1990) and Langeheine and van de Pol (1990).

Although the methodology presented in this chapter can be very effective it is not, of course, without problems. Some of these problems may be overcome, whereas others are yet to be solved. One serious problem that belongs within the first category is model identifiability. For those familiar with log-linear modelling, it may be surprising that a Markov model may turn out to be non-identifiable, even though there are surplus degrees of freedom. Those who are familiar with classical latent class analysis are aware of this problem, however. In classical LC models a latent categorical variable is assumed to explain all associations among the manifest variables. Put differently, all manifest associations vanish, given class membership. For this reason, these models are called local independence models. Markov models differ from classical LC models either by allowing local dependence (association of manifest variables in mixed Markov models) or by restricting local independence to indicators of the same latent variable (latent Markov models). Hence, it should not be surprising that identifiability problems may arise. In general, these may be detected by inspection of the diagnostics provided by the PANMARK program.

In building up the hierarchy of models presented in this chapter we have fitted a number of different models to the brand choice data. On the one hand, this allowed us to demonstrate the strengths and weaknesses of these models. On the other hand, such an exploratory procedure may be denounced as data dredging or as bad science. Those who oppose this approach would argue in favour of using substantive theory as a guide in selecting (potentially rival) models. We do not reject this position. However, it carries the risk of missing a well-fitting model. Each of the many models is a legitimate way to look at the data. One or the other may be better suited to a specific research problem. We would, however, emphasize the important problem of spurious 'change' due to measurement error.

If attention is confined to a hierarchy of nested models, there is a convenient criterion for identifying the preferred model: the log of the likelihood ratio (LR). If non-nested models are to be compared, a more general criterion is needed, such as the Akaike information criterion (AIC) or the Bayesian information criterion (BIC) (see Read and Cressie, 1988). Both of these are a function of the log-likelihood, the number of parameters and (BIC only) the sample size. (In fact, there are many recent publications from different areas of application where authors rely fully on one of these criteria instead of formal goodness-of-fit tests.) For illustrative purposes we have given BIC together with some additional information in Table 8.12 for those models that fit the brand choice data well. If a choice has to be made, then BIC points to the partially latent mover-stayer model.

A problem still to be tackled is the unrealistic assumption that a panel is

Table 8.12 *LR statistic, DF, log-likelihood, number of parameters, and Bayesian information criterion for selected models from Table 8.3*

Model	LR	DF	Log-likelihood	Number of parameters	BIC
pLMS	22.46	24	−2292.83	7	4633.93[1]
One latent, one manifest chain	20.23	22	−2291.71	9	4645.48
LMM, chain-homogeneous resp. prob.	25.29	22	−2294.24	9	4650.54
MS, second order	26.96	22	−2295.08	9	4652.22
LMRr	20.81	21	−2292.00	10	4652.96
MM with chain turnover	23.93	20	−2293.56	11	4662.97
MM, three chains	28.40	20	−2295.79	11	4667.43
MM, two chains, second order	16.38	16	−2289.79	15	4683.02
The data	0.0	0	−2281.60	31	4776.97

[1] Best model according to BIC, which is given by -2 (log-likelihood) $+ q \log(N)$, where q is the number of parameters.

a closed system which no one leaves or joins. Typically, there will be some non-response or attrition at each panel wave. This problem is often circumvented by including in the analysis only subjects with a complete record at the expense of (possibly selective) loss of information from those with incomplete observations. To further complicate the issue, in some panel designs new members join the panel at later points in time.

Little and Rubin (1987: section 11.6) discuss various models for two occasions, including a third variable: (non-)response at the second occasion. Some of these cannot be estimated. In other cases the response variable can be ignored, because the missing cases are 'missing completely at random'. From those models that remain, the 'missing at random' assumption (randomness conditional on some variable) is an interesting option.

For Markov models considered in this chapter, missing values may be handled by introducing 'missing' as another category. For MMLC models with response probabilities, a more parsimonious model will be obtained if no latent class is assumed for the missing cases. This means that the observed scores are assumed 'missing at random' given the relevant latent variable. A test for 'missing completely at random' may be performed by assuming the probability of 'missing' equal for all classes of the relevant latent variable. For MM models such a test involves conditioning on the previous occasion of a variable. Where there are complicated patterns of inflow and outflow of panel members at successive occasions, an LM model for several subsamples (complete cases and several categories of incomplete cases) might be useful to test whether transition probabilities of complete cases may be considered equal to those of incomplete cases.

Finally, some comments about software are in order. As we have mentioned earlier, all models considered in this chapter were fitted by using the PANMARK program. Although PANMARK has been designed especially to fit Markov models, it can be used to fit a large number of classical latent class models that have become quite popular in the social sciences in the 1980s (see Langeheine, 1988 for a recent review). The trick is simply to replace time points, which are the 'variables' in a *T*-wave contingency table, by items or variables of a *T*-way contingency table. PANMARK may then be used to estimate all LC models that can be handled by the probably more widely known MLLSA program of Clogg (1977), and many more including, for example, mixtures of locally (in)dependent classes. In addition, PANMARK provides some information which is lacking in MLLSA but which may be very helpful in assessing the adequacy of a specific model (e.g. standard errors, first-order derivatives, detailed identification test).

Notes

The views expressed in this chapter are those of the authors and do not necessarily reflect the policies of the Netherlands Central Bureau of Statistics.

1 Note that our results differ somewhat from those reported by Bye and Schechter. For the model of all cases, for instance, we find better-fitting parameter estimates than Bye and Schechter did (LR = 3.05 versus LR = 4.75). The same holds for the 'no-no-no' model without equality restrictions between men and women, which was also fitted by Bye and Schechter. This may be due to more iterations performed in our computations or to a better performance of the EM algorithm used in the PANMARK program.

References

Aaker, D.A. (1970) 'A new method for evaluating stochastic models of brand choice', *Journal of Marketing Research*, 7: 300–6.

Bartholomew, D.J. (1981) *Mathematical Methods in the Social Sciences*. Chichester: Wiley.

Blumen, I.M., Kogan, M. and McCarthy, P.J. (1955) *The Industrial Mobility of Labor as a Probability Process*. Ithaca: Cornell University Press.

Bye, B.V. and Schechter, E.S. (1986) 'A latent Markov model approach to the estimation of response error in multiwave panel data', *Journal of the American Statistical Association*, 81: 375–80.

Clogg, C.C. (1977) *Unrestricted and Restricted Maximum Likelihood Latent Structure Analysis: a Manual for Users*. Population Issues Research Center, Pennsylvania State University, Working Paper 1977–09.

Coleman, J.S. (1964) *Models of Change and Response Uncertainty*. Englewood Cliffs: Prentice-Hall.

Converse, P.E. (1964) 'The nature of belief systems in mass publics', in D.E. Apter (ed.), *Ideology and Discontent*. New York: Free Press. pp. 206–61.

Converse, P.E. (1974) 'Comment: the status of nonattitudes', *American Political Science Review*, 68: 650–60.

Davies, R.B. and Crouchley, R. (1985) 'The determinants of party loyalty: a disaggregate analysis of panel data from the 1974 and 1979 general elections in England', *Political Geography Quarterly*, 4: 307–20.

Davies, R.B. and Crouchley, R. (1986) 'The mover-stayer model: *requiescat in pace*', *Sociological Methods and Research*, 14: 356–80.

Dempster, A.P., Laird, N.M. and Rubin, D.B. (1977) 'Maximum likelihood from incomplete data via the EM algorithm', *Journal of the Royal Statistical Society, Series B*, 39: 1–38.

Kelton, C.M.L. and Smith, M.A. (1991) 'Statistical inference in nonstationary Markov models with embedded explanatory variables', *Journal of Statistical Computing and Simulation*, 38: 25–44.

Langeheine, R. (1988) 'New developments in latent class theory', in R. Langeheine and J. Rost (eds), *Latent Trait and Latent Class Models*. New York: Plenum. pp. 77–108.

Langeheine, R. and van de Pol, F. (1990) 'A unifying framework for Markov modelling in discrete space and discrete time', *Sociological Methods and Research*, 18: 416–41.

Lazarsfeld, P.F. (1950) 'The logical and mathematical foundation of latent structure analysis', in S.A. Stouffer, L. Guttman, E.A. Suchman, P.F. Lazarsfeld, S.A. Star and J.A. Clausen (eds), *Measurement and Prediction*. Princeton: Princeton University Press. pp. 362–412.

Little, R.J.A. and Rubin, D.B. (1987) *Statistical Analysis with Missing Data*. New York: Wiley.

Poulsen, C.S. (1982) *Latent Structure Analysis with Choice Modelling Applications* (PhD dissertation, University of Pennsylvania). Aarhus: Aarhus School of Business Administration and Economics.

Read, T.R.C. and Cressie, N.A.C. (1988) *Goodness-of-Fit Statistics for Discrete Multivariate Data*. New York: Springer.

Spilerman, S. (1972) 'The analysis of mobility processes by the introduction of independent variables into a Markov chain', *American Sociological Review*, 37: 277–94.

van de Pol, F. and de Leeuw, J. (1986) 'A latent Markov model to correct for measurement error', *Sociological Methods and Research*, 15: 118–41.

van de Pol, F. and Langeheine, R. (1989) 'Mixed Markov models, mover-stayer models and the EM algorithm. With an application to labor market data from the Netherlands Socio-Economic Panel', in R. Coppi and S. Bolasco (eds), *Multiway Data Analysis*. Amsterdam: North-Holland. pp. 485–95.

van de Pol, F. and Langeheine, R. (1990) 'Mixed Markov latent class models', in C.C. Clogg (ed.), *Sociological Methodology 1990*. Oxford: Blackwell. pp. 213–47.

van de Pol, F., Langeheine, R. and de Jong, W. (1989) *PANMARK User Manual: PANel Analysis Using MARKov Chains*. Voorburg: Netherlands Central Bureau of Statistics.

Wiggins, L.M. (1955) 'Mathematical models for the analysis of multi-wave panels'. PhD dissertation, Columbia University. Ann Arbor: University Microfilms.

Wiggins, L.M. (1973) *Panel Analysis*. Amsterdam: Elsevier.

9

Time-Series Techniques for Repeated Cross-Section Data

Editors' introduction

The analysis of time series is a major and distinct area of study in statistics and there is a large research literature with a number of international journals dedicated to the subject. Much of this prominence is due to the importance of time-series methods for forecasting. Some significant areas of application for time-series forecasting methods lie within the social sciences, including marketing and macro-economics. However, forecasting is beyond the scope of this volume and the time-series example used by Sanders and Ward has the same basic objective as the examples in the other chapters, namely to demonstrate techniques for modelling a temporal process. The response variable is an aggregate measure of UK government popularity, measured monthly. The explanatory variables are measures of consumer confidence and the overall performance of the economy. Particular attention is given to the effects of the Falklands War.

Time-series analysis methods are more problematic in social science research than the other methods considered in this volume. The reasons include the limited information contained in a single time series, the difficulties inherent in formulating models and interpreting results for aggregate processes, and the apparent emphasis in the methods upon errors whereas substantive interest is more concerned with systematic relationships. The generally descriptive and uncontroversial presentations of the earlier chapters could be misleading in these circumstances. Having introduced and illustrated the technical features of time-series methods, Sanders and Ward therefore use their empirical example to provide a perspective on some of the more philosophical and contentious research issues that arise in social science applications. These are areas of debate in which there is only limited consensus but, in this final chapter, it is particularly timely to remind readers that bridging the gap between statistics and social science involves more than the acquisition of statistical skills; social scientists must be prepared to confront the challenges of operationalizing complex theoretical concepts.

The technical language and notation are a serious obstacle to non-statisticians seeking to understand time-series methods. Sanders's and Ward's presentation minimizes this obstacle. Nevertheless an effective introduction to time-series analysis cannot ignore the notation and terminology which are in general use.

The main notational feature which requires explanation is the use of 'operators' to simplify the algebra of time-series models. These operators work in conjunction with subscripts for time. For example if y_t is a time-series observation at time t, then the 'backshift' operator B shifts backwards to the previous observation:

$$By_t = y_{t-1}$$

Similarly, the 'backward difference' operator ∇ gives the difference between the current and previous values:

$$\nabla y_t = y_t - y_{t-1}$$

Squares, cubes and higher powers indicate repeated application of the operator. Thus

$$B^3 y_t = B^2 y_{t-1} = By_{t-2} = y_{t-3}$$

and

$$\nabla^2 y_t = \nabla(y_t - y_{t-1}) = (y_t - y_{t-1}) - (y_{t-1} - y_{t-2}) = y_t - 2y_{t-1} + y_{t-2}$$

The main terms to require explanation are 'autoregressive' (AR) and 'moving average' (MA) models. In an autoregressive formulation, a time-series is a function of its own previous value plus a random error. For example,

$$y_t = \alpha_1 y_{t-1} + \alpha_2 y_{t-2} + \mu_t$$

is an AR(2) model (i.e. dependence is upon the previous two values) where α_1 and α_2 are the AR parameters and μ_t is the error term. In a moving average formulation, a times-series variable is a weighted sum of random errors. Thus

$$y_t = \mu_t + \theta_1 \mu_{t-1} + \theta_2 \mu_{t-2}$$

is an MA(2) model where θ_1 and θ_2 are the MA parameters and the $\{\mu\}$ are independent random errors.

Two autoregressive models are considered in this chapter. The first assumes that the error terms in an otherwise conventional regression model have an AR(1) structure. The second, termed a 'lagged endogenous variable' model, assumes that the response variable has an AR(1) structure. Moving average formulations are rarely used on their own in empirical work but they do have a special role within the autoregressive integrated moving average (ARIMA) approach also introduced by Sanders and Ward. The autoregressive component in this approach applies to the response variable, the moving average component applies to the errors, and the term 'integrated' refers to the differencing method used to remove trends from the data.

Time-Series Techniques for Repeated Cross-Section Data

David Sanders and Hugh Ward

This chapter is concerned primarily with techniques that can be used to analyze aggregate data which describe different individuals over time. Such 'repeated cross-section' data may be drawn from opinion surveys conducted by commercial polling agencies which interview a 'new' random sample of respondents each month in order to ask them the same set of survey questions. Typically, the percentage of respondents who answer a given question in a particular way (for example, the percentage answering 'Conservative' in response to the question, 'Which political party would you vote for if there were a general election tomorrow?') varies over time. This provides the researcher with an aggregate time series which, in principle, can be related empirically either to other attitudinal time series (for example, responses to questions about consumer confidence) or to 'objective' features of the economic and political environment, such as employment, interest rates and inflation.

However, a number of different techniques may be used for analyzing aggregate time-series data, and the choice between the techniques must depend ultimately on the kind of epistemological assumptions about the nature of 'explanation' that the researcher is prepared to make in formulating a statistical model. The first four sections of this chapter review the main approaches to time-series modelling. The subsequent section applies the four techniques to the same data set and shows how the choice of technique can affect the statistical results obtained. The penultimate section briefly reviews the main strengths and weaknesses of the different techniques, concentrating particularly on the different epistemological assumptions that they make.

The four techniques for time-series analysis described below are all based upon the linear model. All allow for the complex multivariate analysis of interval-level data, making provision for the estimation of the effects exerted by a range of continuous and categorical explanatory variables. All can be used for analyzing historical data and for forecasting purposes.

The simple ordinary least squares (OLS) method

The form of the conventional regression (or OLS) model for cross-sectional data is well known:

$$y = \beta_0 + \beta_1 x_1 + \beta_2 x_2 + \ldots + \beta_k x_k + e \qquad (9.1)$$

where y is the response variable, x_1, x_2, ..., x_k are explanatory variables, e is a normally distributed random error term, and the cases may be individuals or social aggregates.

With aggregate time-series data, the OLS model becomes

$$y_t = \beta_0 + \beta_1 x_{1t} + \beta_2 x_{2t} + \ldots + \beta_k x_{kt} + u_t \qquad (9.2)$$

where the t subscripts indicate that the y and x variables are measured over time; u_t defines the error term; and the cases are time points defined by the period for which data are available. The fundamental problem with OLS in this situation is that the u_t tend not to be independent[1], violating an important assumption upon which conventional methods of analysis depend.

The 'serial correlation' in the error may often (but not always) be approximated by a 'first-order autoregressive process' or AR(1) in which

$$u_t = \rho u_{t-1} + e_t \qquad (9.3)$$

where u_t and u_{t-1} are the (systematic) errors from an OLS time-series regression and e_t is an independently distributed error term. Such serially correlated error does not prejudice parameter estimation by OLS regression models but the standard errors of the coefficients will, in general, be underestimated and the R^2 overestimated. As a consequence, the risk of accepting a false hypothesis is increased.

On the other hand, serially correlated error may be a symptom of other misspecifications. These could include the omission of important explanatory variables which are correlated with variables in the model. They could also include failure to represent 'feedback' dependence in which the level of response is dependent upon previous values of the response variable. If OLS methods are used in these circumstances, misleading results may be expected not only for standard errors but also for the parameter estimates.

Autoregressive (maximum likelihood) models

The autoregressive model offers the most immediate and obvious solution to the problem of serially correlated error: if serial correlation is distorting the standard errors of a given OLS model, why not attempt to specify the nature of the distorting 'autoregressive' process and re-estimate the model taking account of that process? This should also result in more efficient estimation of the β parameters. A pragmatic approach is to fit an OLS model and then examine the pattern of intercorrelation among the estimated u_t, u_{t-1}, u_{t-2}, ... If u_t correlates strongly only with u_{t-1}, then the relevant 'error process' can be described as an AR(1); if u_t correlates strongly only with u_{t-1} and u_{t-2}, then the process is an AR(2); and so on.[2] The chosen error process is then incorporated into the estimation procedure; maximum likelihood (or asymptotically equivalent) methods for AR models are available in many standard software packages. If the specified autoregressive structure is correct, the estimation problems associated with OLS largely disappear: estimated standard errors are not deflated and, as a result, significance testing becomes a reliable exercise. This in turn means that the risks of wrongly accepting a false hypothesis (which spuriously links y_t to some x_t) are kept to a minimum. This said, autoregressive models have been criticized on two main grounds.

First, the ρ_k coefficients on the u_t, ..., u_{t-n} terms are often difficult to interpret in substantive terms.[3] Second, models based purely on autoregressive techniques may simply be misspecified; in particular, they may have omitted important exogenous or endogenous variables which need to be included explicitly in the model rather than incorporated implicitly via the 'catch-all' autoregressive structure. These criticisms are all the more potent in the case of 'restricted' autoregressive models where u_t appears to be a function of, say, u_{t-5} but not of u_{t-1}, ..., u_{t-4}. Not only is such a result difficult to interpret substantively, but it also suggests that an additional exogenous variable (operating with a lag of around five time points) should be included explicitly in the model. In response, of course, the advocate of autoregressive techniques can argue that any autoregressive term is simply being employed instrumentally in order to obtain an accurate assessment of the magnitude of the effect of x_{1t}, ..., x_{kt} on y_t, and that the question of the substantive meaning either of ρ_k or of u_{t-1} is therefore irrelevant.

The lagged endogenous variable OLS method

The defining feature of this technique is the inclusion of a term for y_{t-1} on the right-hand side of any equation which tries to predict y_t. This is in addition to the hypothesized effects of any exogenous variables which also need to be included. The basic form of the model is

$$y_t = \beta_0 + \alpha y_{t-1} + \beta_1 x_{1t} + \beta_2 x_{2t} + ... + \beta_k x_{kt} + u_t \qquad (9.4)$$

where y_t is the response (or endogenous) variable; y_{t-1} is the endogenous variable lagged by one time point; x_1, ..., x_k are explanatory (exogenous) variables (which may exert lagged rather than simultaneous effects as shown in this example); and u_t is random error. Specifying the model in this way has two significant advantages. The first is that it frequently circumvents the problem of serially correlated error associated with simple OLS. The second advantage derives from the fact that y_{t-1} summarizes all the past effects of unmeasured variables (that is, variables external to the model) on y_t (see Johnston, 1972: 292–320). This means not only that the effects of measured variables (x_{1t}, ..., x_{kt}) on y_t can be estimated more accurately than would otherwise be the case, but also that the coefficient on y_{t-1} (α) represents the 'discount rate' – the rate at which past influences on y_t decay. This latter feature of the model – that α is the discount rate – is particularly useful for specifying the rate of decay of 'intervention effects', such as the occurrence of particular political events. As shown below, for example, the Falklands War boosted government popularity in May 1983 by some 8.6 per cent. The coefficient on the lagged dependent variable ($\alpha=0.83$) enables us to infer that this effect decayed at a rate of about 0.83 per month thereafter. This implies that the 'May boost' was worth $8.6 \times 0.83 = 7.2$ per cent in June; $7.2 \times 0.86 = 5.9$ per cent in July; and so on. It should be noted, however, that with this sort of model specification the effects of all measured exogenous variables are constrained to decay at the same rate. As discussed below, one significant advantage of Box-Jenkins models is that they permit the specification of a different decay rate for each exogenous variable.

Three other points need to be made about the lagged endogenous variable method. First, as with the simple OLS specification outlined earlier, the estimated coefficients may not be stable over time; that is, they may take on radically different values if they are estimated over different subsets of the entire time series. A series of diagnostic tests for parameter stability are available (CUSUM, CUSUMSQ and recursive coefficient tests) and in general these should be applied systematically if either simple OLS or lagged endogenous variable methods are being used (see Brown et al. 1975). If a particular model fails these tests, then it is probably misspecified and requires either the inclusion of further exogenous variables or a respecification of the ways in which the existing x_{1t}, ..., x_{kt} are hypothesized to affect y_t. Second, even with the inclusion of y_{t-1} in the equation, it is still possible that the error term from (9.4) will be subject to serial correlation. For example, one of the following could be the case:

$$u_t = \rho u_{t-1} + e_t \tag{9.5}$$

$$u_t = \rho_1 u_{t-1} + \rho_2 u_{t-2} + \ldots + \rho_k u_{t-k} + e_t \tag{9.6}$$

$$u_t = \rho u_{t-2} + e_t \tag{9.7}$$

where (9.5) denotes a first-order autoregressive error process, (9.6) denotes a kth-order process, and (9.7) denotes a 'restricted' second-order process. In any of these cases, as with simple OLS, some sort of correction for the error process is required. This can be resolved, of course, by incorporating an appropriate autoregressive error function in the model, although such a strategy carries with it all the limitations of the autoregressive model which were noted earlier.

Finally, it is worth observing that the lagged endogenous variable method described here represents a subspecies of the general to specific 'Hendry' methodology followed by many UK econometricians (see, for example, Hendry, 1983). This approach seeks to specify the short-run dynamics of time-series relationships by moving from a general model specification (which, in addition to y_{t-1}, includes all potential exogenous influences on y_t at all theoretically plausible lags) to a more limited, empirically determined specification which eliminates all non-significant exogenous terms. Thus, for example, a theoretical model which hypothesized that y_t was influenced by x_{1t} or x_{2t}, and in which it was assumed that any changes in x_{1t} or x_{2t} would take no longer than three periods to affect y_t, would initially be specified as

$$y_t = \beta_{00} + \alpha y_{t-1} + \beta_{10}x_{1t} + \beta_{11}x_{1t-1} + \beta_{12}x_{1t-2} + \beta_{13}x_{1t-3} + \beta_{20}x_{2t}$$
$$+ \beta_{21}x_{2t-1} + \beta_{22}x_{2t-2} + \beta_{23}x_{2t-3} + u_t \qquad (9.8)$$

If it turned out empirically that x_{1t} influenced y_t with a lag of one time point while x_{2t} influenced y_t with a lag of two time points, then the final specification would be

$$y_t = \beta_{00} + \alpha_1 y_{t-1} + \beta_{11}x_{1t-1} + \beta_{22}x_{2t-2} + u_t \qquad (9.9)$$

though, as noted before, this specification would have to be checked for both parameter stability and serially correlated error.

Box-Jenkins (ARIMA) methods

Box-Jenkins techniques differ from the regression-based techniques outlined above in two significant respects: (1) in their emphasis upon the need for time-series data to be systematically 'pre-whitened' and the consequences this has for the way in which models are specified; and (2) in their facility for handling complex 'intervention' specifications. We discuss each of these features in turn.

Pre-whitening and model specification

The basic data analytic principle underlying the Box-Jenkins methodology is that x_{t-k} helps to explain y_t in theoretical terms only if it explains variance in y_t over and above the extent to which y_t is explained by its own past values. The application of this principle in turn means that Box-Jenkins methods necessarily place great emphasis on the need to establish the precise nature of the 'process' that is 'self-generating' y_t. This is effected by the use of autocorrelation and partial autocorrelation functions which enable the analyst to determine what sort of 'autoregressive' or 'moving average' process (respectively, AR and MA processes, contributing to the ARIMA mnemonic) is generating y_t.[4] Once the self-generated sources of y_t have been specified, the analyst can then introduce an exogenous variable x_t into the model in the form of a 'transfer function'. The precise lag structure for the effects of x_t is determined by the use of a 'cross-correlation function' which correlates the non-self-generated variation in y_t with the non-self-generated variation in x_t over a range of different lags and leads. If x_{t-k} (that is, x_t at the specified lag or lags) yields a significant coefficient and produces a non-trivial reduction in the 'residual mean square' of the transfer function (in other words, if x_{t-k} adds to the variation in y_t that is explained by the model as a whole), then it can be concluded that x_{t-k} does indeed exert an exogenous influence on y_t.

An important prerequisite of this modelling strategy is that all data which are to be used need to be 'pre-whitened'. This means that, before they are included in any transfer function analysis, all variables must be rendered mean and variance stationary: any trends in the component variables must be removed prior to analysis. This is normally effected by 'differencing', where a first difference of y_t is defined as

$$\nabla y_t = y_t - y_{t-1} \tag{9.10}$$

and where a second difference of y_t is defined as

$$\nabla^2 y_t = \nabla y_t - \nabla y_{t-1} \tag{9.11}$$

Simple linear trends can usually be removed by first differencing; a decline-recovery (or rise-decline) trend by second differencing; and so on (see Appendix).

Given the assumption of pre-whitened data, the form of the Box-Jenkins model is relatively straightforward. Two matters complicate any presentation of it, however. First, Box-Jenkins techniques not only allow for the estimation of the direct effect of a change in x_t on y_t (analogous to the β coefficients in (9.4)), but also allow for the estimation of adjustment to steady state or 'discount' parameters (analogous to the α coefficient in (9.4)) associated with those direct effects. One particularly attractive feature of the Box-Jenkins specification is that it permits, in effect, a different discount rate to be estimated for each exogenous variable. This can be a significant advantage over the lagged exogenous variable specification, which, as noted earlier, constrains the discount rate to be identical for all exogenous variables. What all of this means is that in the Box-Jenkins model there are potentially two parameters associated with each exogenous variable: a ω_k parameter, which measures the direct effect of x_{t-k} on y_t; and a δ_k parameter, which (in general) measures the rate at which the direct effect decays over time.

The second complicating aspect of the Box-Jenkins approach is the highly compressed nature of the notation, which often makes interpretation difficult for the non-technical reader. For one thing, expositions of the method almost invariably employ the 'backshift operator' B, where By_t means y_{t-1}; $B^2 y_t$ means y_{t-2}; and so on. For another, a general statement of the model would require rather more elaboration about the nature of AR and MA processes than can be developed here. We will therefore seek to illustrate the character of the model by the use of a hypothetical example. Consider a situation in which (a) a stationary endogenous variable y_t is influenced by two stationary exogenous variables x_{1t} and x_{2t}; (b) x_t affects y_t with a lag of one time point; and (c) x_{2t} affects y_t with a lag of three time points. The 'compressed' statement of this model would be:

$$y_t = B_0 + \frac{\omega_{11}B}{(1 - \delta_1 B)} x_{1t} + \frac{\omega_{23}B^3}{(1 - \delta_2 B)} x_{2t} + \mu_t \qquad (9.12)$$

Without the use of the backshift operator, (9.12) becomes

$$y_t = \beta_0' + (\delta_1 + \delta_2) y_{t-1} - \delta_1 \delta_2 y_{t-2} + \omega_{11}(x_{1,\ t-1} - \delta_2 x_{1,\ t-2})$$
$$+ \omega_{23}(x_{2,\ t-3} - \delta_1 x_{2,\ t-4}) + u_t' \qquad (9.13)$$

where

$$\beta_0' = \beta_0(1 - \delta_1 - \delta_2 + \delta_1 \delta_2)$$
$$u_t' = u_t - \delta_1 u_{t-1} - \delta_2 u_{t-1} + \delta_1 \delta_2 u_{t-2}$$

and where y_t, x_{1t} and x_{2t} are measured variables; β_0 is a constant; ω_{11} is the direct effect parameter for $x_{1,\ t-1}$; ω_{23} is the direct effect parameter for $x_{2,\ t-3}$; δ_1 and δ_2 are the decay parameters for ω_{11} and ω_{23} respectively; and u_t is a 'white noise' (random) error component. With appropriate software (for example the BMDP-2T program), the estimation of the model described in (9.12), as well as rather more complex models, becomes a relatively straightforward exercise. Evaluating such models is largely a matter of examining the significance levels of the estimated parameters, checking that the transfer function model has a lower residual mean square value than the simple self-generating ARIMA model for y_t, and ensuring that u_t is indeed a white noise term in which no ARIMA process is evident. Provided that the model under analysis satisfies each of these conditions, it may be concluded that the specified exogenous variables do indeed affect y_t, and that the nature of their impact is defined by the appropraite ω_{ij} and δ_i parameters.

Complex intervention specifications in Box-Jenkins analysis

It was noted earlier that 'intervention' effects can be estimated using the lagged endogenous variable method. Using this model, an intervention effect (such as the beginning of a war or the introduction of a new piece of legislation) is operationalized as a dummy variable I_t, which takes the value unity for the single time point when the intervention begins and zero otherwise. For any given y_t, this yields

$$y_t = \beta_0 + \alpha y_{t-1} + \beta_1 I_t + u_t \qquad (9.14)$$

The estimated coefficient on I_t represents the increase or decrease in y_t associated with the intervention; the coefficient on y_{t-1} denotes the rate at which the intervention effect decays.

Box-Jenkins models allow for several additional ways of specifying such intervention effects. In the ensuing review we translate the models into a notation familiar to users of regression techniques.

The gradual-permanent model   In this model an exogenous variable intervenes at some time t^*, firstly, to change y_t immediately by some given amount, and secondly, to further change y_t through time in a way that approaches some upper limit. Compare the two models shown in Figures 9.1 and 9.2. The step function in Figure 9.1 is the standard dummy variable model of classical regression analysis, the dummy variable having the same (positive) impact on $E(y_t)$ (the expected value of y_t) for all values of t greater than or equal to t^*. In contrast, the gradual-permanent model postulates a build-up of the intervention effect over time. Such a gradual build-up frequently seems more theoretically plausible then the 'abrupt' effect modelled by a straightforward dummy: a new piece of race relations legislation, for example, may inhibit discrimination against ethnic minorities to only a limited degree initially, but the effects of the legislation may build gradually over time.

The simplest way of writing the gradual-permanent model is[5]

$$y_t = N_t \qquad \text{for } t<t^* \tag{9.15}$$

$$y_t = \omega \sum_{r=0}^{t-t^*} \delta^r + N_t \quad \text{for } t>t^*, \ 0<\delta<1 \tag{9.16}$$

where y_t is a measured variable; N_t is the ARIMA process self-generating y_t; ω is the initial intervention parameter; and δ is the 'adjustment' parameter. As shown in Figure 9.2:

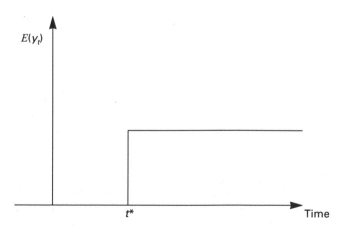

Figure 9.1   *The dummy variable step-function model*

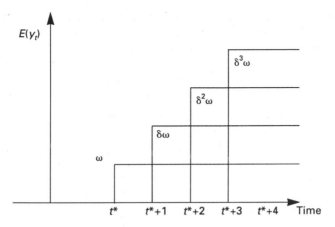

Figure 9.2 *The gradual-permanent model*

at time t^*, $E(y_t) = \omega\delta^0 = \omega$
at time t^*+1, $E(y_t) = \omega(\delta^0 + \delta^1) = \omega + \omega\delta$
at time t^*+2, $E(y_t) = \omega(\delta^0 + \delta^1 + \delta^2) = \omega + \omega\delta + \omega\delta^2$

and so on. Given that δ must be less than unity, successive increments of δ^r become smaller and smaller. As δ approaches unity, the effect grows in an almost linear manner; as δ approaches zero, the growth in y_t tails off more and more rapidly. The value of δ, in short, is a parameter for the rate at which increments to y_t decay. Clearly, since the increments form a geometric progression, if $\delta < 1$ the series will converge on an upper limit of $\omega/(1-\delta)$. If ω is negative, the intervention has a reductive effect on y_t which gradually increases in magnitude.

The abrupt-effect/gradual-decline model   This specification is directly equivalent to the intervention effect associated with the lagged endogenous variable method summarized in (9.14). The model is most easily written as[6]

$y_t = N_t$ for $t<t^*$
$y_t = \omega\delta^{(t-t^*)} + N_t$ for $t>t^*$, $0<\delta<1$

A specification of this sort, for a positive value of ω, is illustrated in Figure 9.3. The parameter δ measures the rate of decay in the initial ω effect; the smaller the value of δ, the faster the effect decays. As t increases, the effect of the intervention approaches zero.

The gradual-temporary model   In this specification the intervention has an immediate effect which builds up thereafter to some maximum value, and then decays gradually to zero. The simplest way of writing the model for the case in which the effect builds up for one period and then decays is[7]

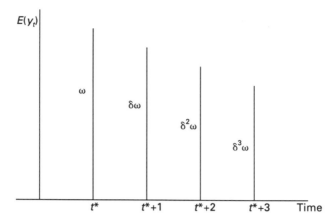

Figure 9.3   *The abrupt-effect/gradual-decline model*

$$y_t = N_t \qquad\qquad\qquad \text{for } t<t^*$$
$$y_t = \omega_0 + N_t \qquad\qquad \text{for } t=t^*$$
$$y_t = \omega_0\delta^{(t-t^*)} + \omega_1\delta^{(t-t^*-1)} \quad \text{for } t>t^* \qquad\qquad\qquad (9.17)$$

where $0<\delta<1$ and where ω_0 and ω_1 both have the same sign. As shown in Figure 9.4, the intervention model here is merely the sum of two abrupt-temporary models, with the first intervention commencing at t^* and the second at t^*+1. As long as ω_1 is greater than $\omega_0 - \delta\omega_0$, the effect of the overall 'summed' intervention increases in the first post-intervention period and then gradually declines.[8]

As these examples show, Box-Jenkins techniques provide a variety of powerful and plausible ways of modelling intervention effects. However, it should be noted that, with the exception of the gradual-permanent model, similar intervention models can be specified using the somewhat simpler lagged endogenous variable technique.

An application of different time series to the same set of data: or how different assumptions can produce different conclusions

The particular example used here involves a problem that has interested political scientists throughout the post-war period: the question of the connections between the popularity of the incumbent government and the state of the domestic economy. The simple theoretical model that is investigated is shown in Figure 9.5. It hypothesizes that economic factors affect government support in two different, if complementary, ways. One set of ('evaluative') effects derives from the objective state of the economy as a whole and it is assumed that the better the overall performance of the economy, the more likely it is that the incumbent government will be rewarded with a high level of popular support. In the model presented here

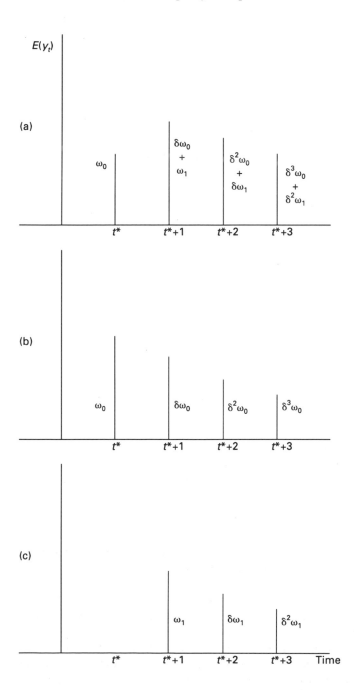

Figure 9.4   *The gradual-temporary model: (a) total effect of ω_0 and ω_1 interventions (b) effect of ω_0 intervention (c) effect of ω_1 intervention*

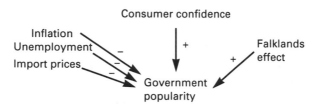

Figure 9.5   *Hypothesized model of the main economic and political effects on UK government popularity, 1979–87. A plus sign denotes a predicted positive relationship, a minus sign a predicted negative relationship; the objective effects are combined to form a single misery index*

we measure the overall strength/weakness of the economy as an aggregate of three variables: inflation, unemployment and import prices.[9] The resultant 'misery index', which in effect measures the weakness of the overall economy, is predicted to exert a negative effect on government popularity. The second set of economic effects is rather more 'subjective' and 'instrumental'. They are concerned with the extent to which macro-economic changes are perceived by voters as affecting their own narrow self-interests. If voters perceive that they are 'doing very well' as a result of current policies, then they are more likely to lend their instrumental support to the party in power. The model assumes that 'instrumental' judgements of this sort can best be measured at the aggregate level by the state of consumer confidence. If electors are optimistic about their own family's financial prospects, then they will be more likely to support the government whose policies produced that optimism in the first place; economic pessimism, in contrast, is likely to be associated with reduced governmental support.[10] Finally, it should be noted that the model also anticipates a political 'intervention' effect: the Falklands War. Given that government popularity increased dramatically in the early months of the war (particularly in May and June of 1982), it makes sense to seek to assess how far the war might have contributed to the Conservatives' election victory in June 1983.

Table 9.1 reports the results derived from estimating the same model using each of the four techniques reviewed above. The data are monthly time series and cover the period June 1979 to June 1987, Mrs Thatcher's first two terms of office as prime minister. The models all assume that while changes in consumer confidence have a near instantaneous effect on government popularity, changes in the objective state of the economy only work through to popularity after a two-month lag.

The simple OLS model (9.18a) at first sight appears to provide some support for the hypothesized model shown in Figure 9.5. Although R^2 is fairly low (0.54), the parameters for consumer confidence and the misery index are both significant and in the predicted direction. And although the

Table 9.1 *Parameter estimates for models of UK government popularity, June 1979 to June 1987 (standard error in parentheses)*

Independent variable	(9.18a) Simple OLS model	(9.18b) Simple OLS model, fewer Falklands variables	(9.19) Autoregressive model	(9.20) Lagged endogenous variable model	(9.21) Box-Jenkins model ω parameter	δ parameter
Popularity $_{t-1}$/AR$_{(1)}$ parameter			0.91 (0.04)	0.83 (0.04)	0.89 (0.05)	
Consumer confidence	0.49 (0.05)	0.50 (0.05)	0.15 (0.05)	0.12 (0.03)	0.13 (0.04)	0.66 (0.19)
Misery index$_{t-2}$	-2.06 (0.38)	-2.10 (0.39)	-0.30 (1.18)	-0.38 (0.20)	0.11 (0.24)	
Falklands-May	5.81 (3.75)	5.68 (3.84)	4.37 (1.61)	8.63 (1.71)	7.98 (1.81)	0.93 (0.08)
Falklands-June	8.10 (3.75)	7.95 (3.84)	5.17 (1.62)	5.54 (1.71)	4.32 (1.76)	0.51 (0.41)
Falklands-July	7.14 (3.75)					
Falklands-August	5.81 (3.75)					
Constant	39.73 (0.48)	39.89 (0.48)	37.85 (2.33)	6.94 (1.73)	38.62 (1.99)	
Residual square	12.89	13.77	3.24	2.68	3.05	
N	95	95	95	95	97	
Durbin-Watson	0.45	0.44	1.95	2.06		
R^2	0.54	0.51	0.88	0.90		
(adjusted R^2)	(0.51)	(0.48)	(0.88)	(0.90)		
Estimated contribution of Falklands boost to government popularity in June 1983	0	0	0	1.35	3.10	

Falklands War coefficients are not all significant, the war certainly appears to have boosted government popularity by around 3 per cent in the early summer of 1982. Dropping the non-significant Falklands dummy variables for July and August has only a very marginal effect on the model (9.18b). However, the very low values of the Durbin-Watson statistics suggests that the models suffer from a serious first-order serial correlation problem, a conclusion that is confirmed by further diagnostic tests which we do not report here.[11]

The three other models, (9.19), (9.20) and (9.21), in their own different ways correct for the problems of serially correlated error.[12] These models have much lower residual mean square values (which is another way of saying that the R^2 values, where they are calculated, are much higher) than the simple OLS models. This is not surprising because (9.19)–(9.21) all include either y_{t-1} or some transformed version of it, in the form of u_{t-1}, in the estimation procedure. There are other consistent patterns in the results for these three models. The coefficient of the consumer confidence variable remains significant, although it is much smaller (between 0.12 and 0.15) than in the OLS models (where it is 0.49 or 0.50). Each of the three models also produces a significant coefficient for the Falklands-May effect, again in contrast to the OLS model which yields a non-significant coefficient for this variable.

Yet in spite of these similarities among the models summarized in (9.19)–(9.21), the results reported also indicate some important differences. The most notable of these is the fact that the lagged endogenous variable method produces a significant (and, as predicted, negative) coefficient for the misery index ($\beta=-0.38$), whereas the autoregressive and Box-Jenkins methods both yield non-significant coefficients (and in the latter case the wrong sign: $\beta=0.11$). In substantive terms, there is clearly a problem here. If we are prepared to believe the results of the lagged endogenous variable model, then we would conclude that the 'objective' state of the economy does exert a direct influence upon voters' support for the government; yet if we believe the results of either the autoregressive or Box-Jenkins models then we would conclude that there was no such role for objective economic factors.

A similar problem emerges when we try to establish what each of these models implies about the impact of the Falklands War on the outcome of the 1983 general election. The OLS model (9.18a) implies that the war had no effect on the subsequent election whatsoever. It boosted popularity substantially in June 1982, but its effects were already statistically non-significant by July of that year (see the non-significant coefficients for the Falklands-July and Falklands-August variables in (9.18a). Similarly, the autoregressive model (9.19) does not include any mechanism whereby the significant May and June 1982 effects may have a continuing impact on the response variable. Both models (9.20) and (9.21), however, suggest that the Falklands effect followed the gradual-temporary intervention model described earlier. Popularity was boosted in May (according to (9.20) by 8.6 per cent, and according to (9.21) by 8.0 per cent); was boosted further in June (in (9.20) by 5.5 per cent and in (9.21) by 4.3 per cent); and subsequently 'decayed' gradually. The rate of decay, however, varies according to the different models. In the lagged endogenous variable model, the decay rate is given by the coefficient on y_{t-1}. This implies that the May boost of 8.6 per cent was worth $8.6 \times 0.83 = 7.2$ per cent in June; $8.6 \times (0.83)^2 = 5.9$ per cent in July; $8.6 \times (0.83)^3 = 4.9$ per cent in August; and so on. The June boost of 5.5 per cent was worth $5.5 \times 0.83 = 4.6$ per cent in July; $5.5 \times (0.83)^2 = 3.8$ per cent in August; and so on. Combining these two sets of effects together, the Falklands War was still worth some 1.3 per cent to the government in June 1983.[13] Given the relative inaccuracy of opinion poll data – even when government popularity is measured, as it is here, by the 'poll of polls' – this result casts considerable doubt on claims (e.g. Norpoth, 1987; Clarke et al., 1990) that the domestic political effects of the Falklands campaign played a decisive role in the Conservatives' election victory in 1983. On the contrary, the importance of the consumer confidence and misery variables in the lagged endogenous variable model support the argument that the 1983 election outcome was the result primarily of economic factors; that the government had secured sufficient economic recovery by the summer of 1983 to ensure its re-election (see Sanders et al. (1987) and Sanders (1991a)).

Yet if (9.20) suggests that the medium-term effects of the Falklands War on government popularity were negligible, the results reported for the Box-Jenkins models (9.21) imply that those effects were a little more substantial. In the Box-Jenkins model, the δ parameters explicitly estimate the rate of decay in their respective ω parameters. The δ parameter for the Falklands-June variable is not significant ($t=1.23$) but the Falklands-May effect was still worth 3.1 per cent in June 1983.[14] The clear substantive implication of this result is that although a Falklands effect of 3 per cent would probably not have been decisive in the circumstances of 1983, it would nonetheless have made an important contribution to the size of the Conservative election victory in June of that year. It is more than twice the effect estimated by the lagged endogenous variable model.

Where does this leave us? Was there a measurable (if modest) Falklands factor at the time of the 1983 election? Should we conclude that the objective state of the economy (as measured by the misery index) had no direct effect on the electorate's support for the government during the first two Thatcher terms? Unfortunately, as the foregoing discussion indicates, these questions cannot be answered independently of the statistical techniques that are employed to investigate them. We can certainly dispense with the conclusions suggested by the simple OLS model, but there is no easy way of resolving the disparities between the autoregressive, lagged endogenous variable and Box-Jenkins methods. The only thing that can be said definitely is that in this particular case – and most likely in others as well – the different techniques produce different statistical results and, by implication, different substantive conclusions. How, then, can we decide between the different techniques?

Which techniques? Assessing relative strengths and weaknesses

Several of the strengths and weaknesses of the different techniques have already been mentioned. Here we summarize and qualify them.

The simple OLS method has the enormous advantage of being easily understood; yet, as noted above, its frequent contamination by serially correlated error often makes it problematic for time-series analysis. This said, from an epistemological point of view, the way in which the simple OLS technique tests a given model does correspond most obviously to what most social scientists would regard as 'testing a causal explanation'. Without wishing to minimize the enormous difficulties associated with the concept of 'explanation', we would argue that a causal explanation of a particular phenomenon or set of phenomena consists in the specification of the minimum non-tautological set of antecedent necessary and/or sufficient conditions required for its (their) occurrence. The simple OLS model, by placing the response variable on the left-hand side, allows the researcher to assess how far a knowledge of the explanatory variables at time t, time $t-1$ and so on, permits accurate predictions to be made about the response variable at time t. If extremely accurate predictions can be made, then it can be concluded that (at the specified level of abstraction) the minimum non-tautological set of antecedent necessary and sufficient conditions required for the occurrence of the response variable has indeed been identified; in other words that an explanation of the response variable has been tested and found to be consistent with the available empirical evidence.

Given the epistemological position of the simple OLS approach, it comes as something of a surprise to discover that many practitioners of time-series analysis reject the use of simple OLS methods out of hand. Where there are strong linear trends in both explanatory and response variables this rejection is entirely justified; the coincidence of the trends usually suggests that some third, unmeasured variable (or set of variables) is operating to produce a spurious correlation between y_t and x_t.

The solution to this problem adopted by the autoregression, lagged endogenous variable and Box-Jenkins techniques (for shorthand purposes we will refer to these collectively as AR-LEV-BJ techniques) is to take explicit account of the extent to which y_t can be predicted by its own values when any attempt is being made to estimate the effects of x_{t-k} on y_t. In the lagged endogenous variable case, the effects of any unmeasured variables are constrained to operate through y_{t-1}; in the autoregressive and Box-Jenkins models the unmeasured variable effects are constrained to operate through whatever autoregressive or ARIMA process appears to determine y_t. By controlling for the unmeasured influences on y_t in this way, the autoregressive, lagged endogenous variable and Box-Jenkins methods not only pre-empt the problem of serially correlated error, but also provide for a more accurate estimation of the effect on y_t that results from a unit change in some x_{t-k}.

As is so often the case, however, resolving one problem serves only to raise another; in this case, an epistemological one. By including the past history of y_t into the estimation procedure, the AR, LEV and BJ methods in effect introduce a version of y_{t-k} on to the right-hand side of the equation for y_t. Yet, if we go back to our definition of a causal explanation, we see that it requires the specification of the 'minimum set of non-tautological antecedent . . . conditions' necessary for the occurrence of the phenomenon in question. Since y_{t-1} is certainly not defined independently of y_t, it appears that the AR, LEV and BJ specifications build a very powerful tautological component into the explanations of y_t that they imply. Moreover, since tautological 'explanations' are not explanations at all – a variable clearly cannot explain itself – it would seem to follow that attempts to explain y_t based upon AR, LEV or BJ model-building procedures can never provide 'real' explanations at all; they are merely refined vehicles for specifying the consequences for y_t of a unit change in x_t. They never allow the analyst to conclude that 'movements in y_t can be (non-tautologically) explained by movements in x_t and the data are consistent with the proposition that y_t is caused by x_t'. Since this, in our view, is one of the main goals of empirical analysis, we believe it constitutes a serious limitation on the AR, LEV and BJ methods.

Not surprisingly, supporters of AR, LEV and BJ techniques respond strongly to these criticisms. They point out that any terms for y_{t-k} can easily be moved across to the left-hand side of the equation so that the right-hand side effectively contains expressions that are non-tautologically related to y_t. In the case of the LEV model, for example, moving y_{t-1} from the right-hand side to the left-hand side of the equation is equivalent to using the change in y_t as the response variable. All that is being done, in short, is to shift the nature of that which is to be explained from the level of y_t to the change in y_t. If we know the 'start' value for y_t, we can easily get back to predicting its subsequent levels. So far, so good.

Yet the epistemological costs of this notational shuffling are more serious than its protagonists imply. This can be seen, firstly, by reference to R^2. With simple OLS (assuming parameter significance and stability), and an absence of serially correlated error) R^2 is a singularly useful statistic: it reveals how well y_t can be predicted purely from movements in (non-tautological) exogenous variables. However, with the AR and LEV models (as their advocates would readily admit), R^2 is highly misleading as a guide to the explanatory power of the non-tautological influences on y_t because it is calculated using an estimation procedure that explicitly incorporates the past history of y_t. Since the AR, LEV and BJ specifications seek to explain only the non-self-generated variation in y_t, what is really required is an R^2 equivalent that measures the extent to which the exogenous variables in a particular model can indeed predict y_t. The statistic that is usually employed in this context is the residual mean square (RMS). As noted earlier, if the addition of a particular x_{t-k} yields a lower RMS value than that obtained by knowing only y_t's past history, then it is inferred that x_{t-k} does affect y_t. What RMS tests of this sort do not reveal, however, is how accurately the non-self-generated variation in y_t can be predicted purely from a knowledge of the exogenous influences upon it. Yet, as discussed above, the only sense in which AR, LEV and BJ techniques explain anything in conventionally understood causal terms is that they can account for the non-self-generated variation in y_t. Curiously, the summary statistics usually associated with these techniques fail to give any clear indication as to the extent to which this objective is in fact achieved. With AR, LEV and BJ methods, in short, not only is the explicandum (the non-self-generated variation in y_t) a much-reduced version of the original phenomenon of interest, but there is also a failure adequately to assess the extent to which that reduced explicandum is indeed non-tauto-logically explained.

A second epistemological cost associated with AR, LEV and BJ methods also derives from their emphasis on the need to take full account of the self-generated variation in y_t. The notion that x_{t-k} only affects y_t to the extent that it explains variation in y_t not explained by y_t's own past history certainly accords with the principle of 'Granger causality'.[15] Unfortunately, it also engenders a serious risk of underestimating the explanatory importance of x_{t-k}. In any given time-series model, it is entirely possible that the self-generated variation in y_t is also capable of being explained by some x_{t-k}. It is highly unlikely, however, that x_{t-k} will predict y_t as well as y_t's own past values will predict y_t. This, in turn, implies that x_{t-k} may appear to exert no influence on y_t simply because it explains the same variation in y_t that is explained by some function in y_{t-k}. In situations such as this, AR, LEV and BJ models are biased towards the underestimation of exogenous effects.

All this discussion of self-generated variation, however, does little to resolve one of the main substantive problems posed in the previous section. If, in a specific case, serially correlated error prejudices a simple OLS model, which of the AR, LEV and BJ class of models should we employ in order to analyze repeated aggregate cross-section data? (The choice of models clearly matters. For example, as we saw earlier, the LEV model found evidence of a significant 'misery' effect on popularity, whereas the AR and BJ methods suggested no such effect.) There is, sadly, no easy or general answer to the question. The researcher must decide which is the more appropriate in the light of her or his particular theoretical concerns. This is not to imply that researchers can simply select the technique which best seems to provide empirical support for their preconceived theoretical suppositions. It does mean, however, that some attempt needs to be made to link the assumptions of the modelling technique to the kind of model of human behaviour that the researcher is seeking to test.

In the context of the government popularity functions used here, for example, we would argue that the entire exercise only makes sense if it is possible at some stage to translate the parameters of a given model into the decision calculus of the individual elector. In our view, this requirement renders the LEV method the most appropriate of the class of AR, LEV and BJ techniques for analyzing government popularity data. In contrast with the AR and BJ techniques, all of the terms specified in the LEV model are directly measured, so that it can be plausibly assumed that the typical elector is in some sense aware of them. The inclusion of the lagged endogenous variable itself can be interpreted as denoting the elector's predisposition to support the government; the exogenous variables denote, obviously, the hypothetical economic and political influences on government popularity.

With the AR and BJ techniques, in contrast, the translation is much more difficult. Although the same sort of interpretation can be made of the exogenous variables as in the LEV case, the substantive meaning of u_{t-1} in the AR model and of the ARIMA process that is self-generating y_t in the BJ model – both by definition phenomena that are not directly observable – is generally far from clear. In these circumstances, it is often difficult to envisage how the coefficients on some of the terms in AR and BJ models translate into what might conceivably go on inside electors' heads.

It is primarily for this reason that we would conclude that the lagged endogenous variable technique is probably the most appropriate for analyzing the sort of data we have described in this chapter. This, in turn, leads us to conclude that, of the various results presented in Table 9.1, the findings reported in (9.20) are probably the most useful for evaluating the theoretical model that was proposed in Figure 9.5. This suggests (a) that both consumer confidence and the objective state of the economy (which may themselves be interrelated)[16] exert direct effects on the level of electoral support for the government; and (b) that the Falklands War was worth just over 1 per cent to the government's popularity by the time of the 1983 election. This is not to imply, however, that the LEV technique is always the best vehicle for handling time-series data. Where the nature of the substantive problem under investigation means that it is unnecessary to translate the parameters of the statistical model into some kind of individual-level decision calculus, it may well be more appropriate to obtain as accurate a definition of the error process as possible; and in these circumstances, AR or BJ methods would probably be more suitable than the LEV technique as it has been outlined here.

Conclusion

In this chapter we have reviewed four different – though related – techniques for time-series analysis. We have also attempted to articulate our doubts, not about the statistical soundness of AR, LEV and BJ techniques, but about their epistemological implications; about the limitations on their ability to evaluate 'explanations' as they are conventionally understood. We certainly do not claim to have provided a definitive analysis of the epistemological difficulties encountered with these techniques, merely to have articulated some genuine sources of concern which, in our view, all practitioners of time-series analysis should at least consider.

Time-series analysis with political and social data is necessarily a highly judgemental process. Apart from the continuing need to avoid models that exhibit serially correlated error, there are few hard and fast rules that must be followed in all circumstances. Indeed, any method that seeks to impose a strict set of rules to be followed will tend to founder on the need for constant interplay between the analyst's theoretical ideas and the way in which they use particular statistical techniques. Time-series analysis with political and social data is not the hard 'science' of the econometricians. It involves the evaluation of causal propositions by reference to concepts that are imperfectly measured and techniques that are rarely altogether appropriate for the task. It is, in essence, art with numbers.

Appendix: effects of differencing on two hypothetical time series

Detrending by differencing can lead to substantively spurious conclusions if the trends in endogenous and exogenous variables are causally related. A familiar paradox is displayed in Figures 9.6 to 9.8. The (hypothetical) y_t and

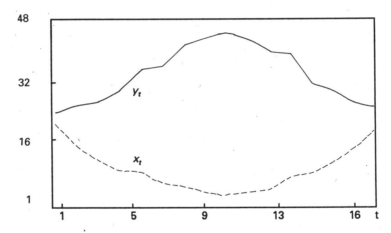

Figure 9.6 *Hypothetical y_t and x_t over time*

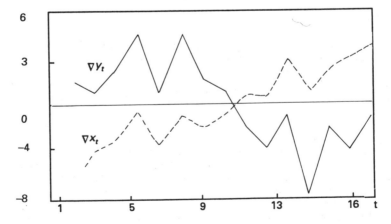

Figure 9.7 *Changes in y_t and x_t (first differences) over time*

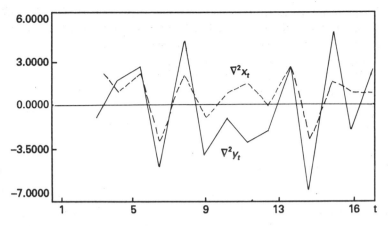

Figure 9.8 *Changes in ∇y_t and ∇x_t (second differences) over time*

x_t variables are clearly negatively related over the long term (each reaches its maximum/minimum at the same point). Yet if both y_t and x_t are differenced to render each series stationary (as in Figure 9.8), the transformed, second-differenced variables appear to be positively related, even though common sense suggests that such an inference is inappropriate. In circumstances such as this, an insistence that all variables must be rendered stationary can produce misleading conclusions. At worst – in situations where there is a considerable amount of measurement error in both y_t and x_t and where the measured variables therefore only track the broad trends in the phenomena under investigation – the removal of trends through differencing can lead to a statistical analysis based almost exclusively on the correlation of measurement error.

Notes

1 Given that with most time-series data, y_{t-1} is generally a good predictor of y_t, it follows that u_{t-1} is likely to be a good predictor of u_t. In other words, u_t and u_{t-1} are likely to highly correlate.

2 If u_t correlates only with, say, u_{t-3} and not with u_{t-1} or u_{t-2}, then this can be regarded as a 'restricted AR(3)' model and estimated accordingly. See Pesaran and Pesaran (1987: 69–70, 150–51).

3 Although ρ_k can be taken to suggest the rate at which the past is discounted, it is still difficult to give substantive meaning to the expression $(u_t - \rho u_{t-1})$.

4 For an accessible introduction to autocorrelation and partial autocorrelation functions, and indeed to Box-Jenkins techniques generally, see Liu (1990). The AR(1) model can be expressed as $y_t = \alpha y_{t-1} + u_t$, where u_t is a disturbance term and α is the parameter of the model. For an MA(1), the model can be written as $y_t = u_t - \rho u_{t-1}$, where u_t and u_{t-1} are disturbance terms and ρ is the parameter of the model.

5 In the Box-Jenkins notation, $y_t = [\omega / (1 - \delta B)] I_t + N_t$.

6 In the Box-Jenkins notation, $y_t = [\omega / (1 - \delta B)] \nabla I_t + N_t$.

7 In the Box-Jenkins notation, $y_t = [(\omega_0 + \omega_1) / (1 - \delta B)] \nabla I_t + N_t$.

8 This model, like the abrupt-effect/gradual-decline model, can be estimated using the lagged endogenous variable method. The model described in Figure 9.4, for example, could easily be estimated with the specification $y_t = \beta_0 + \alpha y_{t-1} + \beta_1 I_t + \beta_2 I_{t+1} + u_t$, where β_1 and β_2 are directly equivalent to ω_0 and ω_1 in (9.17); where α is analogous to δ in the same equation; where I_t is a dummy variable which takes on the value one for the period of the intervention and zero otherwise; and where u_t is a random error term.

9 These variables were selected partly because of their close connections with the overall level of economic activity and partly because the first two at least have consistently received a great deal of media attention in the UK. All three were highly collinear (all bivariate correlations above $r=0.9$ during the period analyzed here), which was why aggregation was considered necessary. The variables were aggregated by standardizing (to give each variable mean zero and unit standard deviation) and summing. The index accordingly gives equal weight to the three component variables.

10 The consumer confidence measure employed here is based on the following monthly Gallup question which has been asked regularly since 1975: 'Thinking about the financial position of your household over the next 12 months, do you expect to be: a lot better off; a little better off; about the same; a little worse off; a lot worse off?' The consumer confidence index is obtained by subtracting the percentage of respondents who think they will be worse off from the percentage who think they will be better off. For a recent examination of the connections between this index and government popularity in Britain, see Sanders (1991b).

11 The standard tests for serially correlated error are available on many econometric packages. See, for example, Pesaran and Pesaran's Datafit program (1987).

12 The lagged endogenous variable model shown in (9.20) was checked systematically for serially correlated error; no evidence of serial correlation was found.

13 As there were 13 months from May 1982 to June 1983, and 12 months from June 1982 to June 1983, the combined effect by June 1983 is given by $(8.6 \times (0.83)^{13}) + (5.5 \times (0.83)^{12})$ = 1.3 per cent.

14 Since the Falklands-May δ parameter estimate is 0.93, the May-boost effect by June 1983 is $7.98 \times (0.93)^{13} = 3.1$. Using the non-significant estimated $\delta=0.5$ to denote the decay rate of the June boost gives a negligible additional effect by June 1983 ($4.32 \times (0.51)^{12} = 0.00$).

15 For an introduction to Granger causality, see Freeman (1983). Granger's notion of causality can be summarized as follows: x_t can be considered to Granger cause y_t if (a) y_t is influenced both by x_t and by lagged values of x_t but x_t is not influenced by lagged values of y_t, and (b) if x_t explains variation in y_t after all self-generated variations in y_t have been taken into account or eliminated.

16 For a discussion of these connections, see Sanders et al. (1987).

References

Brown, R.L., Durbin, J. and Evans, J.M. (1975) 'Techniques for testing the constancy of regression over time', *Journal of the Royal Statistical Society, Series B*, 37: 149–92.

Clarke, H., Mishler, W. and Whitely, P. (1990) 'Recapturing the Falklands: models of Conservative popularity, 1979–83', *British Journal of Political Science*, 20: 63–82.

Freeman, J.R. (1983) 'Granger causality and the time series analysis of political relationships', *American Journal of Political Science*, 27: 327–57.

Hendry, D.F. (1983) 'Econometric modelling: the "consumption function in retrospect"', *Scottish Journal of Political Economy*, 30: 193–229.

Johnston, J. (1972) *Econometric Methods*, 2nd edn. New York: McGraw-Hill.

Liu, L.M. (1990) 'Box-Jenkins time series analysis', in *BMDP Statistical Software Manual*. Oxford: University of California Press.

Norpoth, H. (1987) 'Guns and butter and government popularity in Britain', *American Political Science Review*, 81: 949–59.

Pesaran, M.H. and Pesaran, B. (1987) *Datafit: an Interactive Econometric Software Package*. London: Wiley.

Sanders, D. (1991a) 'Voting behaviour in Britain: lessons of the 1980s', *Contemporary Record*, 4: 2–6.

Sanders, D. (1991b) 'Government popularity and the next general election', *Political Quarterly*, 62: 235–61.

Sanders, D., Ward, H. and Marsh, D. (1987) 'Government popularity and the Falklands War: a reassessment', *British Journal of Political Science*, 17: 281–313.

Index